1936

944

JW(T)

French Society 1789-1970

Georges Dupeux

Professor of Contemporary History,
University Bordeaux

translated by
Peter Wait

LONDON: METHUEN & CO LTD
NEW YORK: BARNES & NOBLE

First published as *La Société Française 1789–1970*
(6th edition 1972) by Armand Colin, Paris
© 1972 Armand Colin

English translation © 1976 by Methuen & Co Ltd
First published 1976
by Methuen & Co Ltd
11 New Fetter Lane, London EC4P 4EE
and Barnes & Noble
a division of Harper & Row
10 East 53rd Street, New York 10022

Typeset in Great Britain by
Preface Limited, Salisbury, Wilts
and printed in Great Britain by
Whitstable Litho, Whitstable, Kent

ISBN 0 416 65250 6 (hardbound)
ISBN 0 416 84410 3 (paperback)

Contents

Introduction

Some years ago it was remarked by a contemporary historian that the social history of France in the nineteenth century was still uncharted territory. Nobody could make such a drastic statement today. In recent years the publication of doctoral theses devoted to social history and some excellent works of synthesis have enormously increased our knowledge of several regions of France, and of much of the nineteenth century. But there are still big gaps and plenty of scope for further research.

There are various reasons for this. One of the principal ones may be the very difficulty of defining the scope of social history. A praiseworthy ambition to describe in detail the daily life of Frenchmen can simply end up with an accumulation of picturesque details without any certainty that they reflect the realities of life for any particular social group. On the other hand simply to describe a series of systematized sociological models, constructed on an *a priori* basis, is to interpose a dark screen between the reader and the events and the people he is reading about.

The conceptual aim of the present work is to provide a history of the various groups that constitute French society, classified according to the position they occupy in the production process and in the social division of labour, of their relationships with each other, and with the way these relationships have changed in the course of time. We have tried to show how certain underprivileged and malcontent social groups have managed to better their social position and even for a time achieve a sort of domination, running the whole course from radical challenge to conservative acceptance, ending with reactionary fears for the future of society; how other groups that once dominated the scene have been totally eclipsed, while others again are emerging from the shadows and demanding their share of the good things of life and even power.

Such a description of social evolution calls for a reference to some of the motive forces behind it. What we may call internal factors belong to the realm of collective psychology and may roughly be called the awakening of consciousness: consciousness of miserable living conditions, of being exploited, consciousness of a technical or intellectual ability that rates a higher rank in the social hierarchy, sometimes a sense of inability to adapt to a society in which the springs of wealth and power had changed.

Other, external, factors are more obviously historical. One is tempted to head the list with the political revolutions with which the nineteenth century is studded; but their importance may be less than contemporaries believed. Wars, on the other hand, had an influence that they scarcely recognized. Technological change had even more. The advance of technology affected both production and consumption; the proportion of the labour force engaged in the primary, secondary and tertiary sectors was drastically changed, while the phenomenon of mass consumption led to that of mass culture. Social evolution moved at a speed that varied with that of technological progress.

Factors whose importance cannot be exaggerated are the fluctuations in the state of the economy. Periods of prosperity ease social tensions, though their benefits may be unequally distributed among social groups: periods of depression exacerbate social malaise, though their ill effects may not hurt everyone equally. There may be gainers as well as losers. So such fluctuations must be treated as historical landmarks, often of greater significance than the key dates of political history.

In a work of this size it is not possible to go very far in detailed analysis. But we hope that the documents, diagrams and tables to be found at the end of each chapter, providing samples of some of the material to be found at the 'cliff face', together with the bibliographical information, will help to satisfy the curiosity of the student who wishes to look beyond our text. In this English edition it has been assumed that the reader will not wish, and in some cases will not be able, to use the rather full bibliographical information that is provided in the French edition. We have, however, cited all those works which are actually referred to in the text, and we have added a list of books in the English language that deal with the more important topics, also a number of French works that we think likely to be found in a reasonably well-equipped history library.

It would be ungrateful not to acknowledge how much we owe to the present generation of French social historians on whose research so many of the conclusions in this work are based. This is especially true of the extremities of our period. Recent work on the Ancien Régime has not only enormously enlarged our knowledge of this period, but has also dispelled an idea that has long dominated French historiography, according to which it is simply the breeding ground of the Revolution. Released from the 'domination of eighteenth century history by the revolutionary event', historians may now take a critical and un-prejudiced look at a society of fascinating complexity.

As to the other extremity — our own time — the steady growth of national prosperity has confirmed the prediction made in the first edition of this book. But, more recently, the violent confrontations of May 1968 seemed at one moment to put at risk all that we had gained. So near to the events it is impossible to measure their significance, impossible for the historian to ignore them, impossible to offer more than a tentative interpretation.

1 People and occupations

Before describing the structure and development of the wide variety of social groups that characterize our period we need to provide some statistical information. This will illustrate the growth in the size of the population and changes in its composition from the eighteenth century to modern times. It will include modifications in demographic structure, in demographic distribution, and in various professional categories too. All these changes were bound up with economic change which it is impossible to examine in detail, but certain fundamental features of which are useful to recall.

1. The changing pattern of population

The population of France has nearly doubled since the end of the eighteenth century, growing from 27 million to 50 million, whereas that of Europe has trebled, growing from 180 million to 550 million. This striking comparison dramatically illustrates the reduction of the French population as part of the population of Europe: from about 15 per cent in 1800, it fell to 7.8 per cent in 1950.

Yet the rate of population growth in France was not always out of step with that of Europe as a whole. Earlier, in the second half of the eighteenth century the growths of France on the one hand and Europe on the other were comparable. The population of France increased by 29 per cent, whereas that of Europe increased by 38 per cent. But between 1800 and 1850 the gap widened (France – 33 per cent: Europe 50 per cent), and whereas Europe, excluding France, maintained this rate of growth between 1850 and 1900 (48 per cent), France did not maintain its previous demographic momentum. The rate of demographic growth fell to 8 per cent, or to 11.5 per cent if one takes into account the loss of Alsace-Lorraine. In the first half of the twentieth century France's population increased by only 7.5 per cent; that of Europe by 33 per cent.

Throughout the nineteenth century there was therefore a significant difference between the more rapidly expanding populations of Western Europe on the one hand and the slower demographic expansion of France on the other: this reveals the unique character of the French demographic experience.

From a dynamic to a static population

The French population increased substantially in the second half of the eighteenth century. A new demographic pattern emerged replacing the older 'pre-Malthusian' pattern. The latter was characterized by two features: 'a certain natural equilibrium and at the same time an occasional large and transient disequilibrium.' The natural equilibrium was the product of high fertility and mortality rates. Fertility was however limited both by social and religious sanctions, and illegitimate births were unusual. Fertility might have been all the greater but for the early death of either father or mother. An integral family — that is, one not sundered by the death of a parent before the mother's childbearing years had come to an end — might produce seven or eight children, while the average family would not produce more than five. This should have been more than enough to assure a full generation replacement rate. Yet child mortality up to the age of four was heavy and usually only half of these children would survive. The population thus remained more or less static with a slight increase of from 10 per cent to 12 per cent over the century.

Yet this delicate balance could easily be upset by formidable demographic crises, which led to sudden leaps in the death rate. These crises were usually connected with extreme scarcity or dearth. Famine and epidemics took their toll among those parts of society already weakened through food shortage and might triple, even quadruple, the normal number of deaths. These outbreaks of mortality would lead to a drop in the marriage rate, perhaps halving it. There would be a consequent drop in births, perhaps by two-thirds. This could lead to an overall population decline of 10 per cent to 20 per cent. Whole generations of potential childbearers might be affected in this way. The effects of such a 'mortality crisis' would thus be both immediate and longlasting.

But all this changed in the second half of the century. Demographic crises almost disappeared. There were several reasons for this — growth in economic resources; lessening of food shortage and possibly also progress in the means of combating illness. An excess of births over deaths became normal, and the increased numbers of young also led to more children when they themselves reached maturity. The population grew swiftly. This was the first stage of the demographic revolution. C. E. Labrousse comments:

The sudden demographic rise which took place in the second quarter of the eighteenth century increased the population by from 30 to 40 per cent. The demographic revolution of the reigns of Louis XV and Louis XVI stands in stark contrast to the static character of French demography under Louis XIV. This demographic revolution was the product, not of a rise in births, but of a decline in deaths, and especially among the masses who had previously been so badly hit by periodic crises. The era of crises of famine — social crises of great complexity accompanied by demographic collapse which often took half a generation to repair — were over.

The first phase of the demographic revolution led to an enormous increase in Europe's population, but in France this phase was of short duration. By the end of the eighteenth century the second phase of the demographic revolution appeared and fertility began to wane. Even after allowing for the decline caused by the wars of the Revolution and Empire, the food scarcity of 1817 and the cholera epidemic of 1832, the evidence is quite clear. In the middle of the eighteenth century there were 35 births per 1,000. In 1801, a good year, there were 33. Apart from the crises already mentioned, the rate never fell below 30 per 1,000 until 1827; after 1829 it never rose above 30. Meanwhile, a decline in the death rate was also taking place: from 27 per 1,000 in the first ten years of the nineteenth century to 23 per 1,000 between 1841 and 1850. Yet this rate of decline seems to have varied in different social groups. If the population of Paris is divided into three according to the amount of rent paid, then it can be seen that among those paying the most rent the mortality rate dropped from 24.9 per 1,000 in 1817 to 18.2 per 1,000 in 1850; in the middle group from 27.3 to 25.1 and in the lower group from 36.5 to 33.7. There was thus a general fall in mortality among all groups, but it was more marked among the rich.

Between 1850 and 1870 the death rate remained more or less static, but after 1870 it began to decline again, and this continued into the twentieth century reaching 13 per 1,000 in 1950. This was chiefly due to a fall in the rate of infant mortality of children under one. At the beginning of the nineteenth century the mortality rate was 187 per 1,000 live births; 179 for the years 1861—5; 167 for 1881—5; 149 in 1900 (Pasteur's work may have had an important influence); 126 on the eve of the first world war. In the years 1935—7 the rate dropped to 66, and to 22 in 1962. Deaths among adolescents (1—15 years old) also declined dramatically from 107 per 1,000 in 1900, to 50 in 1930 and 17 in 1950.

Yet this decline in deaths, which in Europe led to a large increase in the size of the population, did not have the same effect in France. This was because in France the birth rate also declined. France was the first country in which family limitation was widely practised. This had started at the end of the eighteenth century, and its effects were being felt up to the second world war. After 1880 this decline in the birth rate continued rapidly, so much so that between 1886 and 1890 deaths exceeded births. It looked as if the generations would not be able to replace themselves and a period of depopulation would set in.

Table I.1 Net rate of reproduction

Period	France	England	Germany
1896—1810	1.08		
1811—1820	1.08		
1821—1830	1.06		1.31
1831—1840	1.04		1.25
1841—1850	1.01	1.28	1.30
1851—1860	0.97	1.34	1.29
1861—1870	1.01	1.42	1.37
1871—1880	1.04	1.53	1.48
1881—1890	1.02	1.47	1.47
1891—1900	0.97	1.32	1.52
1901—1910	0.96	1.23	1.48
1921—1930	0.93	0.95	0.90
1931—1935	0.90	0.77	0.79
1936—1939	0.89	0.79	0.98

This tendency towards depopulation became even more apparent in France because of other adverse factors. The 1914—18 war accounted for 1,400,000 deaths: one out of every twenty-five Frenchmen, or more specifically two young Frenchmen in ten, lost their lives and in addition there was a decline in the birth rate, giving rise to the phenomenon of 'hollow layers' showing up so clearly in the age pyramid (Fig. 1.3) — half a generation missing. The second influence was the economic crisis of the 1930s. The decline in fertility caused by this crisis coincided with the fall in the marriage rate when the generation born between 1915 and 1919, which had been so reduced in numbers by the war, reached marriageable age. The numbers of births fell so much that after 1935 there was even an excess of deaths over births. This lasted up to the end of the second world war, which itself dealt a further blow — There were 150,000 soldiers killed, 170,000 war victims, 290,000 French who died in Germany and 300,000 other deaths. A total of 900,000 died who, given more normal conditions, would have lived many decades longer.

The demographic revival

In 1946 the number of births in France was 840,000. This represented an increase over the pre-war number of nearly 40 per cent. This change was not peculiar to France. The fundamental question was, how lasting would it be? Demographers have shown that the roots of this change were more deep-seated and went back further than was first thought. The change did in fact prove to be lasting. In the fifteen year period, between 1946 and 1961, France's population increased by more than 5 million, whereas in the previous eighty years it had increased by only 3 million.

After 1940 there were profound changes in French attitudes towards maternity. From then on the birth rate among those couples not split up by the war began to increase. This increase was sufficient to make up not only for the absence of husbands imprisoned or deported, but also for the diminution of the number of marriages. In 1945 the birth rate among married couples was such that this generation was replacing itself, something which had not happened since the end of the nineteenth century.

The net rate of reproduction in France has settled down to 1.12. In Europe, only Portugal (1.34), the Netherlands (1.33), and Finland (1.23) have higher rates. The rate in Spain is 0.99, in Germany 0.97, in Britain 0.95 and in Italy 0.91.

Fig. I.1   Number of children born alive per 1000 marriages

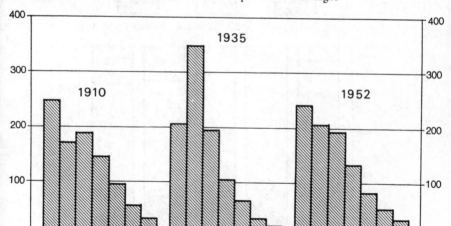

The behaviour of post-war families differs from that of pre-war ones in that the first-born arrive much sooner (though in no greater total numbers); there are more second children in families which already have one; and there is a slightly greater likelihood of a third child being produced in families which already have two. The birth rate among larger families has not increased. As a result the structure of families has slightly changed: the proportion of those without children is the same as it was between the wars; the proportion of those with one child has grown less; that of families with two children has changed little; but the proportion of families with three or four children has increased. The rise in the birth-rate is therefore, above all, due to an increase in the proportion of the middle-sized families.

These changes are too recent to change appreciably the age structure of the population. The ageing of the population is of fundamental significance in French demographic history. In 1851 those over sixty amounted to no more than 10 per cent of the population; in 1901 they amounted to 13 per cent; in 1921 to 13.8 per cent; in 1936, 14.7 per cent, and in 1968, 17.9 per cent. In a century and a half the proportion of the elderly in the population had increased by four-fifths.

Fig. I.2   Relative size of the three main age groups in the French population

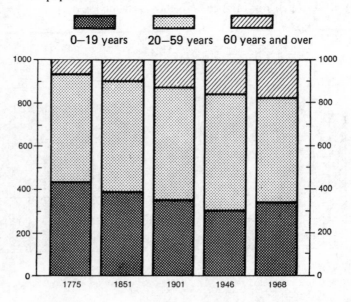

Table I.2 Percentages of French population in three main age groups

Age group	1775	1851	1901	1946	1968
0–19	42.8	38.5	34.3	29.5	33.8
20–59	49.9	51.3	52.7	54.5	48.3
60 and over	7.3	10.2	13.0	16.0	17.9
All ages	100.0	100.0	100.0	100.0	100.0

This phenomenon is the consequence of two basic demographic movements: a decline in the birthrate, (therefore fewer young people), and a decline in the death rate, (at least among the middle-aged and the elderly) since a fall in the mortality of infants or of the young tends to make a population younger. The recovery of the birthrate since 1946 has slightly held back the growth of the proportion of the elderly; but the ageing of the French population will continue for some time to come.

2 Internal migration
The population of France has not only varied in size since the end of the eighteenth century, it has also changed in its geographical distribution. For an overall study of these phenomena one must rely on the date derived from the five-yearly census returns. By comparing these one can arrive at a rough idea of the rise or fall of the population, in each *département* for example, and by taking into account the natural movement of the population it is possible to discover how much is due to births and deaths and how much to local emigration or immigration. However, this method does not allow one to know the real figures for population migrations. Assuming that 100,000 people left a *département* and 200,000 born in another came to it between two census years, the data from the census returns would not indicate the total population movement of 300,000 people, but merely give the impression of 100,000 newcomers. In this case therefore the method underestimates the scale of migratory movements.

Bearing these reservations in mind, and remembering that one can only achieve a partial view of what actually happened, the variations in population in various *départements* may be examined from the beginning of the nineteenth century to the present day. Until 1831 the population grew in every single *département*. After 1836 various *départments* reached their maximum populations and then decreased. The gap between this maximum and the population of 1946 (since the

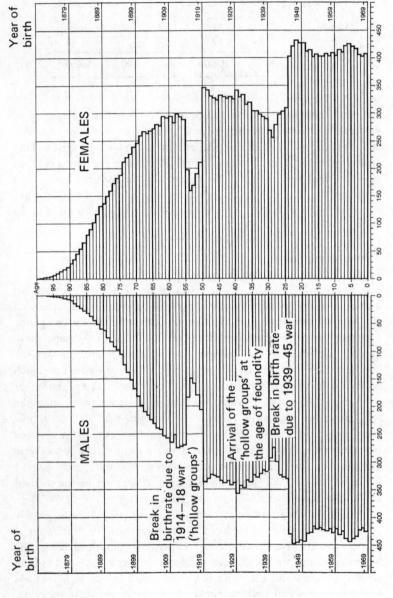

Fig. I.3   French population pyramid, 1 January 1970

immediate post-war revival distorts the figures) indicates those areas where there has been a considerable decrease in population.

The greatest depopulation has been in predominantly agricultural areas: the mountainous regions of the southern Alps, the Jura and the Massif Central; the Aquitaine basin, the southern and western edges of the Paris basin. On the other hand the areas of very slight depopulation, or of population increase, are all areas containing large towns. The most

Fig. I.4 Fall in population of *départements* (1946) from recorded maxima

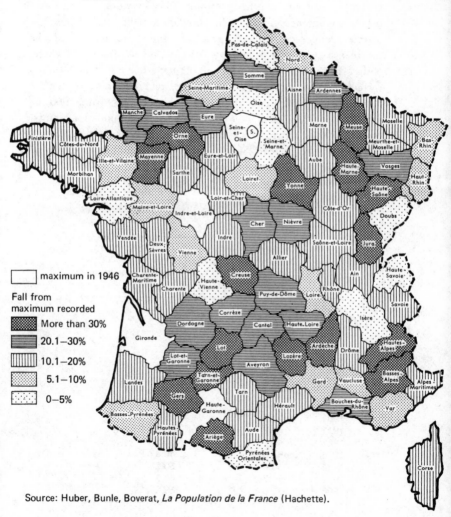

Source: Huber, Bunle, Boverat, *La Population de la France* (Hachette).

notable examples are the *départements* of the Seine and the Seine-et-Oise — the Parisian area. This movement from rural to urban regions is particularly noticeable.

It is possible to give amazing examples of the decline in the vitality of rural areas due to the attractions and the cities. The villages of the Limagne lost their population to the rubber factories of Clermont-Ferrand; in Burgundy the same situation occurred around Le Creusot; population from the villages of Lorraine was attracted to metal-lurgical factories; the rural population of Champagne was attracted to Troyes. But no town had so profound or so widespread an effect on the countryside as Paris. The population of Paris is composed of people from every French province: since the middle of the nineteenth century two-thirds of the Parisians were born elsewhere. Nearly half of the population of the *département* of the Rhône, including Lyon, came from outside the area; the same goes for the *département* of the Bouches du Rhône. Between 1896 and 1906 the urban population of France increased by 1,414,000 inhabitants: only 89,000 of this total was due to an excess of births over deaths: the rest of the increase was due to the effects of the excess of immigration over emigration and amounted to 1,325,000. (Demangeon, *La France économique et humaine*).

Table I.3

	Urban population (*communes* of 2000+) as percentage of total population	Total population of towns of 5000+ as percentage of total population
1836		16.8
1846	24.4	
1851	25.5	17.9
1856	27.3	
1861	28.9	
1866	30.5	24.4
1872	31.1	
1881	34.8	
1891	37.4	
1901	40.9	35.6
1911	44.2	38.4
1921	46.4	41.1
1936	52.4	46.8
1954	56.0	50.2
1962	61.7	55.2
1968	70.5	59.0

These internal population movements can therefore best be followed by distinguishing urban from rural population. This distinction relies on the definition of 1846. According to this, if a *commune* had a clustered population of over 2,000 it was regarded as being an urban community. If this definition is followed the urban population of France increased from 8,674,000 in 1846 to 17,509,000 in 1911 and to 33,000,000 in 1968. However, this definition is quite arbitrary and although in 1846 a population of 2,000 was regarded as an urban population, today this figure seems too low. One might reasonably rate those *communes* with more than 5,000 inhabitants as towns. Even on this basis the table reproduced below shows that the size of the movement remains comparable.

Fig. I.5   French population movement 1846–1968 (logarithmic scale)

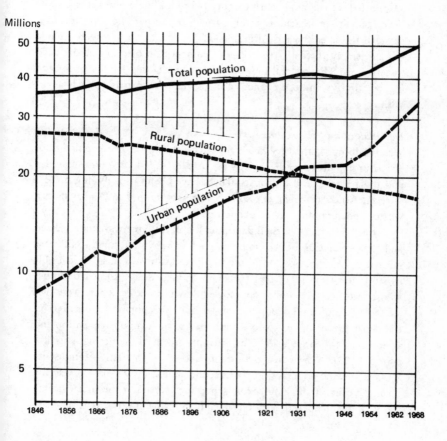

Since the census of 1846 was the first to use this definition of urban population the trend may have started much earlier. It has been estimated that at the end of the seventeenth century urban population only amounted to one-tenth of the total population and that at the end of the eighteenth century it amounted to rather more than one-fifth. Yet in 1846 it only amounted to a little less than a quarter. This indicates that the growth of the 'urban' sector was much less rapid from the Revolution to 1846 than during the course of the eighteenth century. From 1801 to 1831 urban population did not increase any faster than rural population: urban growth only really began to be felt under the July Monarchy and even then only slowly. The reason is that industry had not led to profound changes in population structure: the biggest employer of industrial labour was the textile industry, which was often to be found in the heart of the countryside.

But the internal movements of the population increased in the second half of the nineteenth century because of economic change. The development of machinery for agriculture, especially in threshing, reduced the need for agricultural labour, and rural weavers were finding it increasingly difficult to meet the competition of more modernized installations. This general movement was accelerated by the expansion of the railways and the economic and social transformations it brought with it.

Depopulation of the countryside

We still do not know very much about this shifting of the population of the countryside towards the towns, usually called the 'rural exodus', and its character and its consequences have been variously interpreted. A recent study (Pinchemel) of sixty rural *communes* in Picardy gives a clearer understanding of the phenomenon.

From 1836 to 1872 rural depopulation in this area was still localized and the population of certain *communes* actually continued to increase normally. The peak period of the rural exodus was from 1872 to 1911; it continued from 1911 to 1936 and even increased in some *communes* whilst in others the movement slowed down or ceased. There were two related types of rural depopulation: an 'active' depopulation marked by the departure of people who already had some form of occupation and a 'non-active' depopulation which mainly involved the young. The first period (1836–72) was a period of 'active' depopulation: industrial artisans left the countryside. The second period (1872–1911) was the turning point in the rural exodus because it marked the departure of the young which led to a serious decline in births in rural areas. The last period (1911—36) was again a period of 'active' depopulation, but now not only people with an industrial occupation or who practised home industries were leaving but agricultural workers as well.

So is one justified in speaking of a 'rural exodus'? It has been argued that this is not an accurate description because there had always been departures of the 'surplus' of the population, that is to say of people who for economic or technical reasons no longer found employment in the villages. In Picardy, for instance, their departure had not resulted in land being unoccupied or uncultivated; there had been no extension of waste land and country property was still firmly held. But the picture was different in other depopulated areas: in the southern Alps and in parts of the Massif Central and the Aquitaine basin there were not enough men left adequately to exploit the agricultural resources of these regions.

Rural depopulation allowed those who remained to increase the size of their holdings, and doubtless to enjoy a better standard of living. But it has been argued that the results were not wholly beneficial. In Picardy villages became purely agricultural communities with only a sprinkling of tradespeople or non-agricultural activities. This impoverishment of the socio-professional structure, this 'ruralization' of the countryside dates from the second half of the nineteenth century. The countryside was changing from a place for life to a place for work, with a very narrow outlook. Below a certain density of population, a certain variety of professional activity, the countryside ceases to provide a background for social life, social betterment or any cultural advance. Rural depopulation seems therefore to speed up rural decay.

The growth of towns
The extent of migration to towns is easily demonstrated by the growth curves of various important towns. That there was a sharply defined movement only became clear in 1831: from then on it accelerated and reached its peak between 1851 and 1866. It was less rapid for provincial capitals like Bordeaux and Toulouse whose commercial and administrative functions were more important than their industrial ones than for towns more exclusively industrial like the Lille-Roubaix-Tourcouing group and, even more so, Saint-Etienne. The development of this town was, in the French context, prodigious — the 'take-off' started in the early years of the nineteenth century. Its population doubled between 1801 and 1831 and increased six-fold in little over sixty years, (1801—66) and in 1921, despite the slower pace of the years 1901—11, the population of Saint-Etienne was ten times what it

Fig. I.6   Population growth of certain towns since 1801

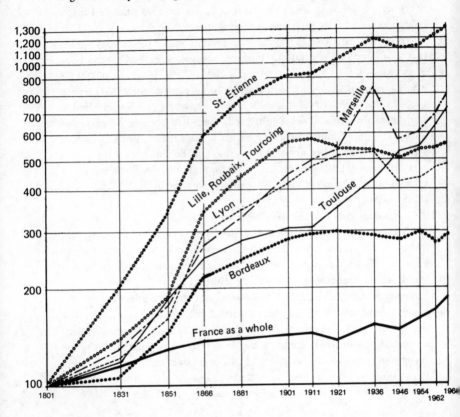

had been in 1801. This is a good example of the connection between urbanization and industrialization.

Analysis of census figures shows that the most rapid years of urban growth were between 1851 and 1866 and that growth after this time was much slower in most large towns and a ceiling seems to have been reached in the early years of the twentieth century. Yet the movement of population from the countryside was still continuing, a fact which is explained by administrative distinctions within these great urban conglomerations: the urban *commune* is the census unit, but at the beginning of the twentieth century it only represented a part of the conglomerations, a part which had absorbed its full quota. The immigrants had settled in neighbouring *communes* which became

Fig. I.7 Population growth in the Paris conurbation since 1801 (and 1851)

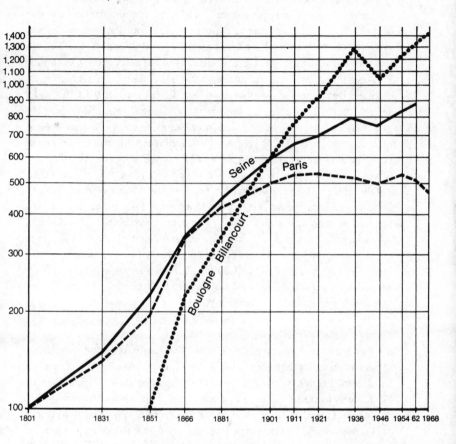

suburbs. It is because these suburbs do not figure in the graphs that the move towards urbanization seems to falter and almost cease, when in fact it is proceeding at an even pace. The most extreme case was Paris where the actual city's population reached saturation point by 1911, but the movement of immigrants continued, as the curve for the *département* of the Seine indicates (and the curve for just one suburban *commune*, Boulogne-Billancourt, shows even more strongly).

This concentration of people in the Paris region is an important fact in the history of the French population: today nearly one-fifth, (18.4 per cent) of the whole population lives in this area, more than a quarter of the total urban population of France. This is a development which has taken place during the last hundred years. In 1801 Paris had approximately half a million inhabitants and they amounted to about 2 per cent of the population: even in 1851 the population of Paris was only 3 per cent of the national total. The Parisian industrial agglomeration in its full modern sense began only under the Second Empire, with metallurgical and chemical industry developing alongside the traditional professions, concentrations of manpower in big organizations alongside the workshops of small-scale industry in the older suburbs and the proletariat joining the craftsman and journeymen. In 1881 7.5 per cent of the population of France lived in the *département* of the Seine; in 1911 this proportion had increased to more than 10 per cent and was almost 12 per cent in 1931. By this date the great Parisian urban complex, (which reached into the *départements* of the Seine-et-Oise and the Seine-et-Marne), accounted for 14 per cent of France's population; today it accounts for 17 per cent. This concentration of a large amount of the population in one area is explained by the diverse activities of the capital. It is a rare phenomenon (London is perhaps another example) and the tendency still exists. The population of this area is always increasing (120,000 families per year on average). It leads to a disturbing kind of disequilibrium which evoked the censorious contrast 'Paris and the French desert'.

3 Professional migrations
By this is meant movements among the working part of the population between trades, or between jobs in the same trade. This was a marked feature of French society after 1789. The professional structure of France was unstable. This can be seen in a simple but effective way if one remembers that on the eve of the Revolution more than two-thirds of France's inhabitants worked on the land – whereas only approximately one-fifth do so today. Our information on this problem is incomplete, imprecise and at times unreliable. Only for 1851 is there a census which gives information on the professions of the population but even then the census methods were not always particularly sophisticated and they only improved towards the beginning of the twentieth century. The criteria for deciding who belonged to what profession were not consistent. The results obtained from the use of such records must be accepted only with the greatest caution.

From the middle of the nineteenth century to 1921, the working population increased from 14 million (1856), to 20 million (1921). It remained more or less stable for a decade and then decreased by 1,200,000 between 1931 and 1936. This was a consequence of the economic crises of the 1930s. After the second world war the working population remained constant, and later increased to about 21 millions in 1969.

The percentage of the working population has varied: the proportion of workers remained more or less constant in the second half of the nineteenth century, (40–43 per cent of the total population); it increased from the turn of the century to the eve of the first world war (51 per cent in 1911), dropped during the economic crises (47 per cent in 1936) and continued to decrease until modern times (41 per cent in 1968). It is sometimes thought that this drop in the percentage of the active section of the population was due to a decline in the number of women who went out to work, but this is not so: the proportion of women to men among the active population has not changed greatly (in 1886, 31 women to 69 men; in 1968, 35 women to 65 men). It seems more likely that the drop is due to the later age at which the young started work and the increasing tendency for those over sixty-five not to work because of the social benefits they now receive. At the end of the nineteenth century two-thirds of men over sixty-five were engaged in some job or other; in 1954 only one-third were still working. The number of those living on state welfare has therefore increased.

Until recently the largest group in the working population was that involved in agriculture. However, its relative size has been decreasing since at least the eighteenth century. It is difficult to be at all precise about this decline because of the nature of the sources and the variations in census methods. Also, the considerable element of female help has not been measured at all. However, it seems that around the middle of the nineteenth century those engaged in agriculture amounted to more than 52 per cent of the active male population. The numerical figures, probably inaccurate, show a decline from 7,800,000 in 1851 to a figure between 5,100,000 and 5,800,000 between 1856 and 1891, i.e. about 45 per cent. This phenomenon has accelerated in the twentieth century. In 1896 there were 5.7 million working in agriculture, in 1921 there were 5 million, 4.5 million in 1931, and 4.2 in 1936 and 1946, falling to 2 million in 1968, or 15 per cent of the whole active male population. Between 1954 and 1962 the fall in numbers of the working agricultural population was very rapid (an average of 3.5 per cent annually); since then it has become still faster, falling at the rate of 3.8 per cent annually. This movement has involved both wage-earners and non-earners and expecially the young: a disturbing factor emphasising the lack of demographic balance in the countryside.

Between 1856 and 1891 the number of men and women employed in the industrial sector remained more or less constant (about 4.5 million). The number grew proportionately with the total population from the end of the nineteenth century onwards to reach 7 million in 1931 – an increase of two-thirds since the middle of the nineteenth century. Between 1931 and 1936 – the period of the economic crisis – there was a fall of 18 per cent but the tendency to increase appeared again after the second world war: according to the 1962 census industrial workers numbered 7.3 million or 38.5 per cent of the total working population; in 1968 they were nearly 8 million (38.6 per cent). The number of women workers reached its maximum in 1906 (2 million), but fell after that date, reaching 1.8 million in 1968 – about equal to that of 1876. Hence the number of men involved in industrial work has increased. There was a high peak of 5 million in 1931 but by 1962 this figure had increased to a record 6 million.

There have been movements within industry itself indicating progress or decline in one particular industrial sector. The census returns do not give sufficient information for a detailed picture to be drawn but they do allow the broad outlines of the evolution of various industries to be known. The number of those engaged in mining, almost all being men, increased steadily from the middle of the nineteenth century until 1931: there were 33,600 miners according to an official mining source in 1851, and 292,000 in 1930. During the economic crisis of the 1930s the numbers decreased temporarily but after the Liberation they increased again – possibly owing to the great effort made to increase output in the power industries. Progress in the mechanization of the mining industry subsequently led to an appreciable reduction in the amount of manpower employed. This was especially true in the coalmining industry where the output per worker increased sharply.

Greater still was the progress in the metallurgical industries: in 1886 they accounted for less than 400,000 workers; but this figure had increased to 900,000 by the beginning of the twentieth century and to 1,650,000 in 1931. Again the economic crisis of the 1930s led to a recession but the industry advanced after the second world war and in 1962 its total strength reached nearly 2.5 million – 33 per cent of the active industrial population. The iron and steel industries hold the key to this progress – their total labour strength was multiplied by 2.3 between 1896 and 1936 but during the same period the total labour strength of the non-ferrous industries tripled. This then is a sector of industry in full momentum: the same goes for the chemical industries whose total labour force more than tripled between 1896 and 1921 and almost doubled again between 1921 and 1954. Although the petroleum and motor fuel branches only employ a relatively small labour force, they have made the most rapid progress.

The development of consumer industries has been quite different. In the middle of the nineteenth century the textile industry employed more workers than any other. The maximum number employed was in 1866 when there were more than one million workers, (64 per cent of whom were men). The number of men employed then decreased: in 1936 there were fewer than 300,000. The number of women employed remained constant until 1921 when their numbers also began to decline. From 1926 to 1954 the total labour force decreased by 32 per cent. The pattern in the clothing industry was rather different: an increase in the labour force until 1906, and then after the first world war a decrease which has lasted until present times (a reduction by about two-thirds). Change in habits, improvements in production methods, a move from 'tailor-made' to 'off-the-peg', account for this. The same kind of pattern emerges in the leather industry, although the reduction in the labour force was slower, being only 30 per cent between 1901 and 1954. The only consumer industries whose labour force has continued to increase are the printing industries and the food industries.

Changes in methods of transport involved an ever increasing work force. The transport revolution was only beginning in the middle of the nineteenth century. The 1866 census indicates 264,000 employed in the transport and food-supply industries, and of these 107,000 were employed on the railways. In 1930 the largest number ever recorded of those working on the railways was reached: 550,000. The introduction of more modern methods and productivity increases had reduced this to 360,000 by 1959. Developments in road, air and sea transport increased the total transport labour force to 723,000 in 1936 and 800,000 in 1968. In about a hundred years the total transport labour force had at least tripled.

In the distributive trades the number of employees increased rapidly from 1866 (973,000) to 1936 (2,833,000), then more slowly (3,400,000 in 1968): a threefold increase. The proportion of men to women employed has fallen from 2:1 in the nineteenth century to about as many women as men today. All the distributive trades have been affected by this increase in the labour force but in differing degrees: in the drink and hotel sector an increase of 24 per cent between 1896 and 1936; 62 per cent in the food sector; 175 per cent in the cloth and clothing sector; 236 per cent in the sale of books and 450 per cent in banks and insurance, where women predominate today (whereas in 1869 they only accounted for 5 per cent of the labour force).

In the liberal professions, where the role of women has also increased, the total labour force employed has increased too: 900,000 in 1851 to 2,270,000 in 1954. But the term 'liberal professions' is too vague: its constituent elements need more careful analysis. The number of those engaged in the legal profession has not increased significantly over the past hundred years; lawyers, solicitors, bailiffs are all in professions where one man replaces another. The number of painters and writers has hardly changed in a century. But there are more and more engineers; just how many is hard to establish, since the census groups many of them under the branches in which they specialize. The number of those employed in the medical professions has greatly increased: from 40,000 in 1851 to 400,000 in 1951. This remarkable rise is only outstripped by the increase in the number of students (only a temporary profession, it is true): 17,000 in 1890, 30,000 in 1900, 135,000 in 1950, 400,000 in 1965, 700,000 in 1970.

The census returns consider those employed in the public services as belonging to the liberal professions. The number of civil servants has increased from 130,000 in 1839 to 500,000 in 1914, 682,000 in 1936 and 950,000 in 1946. The rapid rate of increase of the years 1936—46 has not been maintained, despite the increase in the number of teachers which followed the demographic upsurge of the post-war years: 65,000 in state schools in 1866, 150,000 in 1914, 186,000 in 1936, 224,000 in 1946 and 313,000 in 1956. At this time those employed in teaching or in the postal services accounted for half of all civil servants. By 1970 the distribution of civil servants among the various ministries was as shown in Table 1.4.

The character of change in the domestic service sector is quite different. The number of servants (not counting farm 'servants', really labourers) was very high in the nineteenth century. The maximum seems to have been reached by the end of the century, the census of 1891 indicating a total of 1,156,000, of whom 70 per cent were women. In 1931 the number had fallen to 800,000, by 1968 to 530,000, of whom 94 per cent were women. There has also been a change in the character of domestic employment. The servant who lived in has been progressively replaced by the 'daily'. There are various different reasons for the transformation of this sector: change in habits,

Table I.4 Officials in government service (in 000s, on 31 December of each year)

	1952	1960	1968	1970	Percentage change 1970/1952
Foreign affairs	12.4	26.2	15.3	15.4	124
Social services	19	18	26.2	25.6	135
Education and cultural affairs	263.2	430.7	649.3	750.2	285
Post office and savings banks	201.3	235.2	283.5	297.4	148
Finance and economic affairs	104.8	114.1	130.9	136.9	130
Home affairs	79.5	77.9	109.6	114.5	144
Housing and transport	94	86.1	80.5	81.9	87
Agriculture	14.6	17.2	22	25.5	175
Justice	17.7	16.4	23.7	25.5	144
Various	12.2	9.3	9.6	11.6	95
Civilian officials in service establishments	194.1	172.7	146.9	145.6	75
Armed forces	495.3	426	284.0	283.7	57
TOTAL	1 508.1	1 629.8	1 781.5	1 913.1	127

Source: Ministère de l'Economie et des Finances.

economies on the part of employers and a desire on the part of employees to be more independent in their work.

A general idea of the changes in the character of the population which have taken place during the last hundred years can be realized by using the methods of classification and terminology of Colin Clark. He distinguishes three areas of activity: the primary sector (agriculture, forestry and fishing); the secondary sector (mining, processing and manufacturing, building, public works, water, gas and electrical industries) and the tertiary sector which includes everything else — distributive industries, public services and all other activities which do not materially produce anything. In France the evolution of these three sectors has been as follows:

Table I.5 Workers in the three main sectors (in percentages)

Années	1851	1881	1901	1921	1931	1936	1954	1962	1968
Primary	53	48	42	43	37	37	30	22	16
Secondary	25	27	31	29	33	30	34	37	40
Tertiary	22	25	27	28	30	33	36	41	44

A hundred years ago there were two agricultural to every one industrial worker, and one worker in the tertiary sector. Today the preponderance has passed to the tertiary sector which is slightly ahead of the secondary sector and leaves the primary sector well behind. The reduction in the primary sector (two-thirds) is very considerable; and there has been a drift of population towards the secondary sector (an

Fig. I.8 Proportion of working population per sector

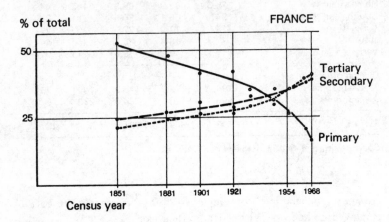

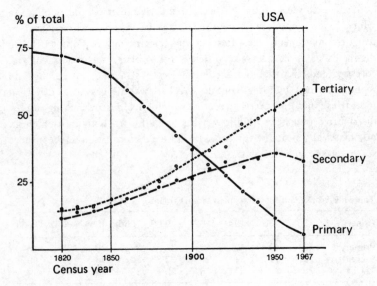

Source: Friedmann-Naville, *Traité de sociologie du travail* (A. Colin).

increase of more than half) and especially the tertiary sector (more than a twofold increase). These phenomena are characteristic of the development of industrial societies, although particular details may differ. France's development lies between that of Italy, where the primary sector still accounts for around 40 per cent of the active population, and that of Germany, where the drift towards the secondary sector has been much more definite, and England where more than half of the active population belongs to the secondary sector and nearly two-fifths to the tertiary sector. But these advanced European countries lag behind the development of the USA where as early as 1920 the active population was evenly distributed between the three sectors and where, by 1930, the tertiary sector was preponderant.

Nevertheless the structure of the French working population is still changing rapidly. A study undertaken by the INSEE which investigated changes which took place between 1954 and 1960 indicated a loss of 14 per cent in the primary sector whilst the number of industrial workers increased by 6 per cent. But the most prominent changes have taken place in the professional and managerial sector – an increase of some 31 per cent. Although this group only contains a very small proportion of the total working population, less than one-tenth, the remarkable increase is possibly an indication of a profound change in French society.

4. The development of the economy

The changes in the structure of the French population since the eighteenth century which have just been discussed were caused by changes in the economy. These changes have been described as an 'industrial revolution' – although they were slow and possibly amount more accurately to an industrial 'evolution'. They have been classified as three industrial revolutions according to the new type of power employed. The first is said to have come with the use of coal and the steam engine, the second with the use of electricity, oil and turbine power and the third with the use of nuclear power. But industrial change is characterized not only by the nature of new forms of energy but also by the change from manual labour to machine labour, followed by the development of newer machines, from the power loom to the automatic loom, via the Bessemer process.

Innovation

The first industrial revolution involved the harshest upheaval, the exchange of the natural environment, in which man had worked since the days of Adam, for a technical environment. Meanwhile the natural economy, characterized by agriculture predominantly geared for home consumption, yielded to a market economy. This resulted in an increase in the size of the secondary and tertiary sectors of the population at the expense of the primary sector.

There were various stages in the first industrial revolution. A description of these helps explain its character. There was firstly technical progress, the impetus for which came largely from England. Newcomen (1710) and Watt (around 1770) were pioneers in the use of steam power. In 1779 Watt supplied the Périer brothers with the Chaillot steam pump, used by the water supply service of Paris. At the beginning of the Revolution there were only ten steam engines used to pump out water from coal mines, and only in 1803 was a steam engine used for power in a spinning mill. In 1816 there were between 150 and 200 steam engines but only fifty of these were of French manufacture. There was slow but fairly steady progress between 1820 and 1827 which slowed down between 1827 and 1832 but rapidly quickened after 1833. Thereafter the use of steam engines increased rapidly in France throughout the nineteenth century until the first world war.

Again British influence was important in the mechanization of French industry. The most rapid mechanization took place in the textile industry, which was much more labour-intensive than metallurgy, and because mechanization in this industry was rather easier and less costly to instal. Within the textile industry itself spinning was more labour-intensive than weaving and probably as a result modernization was much more rapid in spinning. The textile machinery introduced into France was almost exclusively of English origin coming through foreign entrepreneurs or exiles such as the Englishmen John Holker and Edward Milne and the Swiss Oberkampf. Among French entrepreneurs those of Alsace were almost the only ones to convert their equipment.

The cotton industry proved to be a fertile area for the introduction of innovations — possibly because it was a new industry which escaped much governmental regulation. Spinning-jennies, perfected by Hargreaves in 1765, were introduced into France after 1771. Arkwright's frame (for spinning) was introduced by Milne around 1787, and the mule-jenny was introduced after 1789. But the use of these machines was not widespread and their introduction was, in effect, slow to progress. Only under the July monarchy was the cotton spinning industry completely and efficiently mechanized, since early mechanized spinning had not always produced satisfactory thread. The mechanization of weaving was even slower. Yet the flying shuttle had been

Fig. I.9   Technical advance, 1825—1965

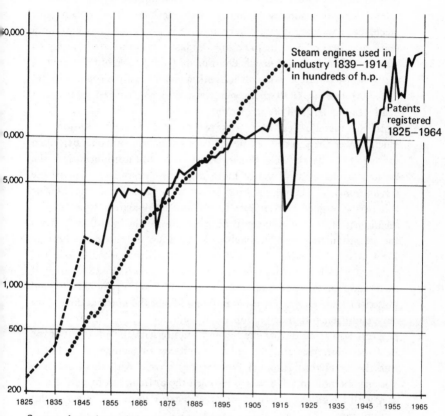

Source: *Annuaire statistique de la France* (Presses Universitaires de France).

invented by John Kay in 1733 and he had himself introduced it into France in 1747 when forced to leave his country; but it only knew a real success in the early years of the nineteenth century. Ternaux, a French entrepreneur, used it in his factories, but it was not used in Roubaix before 1820, Normandy before 1825 and Alsace before 1830.

The mechanization of the woollen industry followed, but twenty years later. The jenny was being used for spinning before the Revolution, but the use of Cartwright's wool-combing machine invented in 1784 was only really widespread after 1825. The problem of mechanizing the carding of wool was not really solved before 1830. The handloom maintained its dominance for a long time because of the tendency to produce only high-quality cloths, and mechanical weaving only made widespread progress under the Second Empire.

In the silk industry spinning was mechanized early on, but mechanized weaving did not start until 1830 and was widely used only under the Second Empire. The linen industry was the last industry to have its spinning mechanized. Philippe de Girard took out a patent as early as 1810 but the value of his work was only really recognized after 1830. As late as 1848 there were only 600 mechanized looms, and hand-weaving was still preponderant.

In the metallurgical industries the process of mechanization was much slower than in the textile industries. Smelting by coke, perfected towards 1713 by the Englishman Darby, was only introduced into the Wendel foundries at Hayange more than fifty years later. During the Revolution and Empire smelting by wood remained the rule. During this period France was cut off to a considerable extent from English technological developments and did not know of the 'puddling' process for decarbonizing iron through coke-smelting, invented by Cort in 1784. After the peace of 1815 French industrialists visited Britain and returned with information about the latest processes. In 1819 some of them adopted the 'puddling' process — Wendel in Lorraine, Manby and Wilson in Le Creusot. Yet even in the middle of the nineteenth century only one French foundry in four used 'puddling' and rolling. Important progress was made during the Second Empire with the adoption of the Bessemer converter and the reduction process of Siemens and Martin. But the 'steel revolution' in France only arrived with the Gilchrist—Thomas method in 1878 which lessened the difficulties of treating iron ores with a high phosphorus content such as are found in the iron fields of Lorraine.

Technological progress had been slow, especially if compared with the progress made in England after the middle of the eighteenth century. According to Charles Ballot the years 1780—92 were 'years of effort, of scattered initiatives without any attempt at overall planning, and which whilst changing some methods of production, made no profound impact on the character of the economy as a whole'. According to the American A. L. Dunham the period of the Revolution and Empire was one of stagnation and 'the period 1815—48 marked the first phase of the industrial revolution in France but not the period of its fullest development, which began only after 1860'. But even after 1860 the difference had not been made up. According to Rondo Cameron 'between 1815 and 1914 total real income and individual incomes rose slower in France than in any other large industrial nation.

The same holds true in respect of the formation of capital, industrial production and other indices of economic growth'.

It is difficult to discover the various and probably numerous causes of what had been called French 'industrial retardation'. One cause seems to have been the reluctance of certain factory owners to use coal, at least in the early stages of the industrial revolution. In the eighteenth century foundry owners did not accept the need to abandon the use of wood and replace it by coal. Forest owners undoubtedly put pressure on the government to prevent the importation of foreign coal, and thus to defend their own financial interests. French coal was generally difficult to mine — it was, on the whole, a more costly process than in England. Before the construction of the railways the cost of transport made coal expensive and limited its use and this was the most important factor preventing its more widespread adoption. During the time of the Restoration transport costs raised the price from eight to ten times what it was at the pit head. Towards the end of the nineteenth century the average price of coal per metric ton was 12 francs in France. In Germany it was 9.16 francs, in England 8.6 francs and the USA 5.69 francs.

Historians have frequently emphasized the important role of the state in the industrial revolution. At the end of the eighteenth century the government encouraged the diffusion of technical improvements, often sending French industrialists to England to study new processes. The French government even encouraged industrial espionage. In the nineteenth century an active contribution was made by the administration, and in particular by the *Corps des Ponts et Chaussés* (Administration of Bridges and Roads) and the *Service des Mines* (Mining Authority). The concern of the state to do something underlines the indifference of the greater majority of French entrepreneurs towards innovations. This is sometimes ascribed to their spirit of individualism — a spirit found among all those involved in the economy, from the head of an industrial enterprise to the lowest worker. The origins of this 'spirit of individualism' still prevalent in the nineteenth century were old and were characteristic of a not very distant peasant past.

Some historians consider that the protectionist customs system — which was strengthened by the laws of 1821—2 was a kind of cancerous growth on the economy which damaged both the export and the home market, and discouraged progress and initiative. But others consider it did not impede innovation and that the bolder entrepreneurs were enabled to develop their experiments under the shelter of the protectionist system. There is more agreement over the serious effects of lack of investment. There was plenty of capital available for investment in productive enterprise. But savings were more usually invested in state loans or loans to local bodies, for housing schemes and, more frequently, for the purchase of land. Land had two attractions: firstly it was considered to be a safe investment, and secondly it brought with it increased social status. During the second half of the nineteenth century holders of capital placed some of it abroad. Investments in landed property, or in annuities, although yielding less, were preferred to industrial investments. On the other hand others preferred foreign debentures, which although more risky, could yield much more.

The French financial system did not favour investments either. During the nineteenth century the level of state revenue and state expenditure per head was higher in France than in any other country. This fiscal system might have been justified if some of the revenue had been used to promote economic development, but the costs of raising the revenue proved to be excessive. In 1863, for example, 514 million francs of direct taxes were levied but the wages of the staff of the Ministry of Finance came to 126 million, a quarter of the sum gathered in. This kind of situation revealed the weaknesses caused by far too many civil servants. In addition military expenditure, including repayment of war debts, consumed nearly half of the estimated receipts.

It has been calculated by R. E. Cameron that between 1820 and 1900 investments in industry and agriculture did not exceed 50—60,000 million francs — an annual average of 600 million. Cameron maintains that the growth of French industry lagged behind the growths of the industry of its neighbours because of this lack of investment. But this lack of investment may have causes of its own. The slow rate of demographic growth did not make the need for investment so apparent, and the technical apparatus necessary for the development of investment hardly existed at the beginning of the nineteenth century. The Paris financial market was only of limited importance. The Bank of France had only functioned in time of war. The law of 1816 which reorganized the stock exchange limited the number of stockbrokers to sixty. Dealings in industrial shares took place outside, and their brokers had no acknowledged legal existence. The issue price of these shares was usually very high (5—10,000 francs). At first the stock exchange concerned itself almost exclusively with government bonds, then with various sorts of insurance, some public services such as the Royal

Transport services and one or two gas companies. Later, under the July Monarchy it quoted the stocks and shares of canals, bridges, the most important coal mining concerns, metallurgical factories, some textile companies and, of course, the railway companies.

Progress had been made by the middle of the nineteenth century, but there was still a long way to go. The Bank of France had managed to overcome popular distrust of its bank notes now circulating throughout the country, but would only rediscount bills if they were less than three months from first issue and only then if guaranteed by the signature of a recognized discount house. The Bank had opted for 'Malthusian conservatism founded on the high price of capital' (Palmade). High finance therefore looked after the placing of state loans, advancing capital towards government stock and therefore not towards commerce and industry. Lafitte had hoped to encourage investment in commerce and industry through the creation of a large association for the financing of industry (*Société commanditaire de l'industrie*) in 1825 whose object would have been 'to contribute funds towards and have an interest in the success of any enterprise and any invention and any method of improving industry, agriculture and commerce'. But this project did not receive the necessary governmental authorization. Lafitte revived the idea in 1837 by creating a bank for commerce and industry (*Caisse générale pour le Commerce et l'Industrie*) which had several imitators in Paris and the rest of France. But none of them weathered the crisis of 1848 and they disappeared with that crisis.

Decisive progress in the liberation of capital was made under the Second Empire. High finance began to make long term investments in industry but the most important factor was the appearance of new banking establishments. The *Crédit Mobilier*, set up in 1852, was an investment bank which aimed at mobilizing French capital through bonds open to public subscription, and the capital would then be placed at the service of commerce and industry. It had some success, but disappeared along with the Empire in 1870. Deposit banks however became more firmly established. There were several such as the *Comptoir d'Escompte de Paris* (which became a private bank in 1853); the *Crédit industriel et commercial* (1859); the *Crédit Lyonnais* (1863) and the *Société Générale* (1864). These developed short-term credit but also went in for more ambitious transactions which were not without dangers, as several crises were to reveal. Commercial banks, which were rather better equipped to deal with long-term financing of industrial enterprises, appeared a little later: the *Banque de Paris et des Pays Bas* (1872); the *Banque Parisienne* (1874, becoming the *Union Parisienne* in

1904); the *Banque de l'Indochine* (1875) and the *Banque Française pour le commerce et l'industrie* (1901).

At the end of the nineteenth century France was therefore armed with a satisfactory banking system and a mass of available capital. Yet for various reasons the tendency was for this capital to be invested abroad, and not in national enterprises. External investments represented 25 per cent of total investments in 1880, and on the eve of the first world war stood at 45 per cent. There were undoubtedly economic and political advantages to be derived from such investments but it is possible that this heavy export of capital explains in large measure the slow development of French industry, depriving it of the possibility of maintaining its previous rate of growth and of keeping up with the rate reached by the rest of the European powers, not to mention the USA. The problem of 'growth' must be analysed a little more.

Economic growth

Research into the growth of the French economy is only just beginning and is handicapped by weakness in the means of measuring economic growth. One possible way of doing this is to study the development of the national income. This has been done by F. Perroux. It is impossible to plot the national income in a chronological series because there is no one single source from which to derive information. But by using the views of contemporaries on the question in conjunction with the partially continuous series of estimates they drew up themselves, it is possible to achieve an outline of its development. On the whole the national income seems to have grown at an even rate between 1789 and 1914. It seems to have doubled between 1789 and 1850, increasing from 5,000 million to 10,000 million; it doubled again between 1850 and 1880 and only seems to have increased by half between 1880 and 1914. For the whole period 1789–1914 annual growth of national income seems to lie at slightly less than 2 per cent.

Since the first world war its development has been much less even. The series of figures worked out by Sauvy (national revenue calculated in fixed francs) show that the pre-war level was only regained in 1923. From 1923 to 1929 it grew by 38 per cent: from 1930 to 1936 a fall of 18 per cent reduced it to the 1924 level. From 1936 to the war the national income stagnated and then slumped until 1944. The 1938 level was only regained ten years later. After this there was a vigorous development which raised the national income to a very high level: between 1948 and 1960 the national income almost doubled (85 per cent). It doubled again between 1960 and 1970.

Fig. I.10   Estimates of national revenue

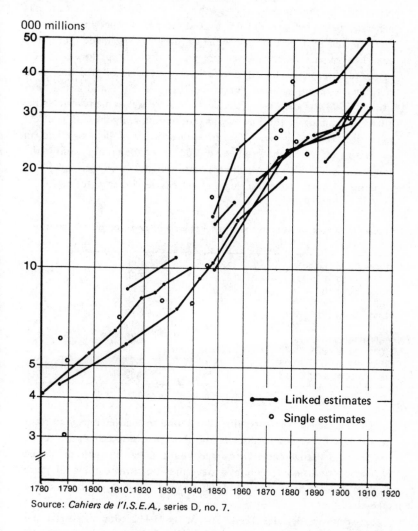

000 millions

Source: *Cahiers de l'I.S.E.A.*, series D, no. 7.

J. Marczewski's recent study of the growth of the economy again uses composite sources and sources of unequal value, and these difficulties obviously affect the reliability of his conclusions, but these conclusions do allow the question of growth to be studied more closely. The growth of national domestic output has been estimated by calculating the agricultural output and the industrial output averaged out over ten year periods.

The data of the gross primary agricultural product have been calculated by volume. The growth of agricultural production has generally been slow and did not exceed 1.5 per cent per annum during any one ten year period. The quickest progress was made during the first half of the nineteenth century; but after the period 1855–64 agricultural growth slowed down, largely because of overseas competition. A severe agrarian depression began in 1873 and lasted until around 1896. At the end of the century there was some revival lasting till the beginning of the first world war, undoubtedly due to the effect of a protectionist policy. Yet this protectionist policy also had an enervating effect on the productive capacity of the country and in the long term slowed down French economic growth as a whole.

Gross national manufacturing product has developed as follows:

Table I.6 Annual growth rate (geometric) of gross domestic product & industry and handicraft

1781–90 to 1803–12	(22 yrs)	1.98
1803–12 to 1825–34	(22 yrs)	2.86
1825–34 to 1835–44	(10 yrs)	3.52
1835–44 to 1845–54	(10 yrs)	2.45
1845–54 to 1855–64	(10 yrs)	2.76
1855–64 to 1865–74	(10 yrs)	2.72
1865–74 to 1875–84	(10 yrs)	2.75
1875–84 to 1885–94	(10 yrs)	2.20
1885–94 to 1895–1904	(10 yrs)	2.47
1895–1904 to 1905–13	(9.5 yrs)	2.85

An analysis of these results allows one to answer one important question: to use the expression of the American economist W. W. Rostow, did France experience an economic 'take-off' which marks the passing of traditional economic structures and the coming of more modern ones, where industry predominated? And if so, when did it take place?

Between the decades 1781–90 and 1803–12 total industrial and artisanal output increased by an annual amount of around 2 per cent (1.98), between 1803–12 and 1825–34 the average had reached 2.86 per cent, and between 1825 and 1835–44, 3.52 per cent. Therefore the rate of growth in this latter period is the greater, and it would seem that a 'take-off' took place around 1830. Yet Marczewski does not take this view himself, and comments, 'One must not forget that the curve which represents the growth of output in the periods 1781–90 and 1803–12 is actually a 'U' shape, whose minimum point corresponds to about the year 1796. The rate of growth of industrial output between 1796 and 1812 is thus much faster than the average rate for the whole period and must reach an annual rate of around 3 per cent, which is quite comparable with the rates reached in the periods which follow. According to these figures therefore the first forty years of the nineteenth century are a consistent period of rapid industrial growth of between 3 and 3.5 per cent per annum. At first the cotton and silk industries were the 'motive industries', the nerve centre of industry as a whole. That is to say they were important from the point of view of their relative share in industry as a whole and because they had a high rate of growth. They still held this vital position in industry in the period after 1825, but after this date the coalmining and the

Fig. I.11   Growth of national revenue since 1901 (*in fixed francs*)

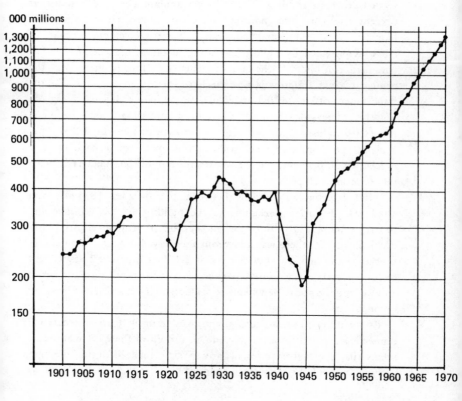

metallurgical industries began to assert themselves and the metal processing industries began to appear among the 'motive industries'. The setting up and equipping of an extremely important metallurgical industry between 1825 and 1830 led to the re-equipment of the older textile industries and gave the French economy a powerful stimulus.

Between the decades 1835—44 and 1845—54 the rate of growth of gross industrial output fell to 2.45 per cent. The cotton industry was no longer a 'motive' power in industry. Silk still was, though its rate had slowed up. A newcomer, the chemical industry, announced its presence by a very high growth rate (15 per cent) although its relative weight was still light. Headway was still being made in the coalmining and metallurgical industries but the tempo of production was moderate. 'All in all', comments Marczewski, 'this was a period of transition between the period of expansion of the cotton and silk industries now losing its momentum and the development of the railways, which had its full effect only after the 1850s.'

Between the decades 1845—54 and 1875—84 the rate of growth settled down to about 2.7 per cent per annum. The textile industries (except the new jute industry) were no longer motive powers in industry. The building and food industries were developing because of stimulus provided by rapidly increasing incomes; the chemical industries had consolidated the progress they had already made. But the principal agent of growth was the construction of the railways: the importance of those industries whose activities depended on the railways increased strikingly. Coalmining, metallurgy and the metal processing industries reached a rate of growth of between 3 and 6 per cent; the production of steel, still in its infancy, even reached a rate of more than 10 per cent, and the working of non-ferrous metals reached a rate of around 20 per cent.

After a downward trend between the decades 1875—84 and 1885—94, due to a slackening in the building of the railways and general economic depression, when the rate of growth fell to 2.2 per cent per annum, there was a vigorous recovery during the two decades preceding the first world war: rates of 2.47 per cent and 2.85 per cent respectively. This was caused by expansion of the mechanical industries and the appearance of new industries, amongst them artificial fibres and rayon.

By combining the agricultural and maufacturing figures the national domestic output may be calculated. As a result of these calculations, it seems that the highest rates of growth were realized during the first seventy years of the nineteenth century and during the period 1896 to

1913. The agricultural depression seems largely responsible for the slowing down of growth between 1875 and 1896, since industrial output only slackened after 1885. The decades of highest growth occurred between 1825−34 and 1835−44, between 1845−54 and 1855−64 and between 1895−1904 and 1905−13. These peaks of acceleration occurred at times which contemporary opinion regarded as periods of particularly rapid development; the early years of the July Monarchy and of the Second Empire and the 'Belle Epoque' of the 1900s.

The first world war had not only an immediate slowing down effect on the rate of growth but also had a more lastingly destructive impact. The pre-war level of growth was only regained in 1923 − for example in 1919 it was only about half of what it had been in 1913. But the period from 1923 to 1930 was a period of vigorous growth − 1.8 per cent in agriculture and 4 per cent in industry. 'France stood at the head of European industrial development. These results were not only caused by French economic vitality, but also by stagnation in Great Britain and the relatively slow recovery of Germany.' (F. Walter)

But this distinguished era was followed by one of disaster. 'The international crisis of 1929 reached France later than other countries but its effects were longer-lasting. In 1938 the total steel production for ninety *départements* was lower than it had been in 1913.' Metal processing was at a rate barely 2 per cent more than in 1913 and textile production had fallen by 17 per cent since that date. For industry as a whole there was a decline of 14 per cent whereas in the rest of Europe there was a rise of some 25 per cent. (Walter)

There was a slow decline in production during the second world war and the period of German occupation: in 1945 the yield of the harvest was less than 60 per cent of its pre-war level and industrial production scarcely reached 55 per cent of its 1938 figure. Besides, industrial equipment tended to be worn or out of date − some of it needed replacing, some had not been properly maintained. The shortfall of investment in the ten years preceding the war only helped to worsen this situation.

The Monnet Plan

But the new economic policy pursued after the liberation of France made a notable impact on economic growth. The plans (starting with the Monnet Plan, 1957−61, followed by a series of plans for modernization of plants and production methods) have gone all out for economic growth, with a policy of massive and judiciously applied investment, fiscal and budgetary action, and systematic intervention over prices to encourage industrial productivity. After concentrating initially on the re-establishment of the key sectors, coal, electricity, oil, iron and other mining, the planners went on to deal with basic industrial products, iron products, cement, the chemical industry. Finally they moved on to the manufacturing and processing industries, especially the emergent, rapidly developing ones such as electronics, radio, artificial fibres, plastics. In every case the *Commissariat du Plan* used only tact and persuasion on sometimes rather hidebound management and employees alike, making no demands, only suggestions, with the sole aim of expanding production, helping by the injection of capital, to modernize plant and lower costs. Gradually the norms and quotas progressively set by the Plan came to be accepted by the main branches of national industry because they found it paid them to do so. Gradually the employers, resentful of any sort of control, came to accept the 'new order' and learned to subordinate notions of immediate profit to long term plans conducive to industrial growth and hence to national advantage. At the same time the members of the *Administration du Plan*, few in number but highly intelligent and dynamic, were stepping up their support of scientific and technological research as the basis of their policy of modernization and expansion.

By 1947 industrial production had reached the 1938 level; by 1949 it had even equalled the record year 1929. Since 1949 the annual rate of increase has reached 6 per cent per year — an entirely new phenomenon in France. Possibly the 'take-off' of the economy usually placed during the first half of the nineteenth century could more satisfactorily be placed around the year 1950. The consequence of the increased importance of industry in the gross national product, of accelerated technical progress and the policy of development pursued by the government may have an enormous effect on the future development of French society.

documentation

Table I.7 French population growth since 1791

Year of census	Total (in 000s)	Total increase	Annual increase per 100 inhabitants
1791	27 190		0.005
1801	27 350	160	0.56
1821	30 462	3 112	0.69
1831	32 569	2 107	0.59
1836	33 541	972	0.41
1841	34 230	689	0.68
1846	35 400	1 170	0.21
1851	35 783	383	0.14
1856	36 039	256	0.74
1861 (a)	37 386	1 347	0.36
1866	38 067	681	
1872 (b)	36 103		0.55
1876	36 906	803	0.41
1831	37 672	766	0.29
1886	38 219	547	0.06
1891	38 343	124	0.09
1896	38 518	175	0.23
1901	38 962	444	0.15
1906	39 252	290	0.18
1911	39 605	353	
1921 (c)	39 210		
1926	40 744	1 534	0.78
1931	41 835	1 091	0.53
1936 (d)	41 907	72	0.03
1946	40 503		
1954	42 777	2 274	0.70
1962	47 558	4 781	0.80
1968	50 105	2 547	0.70

(a) Including Nice and Savoy (669 000 inhabitants).
(b) Without Alsace and Lorraine (1 500 000 inhabitants).
(c) Including Alsace and Lorraine (1 710 000 inhabitants).
(d) An overestimation of about 400 000 (200 000 for Bouches du Rhône, 100 000 for Rhône and 100 000 for Corsica).

Table I.8 Marriages, births, deaths, 1806—1969

	Mean annual total (in thousands)				Totals per 10 000 of population			
	Marriages	Children born living	Deaths	Excess of births over deaths	Marriages	Children born living	Deaths	Excess of births over deaths
1806—10	229.0	921.9	767.5	+154.4	157	317	263	+54
1811—15	250.5	930.7	789.3	+141.4	171	317	269	+48
1816—20	218.5	955.1	757.0	+198.1	146	319	253	+66
1821—25	240.3	971.8	765.2	+206.6	155	314	247	+67
1826—30	254.3	976.6	815.5	+161.1	159	305	255	+50
1831—35	259.7	975.0	856.2	+118.8	158	296	260	+36
1836—40	273.0	959.4	799.8	+159.6	162	284	237	+47
1841—45	282.3	976.0	786.0	+190.0	163	281	227	+54
1846—50	277.6	949.6	848.3	+101.3	156	267	239	+28
1851—55	280.6	939.8	867.2	+72.6	156	261	241	+20
1856—60	294.9	967.4	866.2	+101.2	162	266	238	+28
1861—65	301.8	1 004.9	861.7	+143.2	160	267	229	+38
1866—70	291.0	998.8	934.0	+64.8	152	261	244	+17
1871—75	320.7	981.0	949.6	+31.4	169	258	250	+8
1876—80	292.3	993.6	874.2	+119.4	151	257	226	+31
1881—85	294.3	983.8	879.4	+104.4	149	250	223	+27
1886—90	286.3	930.0	879.4	+50.6	143	233	221	+12
1891—95	297.9	905.6	893.9	+11.7	149	226	223	+3
1896—1900	305.3	899.6	835.1	+64.5	151	222	206	+16
1901—05	312.2	883.5	800.9	+82.6	153	216	196	+20
1906—10	323.6	833.4	787.3	+46.1	157	202	191	+11
1911—15	250.0	721.5	891.1	−169.6	121	174	215	−41
1916—20	336.5	519.8	868.5	−348.7	171	132	221	−89
1921—25	380.7	771.2	686.6	+84.6	191	193	172	+21
1926—30	339.4	748.1	690.0	+58.1	165	182	168	+14
1931—35	308.0	690.2	658.4	+31.8	147	165	157	+8
1936—40	252.7	606.5	684.3	−77.8	121	145	159	−14
1941—45	262.0	595.0	673.0	−78.0	133	151	171	−20
1946—50	397.4	860.1	537.2	+332.9	194	210	131	+79
1951—55	313.8	810.4	534.9	+275.5	147	190	126	+64
1956—60	311.0	813.0	518.0	+295.0	139	182	116	+66
1961—65	333.0	852.2	529.1	+323.1	140	179	111	+68
1966—69	355.6	842.5	546.2	+296.3	143	169	110	+59

Table I.9 Foreigners in France

| Year | Legal population or habitual residents | | Actual population | | | |
| | | | Foreigners | | Naturalized | |
	Thousands	Totals per 10 000 inhabitants	Thousands	Totals per 10 000 inhabitants	Thousands	Totals per 10 000 inhabitants
1851	379	106				
1861	506	135				
1866	655	172				
1872	741	205				
1876	802	218				
1881	1 000	266	1 001	267	77	21
1886	1 115	292	1 127	297	104	28
1891	1 102	287	1 130	297	171	45
1896	1 027	267	1 052	275	203	53
1901	1 038	267	1 034	269	222	59
1906	1 009	156	1 047	270	222	57
1911	1 133	286	1 160	296	253	64
1921	1 550	396	1 532	395	254	66
1926	2 505	615	2 409	599	249	62
1931	2 891	691	2 715	658	361	88
1936	2 454	585	2 198	534	517	125
1946	1 672	412	1 685	424	853	214
1954	1 452	340	1 558	364	1 082	253
1962			2 170	456	1 284	276
1968			2 664	531	1 316	262

Table I.10 Population movement in the Paris region

Census years	Districts included in the boundaries fixed before the revision of 1860	Suburban *communes* absorbed in 1860	Total population of Paris and of former suburbs	*Département* of the Seine
1801	546 856			631 585
1811	622 636			
1817	713 966			
1831	785 866	75 574	861 440	935 108
1836	899 313	103 320	1 002 633	
1841	936 261	124 564	1 059 825	1 194 603
1846	1 053 897	173 083	1 226 980	1 364 467
1851	1 053 261	223 802	1 277 063	1 422 065
1856	1 174 346	364 257	1 538 603	1 727 419
1861			1 696 141	1 953 660
1866			1 825 274	2 150 916
1872			1 851 792	2 220 060
1876			1 988 806	2 410 849
1881			2 269 023	2 799 329
1886			2 344 550	2 961 089
1891			2 447 957	2 141 595
1896			2 536 834	3 340 514
1901			2 714 068	3 669 930
1906			2 763 400	3 848 618
1911			2 888 100	4 154 042
1921			2 906 500	4 411 691
1926			2 871 400	4 628 637
1931			2 891 000	4 933 855
1936			2 829 746	4 962 967
1946			2 725 374	4 775 711
1954			2 850 189	5 154 834
1962			2 753 014	5 575 288
1968			2 590 771	6 424 751

Source: L. CHEVALIER, *La Formation de la population parisienne au XIX*e, (Paris, Presses Universitaires de France) p. 284; *Annuaire de la France*, (Paris, Presses Universitaires de France, 1961).

Table I.11 Relative population of *communes* in 1968

	Number of *communes*		Population of *communes*	
	Actual	As percentage of all	Actual	As percentage of all
100 000 and more	37	0.1	9 641 471	19.0
80 000 less than 100 000	10	ϵ	897 750	1.8
50 000 less than 80 000	50	0.1	3 043 475	6.0
30 000 less than 50 000	100	0.3	3 911 758	7.7
20 000 less than 30 000	137	0.4	3 347 322	6.6
10 000 less than 20 000	345	0.9	4 713 885	9.3
9 000 less than 10 000	69	0.2	652 492	1.3
6 000 less than 9 000	327	0.9	2 380 872	4.7
5 000 less than 6 000	246	0.6	1 342 895	2.6
4 000 less than 5 000	312	0.8	1 381 232	2.7
3 500 less than 4 000	234	0.6	870 046	1.7
3 000 less than 3 500	331	0.9	1 068 283	2.1
2 500 less than 3 000	392	1.0	1 071 161	2.1
2 000 less than 2 500	669	1.8	1 487 233	2.9
1 500 less than 2 000	1 134	3.0	1 948 196	3.8
1 000 less than 1 500	2 484	6.6	2 991 699	5.9
700 less than 1 000	2 860	7.6	2 359 360	4.6
500 less than 700	3 964	10.5	2 316 167	4.6
400 less than 500	2 776	7.4	1 233 312	2.4
300 less than 400	4 018	10.7	1 387 331	2.7
200 less than 300	5 822	15.4	1 428 675	2.8
100 less than 200	7 514	19.9	1 111 813	2.2
50 less than 100	2 895	7.7	221 049	0.4
Less than 50	982	2.6	33 100	0.1
TOTAL	37 708	100.0	50 840 577	100.0

Source: 1968 census.

Fig. I.12   Nineteenth-century migration to Paris

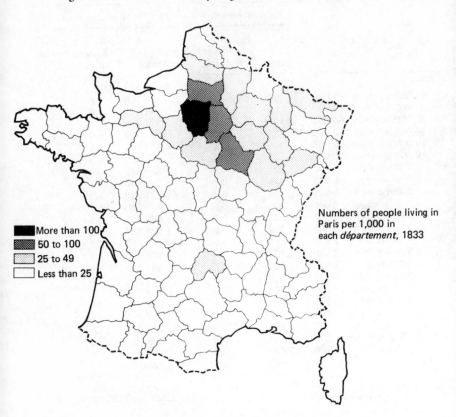

More than 100
50 to 100
25 to 49
Less than 25

Numbers of people living in
Paris per 1,000 in
each *département*, 1833

Fig. I.13   Nineteenth-century migration to Paris

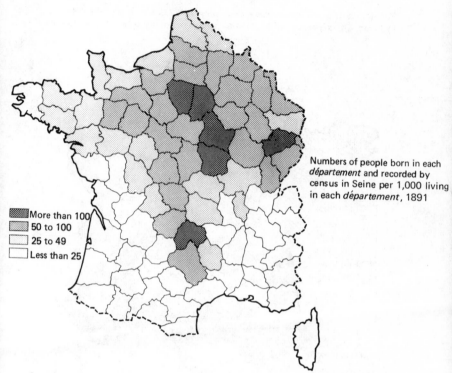

Numbers of people born in each *département* and recorded by census in Seine per 1,000 living in each *département*, 1891

More than 100
50 to 100
25 to 49
Less than 25

Source: L. Chevalier, *La Formation de la population parisienne au XIXe siècle.*

Fig. I.14   Size of urban population in 1968

Population of urban *communes* (*communes* with 2,000 or more inhabitants included with *département* capitals) as percentage of *département* populations

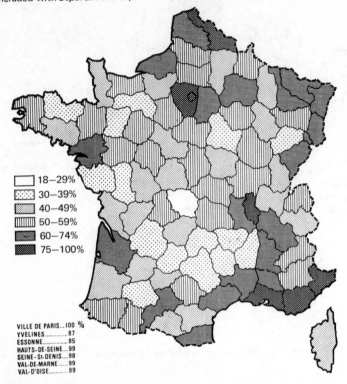

18—29%
30—39%
40—49%
50—59%
60—74%
75—100%

VILLE DE PARIS...100 %
YVELINES...........87
ESSONNE..........85
HAUTS-DE-SEINE...99
SEINE-St-DENIS....98
VAL-DE-MARNE......99
VAL-D'OISE..........89

Fig. I.15 The growth of French agricultural production in fixed francs (*base: 100 in 1892*), *logarithmic scale*

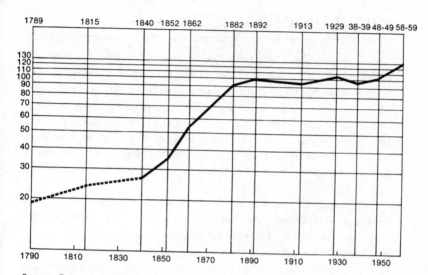

Source: Pautard, *Les Disparités régionales dans la croissance de l'agriculture française*, p. 41.

II French society at the end of the Ancien Régime

Although the monarchy of the Ancien Régime proclaimed the juridical sovereignty of the state, the clergy, the nobility, the bourgeoisie and various other bodies all had autonomous juridical systems of their own. The monarchy made little headway, even when exerting itself, in eliminating these. There were various sorts of law: canon law, feudal law, manorial law, guild laws and collective obligations in rural areas, many of which existed side by side. In the society of the Ancien Régime men were neither born 'free', nor were they born 'with equal rights'.

Privilege and custom were the basis of that society. There were privileges everywhere: the 'estates' or 'orders' had privileges; the provinces had certain 'immunities' or privileges; there were corporate privileges (some office holders in the judiciary or in finance were exempt from the *taille* and guilds had the monopoly of a particular rade or manufacture); there were privileges attached to a place of abode (the right of *bourgeoisie* carried with it certain fiscal exemptions). All these meant that there was a considerable amount of inequality; that society was compartmentalized and that France was 'divided territorially and socially'.

1. The vertical structure of society — a society of 'orders'

French society at the end of the eighteenth century still kept many of its original features, and in particular the idea which persisted that the owners of land (that is to say, in effect, the wealthy, since the real source of wealth was still land) were the masters of those who worked it and lived by their work on it. These landowners had been deprived by the monarch of all political power (except certain rights in the exercise of justice) but had managed to retain their privileges. The clergy had similarly been subjected to royal authority, yet in effect maintained a surprising degree of independence and were subject to their own corpus of law. Those belonging to neither of these two 'orders' were the third estate (*tiers état*). The 'society of orders' thus consisted of the clergy, (the first estate), the nobility, (the second estate) and the rest, (the third estate). Custom had hardened these divisions and the distinction based on the three 'orders' or 'estates' had become a fundamental law.

The clergy

The clergy was the first order in the state and had very extensive privileges. First, it had honorific privileges which gave it precedence over the other orders. The article 'Clergé' in the *Encyclopedié* commented 'The clergy has precedence over every layman, over the *parlements* and other secular courts, in church and all religious processions and ceremonies. In political assemblies ... the clergy precedes the nobility and the third estate, and has the right to speak first in deputations to the King ...'. It had judicial privileges, having its own courts, the *officialités*. In addition it had fiscal privileges since it paid no taxes direct to the government and it was even able to determine itself the amount of taxation it did pay. This was the 'free gift' which it granted to the king every five years. It even had its own assembly – the only order to have one – which met every five years and in addition had its own administration, the *Agence Genérale*. It was therefore the most honoured, the least weighed down with imposed taxation and the best organized of the orders.

It was also a very rich order, with wealth derived from several sources: first, the *dîme* (tithe) which it levied on produce from the land. The *dîme* affected everyone – all property, even the King's. It was levied on the actual produce of the land, (*grosse dîme* on grains; *menue dîme* on the other produce) so that the value of the *dîme* was linked with the yield and price of agricultural produce, and therefore varied from year to year. The amount of the crop actually taken was not exactly one-tenth – sometimes one sheaf in twelve or less. The average over the whole country was probably one-thirteenth and the annual revenue derived from this source, amounted on average to 100 million livres. The Church therefore profited from rises in food prices since it was always assured of the same percentage of the crop.

About the same amount of income was derived from the second source of revenue, landed poperty – property owned by the clergy in both town and country. In the towns, the clergy and especially the regular clergy owned many tenement houses, enclosed plots and gardens, but the actual extent of this property remains unknown; the extent of rural property is little better known: it was not as extensive as contemporaries often claimed. In some regions it was considerable (as much as 40 per cent of all land in the Cambrésis): in the west and in mountainous areas the amount was small and in the south it was negligible. Overall it probably did not exceed 10 per cent. These lands do not seem to have been well looked after or well-cultivated and did not therefore yield a great deal of revenue. The under-exploitation of these lands strengthened and even, on the grounds of general utility, justified the covetous looks which were cast on them.

A third source of revenue was the *droit de casuel:* fees received for services rendered, such as registration of births and deaths, revenue from offertories and endowments. The actual value of this revenue is difficult to estimate but was certainly lower in the countryside than in the towns.

Yet it must be remembered that the clergy had to meet certain financial obligations. The heaviest of these was the *don gratuit;* the free gift, which by the end of the eighteenth century was averaging 6 million livres per annum, and the interest on the loan for the Hôtel de Ville which it paid on behalf of the state, which totalled nearly half a million livres. Some of the revenue was used to maintain places of worship, although parish authorities might give some aid towards this. The clergy also had an important function in the organization of charity: poor relief, distribution of alms, and the running of hospitals. Yet in times of extreme crisis the state might also do something for the poor, such as in organizing work in the form of the *ateliers de charité*, exercising a kind of general control over charitable institutions and founding new institutions for the poor and sick (*hospices*).

The clergy were also in charge of certain public services such as the keeping of the registration of births, marriages and deaths. They supervised public schools maintained by parishes and private schools run by individuals; they heavily subsidized schools in poor parishes; and they founded schools. Some clergy were exclusively devoted to teaching, the Frères des Écoles Chrétiennes (called 'Ignorantins' because they did not teach Latin), the Lazaristes, and for girls, the Ursulines. Secondary schools were largely under the care of monastic communities: at first the Jesuits, later the Oratorians and the Benedictines. Subjects taught were largely the humanities, classics and mathematics and they produced in their pupils clear thinking and experience in the art of speaking. The orators of the French Revolution were products of these schools.

In return for the contribution it made to the monarch he, for his part, gave the Church aid and protection. Roman Catholicism was the only religion recognized by the state and since the Revocation of the Edict of Nantes the only Church officially allowed to hold services. The King had to expurgate heresy and on the day of his anointing and coronation swore to do this. It was his duty to see that religious instruction was on orthodox lines and for this used censorship. Royal censorship was confined to the *Direction de la Librairie*.

The Sorbonne (which was at that time the Faculty of Theology) could also censor books, as could the *parlements*. Crime against religion such as blasphemy and sacrilege was punished. The King had to make sure that religion was being observed and that religious festivals were being respected by enforcing Sunday rest, by nominating representatives in religious processions, and by forbidding the sale of meat during Lent. He ensured that the Church hierarchy was respected by putting his own right of constraint at the service of the bishops. The bishops could send recalcitrant clerics into a monastery for three months without giving any reason and with the aid of the public authorities.

The clergy was not a united order — it was, according to the article 'Clergé' in the *Encyclopédie*, 'a body of individuals dedicated to God by either religious faith or because of being in holy orders. In England a distinction is made between upper and lower clergy. The same situation exists in Fance, but the names are different. In France they are called the first and second orders.'

There were almost equal numbers of regular and secular clergy: about 70,000 male secular clerics, and about 60,000 regular clerics, male and female. They only amounted to about 0.5 per cent of the total population. There was considerable disproportion in the numbers of upper and lower clergy. Heads of monastic establishments, bishops and cathedral canons amounted to less than 4,000, whereas there were over 125,000 lower clergy.

The number of regular clergy had declined during the eighteenth century. Public opinion was generally hostile to them. Recruitment, especially of men, was becoming increasingly difficult. The attacks of writers such as Voltaire had done the reputations of the monasteries harm: the monastic life was regarded by many as fruitless and purposeless and so therefore were lifelong vows. The suppression of the Jesuits led the General Assembly of French clergy to reform the rest of the regular orders in 1765. A Commission for Reform was still working in 1789 and some of its reforms, by raising the age of men taking perpetual vows to twenty-one and women to eighteen and by suppressing some monastic communities, reduced the number of monks and nuns by several thousand. In 1790 there were, according to different sources, 18,000-23,000 monks and 37,000 nuns. The physical and moral condition of the regular clergy as a whole was also in need of reform. Physical, because the King donated to most of the monasteries and all too frequently his choice fell not on the rightful recipients, the monks, but 'in commission' either to prelates to increase their income, or to just anyone who had a tonsure, generally a nobleman. Such 'in commendam' abbots pocketed half or two-thirds of the revenue, leaving only what was left for the upkeep of the monks. Moral, because within the monasteries discipline was often slack — especially in men's 'communities' and in the contemplative and mendicant orders. Only the new communities of women involved in teaching or in charity escaped the discredit which had fallen on their fellows, and of which one reads so much in the *cahiers de doléances.*

The upper secular clergy comprised the 138 archbishops and bishops (the three bishops of Corsica were subordinate to the Archbishop of Pisa), and 2,800 coadjutors, vicars-general and cathedral canons. In the seventeenth century some commoners, most notably Bossuet, had managed to penetrate the ranks of the upper clergy but this was no longer possible in the eighteenth century — the upper clergy was a closed shop, and practically a preserve of the upper nobility. Certain families managed to collect several such dignities. On the eve of the Revolution, among the bishops there were three members of the La Rochefoucauld family, two of the Rohan family, two of the Cicé family and four of the Castellane family. For the younger sons of these families entry into the upper clergy presented few problems. 'Deacon, then abbot; two years a priest, then vicar-general, then bishop'. Talleyrand complained when he was thirty-four that he was not yet a bishop, but he became one at the age of thirty-five. The office of vicar-general was intended to serve as training for candidates to bishoprics, but they learned little, since a bishop often appointed as many as fifteen or twenty vicars-general whose company might alleviate the boredom of the visits he was obliged to make to his diocese; they were men from the same social background. But the administration of the diocese was left to those keen to do it and to commoners, such as the abbé Sieyès, or the abbé Maury, if they could be found. The bishops' style of living depended on their incomes, and has, of course been the subject of exaggeration. It was said that their income was 100,000, 200,000, 300,000 and even 800,000 livres. This was perhaps not true of all of them, but some had vast wealth — notably, Brienne of Toulouse, Dillon of Hautefontaine and above all Rohan of Saverne. Some of these bishops were diligent and carried out their duties conscientiously. Boisgelin, the Archbishop of Aix and a significant Church leader at the time of the Revolution, owed his reputation to the dignity of his way of life and his unerring faith, but the less serious, even 'showy' clerics were typical of all in the public imagination. These were the bishops who led a worldly court life and were absent from their dioceses, where they would leave administrators — popularly called 'boy-bishops' — in their place; they rarely preached, seldom administered the sacraments and rarely bothered to make pastoral visitations to their parish priests whom, in any case, they held in contempt. 'I am in the throes,' wrote one, 'of visiting these brothers, these teachers of the people, whom I heap with compliments. Fénelon's sort of talk is all very well, but these people hardly understand any of the nice things one may say to them. They are coarse, dirty, ignorant, and to enjoy the company of these mediators between heaven and earth one has to be very fond of the pestilential stink of garlic'.

The condition of the 60,000 parish-priests, curates and other secular clergy was by no means the same as that of their superiors. Their family background was quite different: most came from plebeian backgrounds, from the middle classes in the towns, and from the peasantry and lower middle classes in the countryside. Their education reflected the low standards of seminary teaching. Their standard of living was inferior. There is of course the traditional picture contrasting rich, well-heeled, idle, pleasure-seeking high clerics and idle monks with lower clergy devoted to their parishioners, dwelling in pious poverty: a picture often encountered in the *cahiers de doléances*. Recent studies considerably modify this view, emphasizing the wide divergences to be found in clerical life. Some parish priests were quite well off (some in the pays de Caux, Normandy, had an income of 20,000 livres and in the Medoc the curé of Saint-Estèphe earned 11,000 livres in the years 1772–3, and the curé of Cantenac 13,380) either because their parish was rich and the revenues due to the parish priest were large, or because the tithe was handed over to them intact or because they earned a good income from fees. Recent research shows that between the upper and the lower clergy there was a sizeable middle class capable of playing a major role in times of trouble.

This is not to suggest that there was no clerical poverty. All too often the tithe was farmed off, in the hands of 'gros décimateurs' (middle men) who only allowed the parish priest the *portion congrue*, the 'agreed share', for long fixed at 300 livres, raised to 500 in 1768 and finally to 750 in 1786. These last two sums are not negligible. Increases of this order would have ensured a significant easing of the hardship of working-class life. But parish priests had a different standard of living to maintain (almsgiving, the need for a servant), which is why life was hard for those who lived on the 'agreed share'. The lot of curates, 'a real ecclesiastical proletariat' in the words of Henri Sée, was often pitiable. The majority had no hope of achieving a living and earned no more than the 'agreed share' of 300 livres. Unbeneficed priests who worked for institutions and the fee for an occasional mass were no better off.

Nevertheless the mutual hostility of higher and lower clergy did not arise from the latter's poverty. The resentment felt by parish priests, often very bitter on the eve of the Revolution, sprang from other causes, partly social, partly ideological. The contrast between their way of life and the dazzling pomp of that of numerous prelates offended them; the absenteeism and inefficiency of their bishops shocked them. Often they were motivated by the worry of how better to perform their duties to their flock on the pittance allotted to this primal end; perhaps above all their strongest impulsion came from a kind of strong but unavowed Jansenist hangover: in many dioceses the parish priests wanted to play a more active part in administration. This almost amounted to a desire for ecclesiastical democracy, which in spite of the royal veto of 1782 led to public meetings and the publication of demands. This is why the bishops so often failed to get their own candidates adopted at the election of 1789.

Born of the bourgeoisie the lower clergy were imbued with the ideas of their class. When in 1789 a number of their deputies to the Estates General joined up with those of the Third Estate it was neither accidental, nor the action of a few leading personalities, but simply arose from the logic of the situation.

The nobility

The nobility were only the second estate — yet they were more conscious of their descent and especially of their privileges and rights than the clergy. Sieyès said they were less an order than a profession. Vocation, not birth, was ideally the motive for entering the priesthood: it was a life-long commitment, and as it was a commitment to celibacy the ranks had to be totally renewed every generation. But it was birth that set the nobility apart. It was the nobleman's blood that assured his superiority over the commoner. This superiority was alleged by the theorists of the aristocratic idea to be racial. They claimed that the nobles were the descendants of the Franks, who had established by conquest their feudal rights over the persons and property of the Gallo-Romans, and hence their legal pre-eminence in the state.

Yet this *noblesse de race*, this ancestral nobility (entry to which could be gained only by proving four generations of ancestors) was only a very small proportion of the 'order' as a whole. They had excessive pretensions, but with little justification. The Talleyrands claimed they were descended from Hugh Capet, but yet could only prove that one of their ancestors was ennobled by Francis I. The nobility depended upon ennoblement for its continuance. This could be gained by royal favour, or by the tenure of certain public offices. The King might grant letters of nobility (*lettres d'anoblissement*) which conferred either gradual or personal nobility for life, or in perpetuity. The monarchy thus had at its hands a means of recruiting an élite, but though in the past it had been lavishly used, pressures from the nobility itself had resulted in its near abandonment in the second half of the eighteenth century. In the reign of Louis XVI less than 300 officers, a few engineers and doctors, a handful of merchants, a few industrialists, such as Holker and Oberkampf, and a few bankers were ennobled. The monarchy had missed a chance, one of its last, to adapt the régime to a new era and ensure its survival. Public offices conferring nobility were more numerous.

There were many such positions which brought with them hereditary nobility such as chancellor, keeper of the seals, secretary of state, provincial governor, president of a high court; the highest ranking posts in the magistrature conferred nobility for life, but those posts having themselves become practically hereditary confirmed hereditary nobility on their incumbents. There were, too, the offices of secretary to the king, involving no work, but costing 80,000 livres. These had multiplied (more than 900 according to Necker) and provided another means for commoners who had made their pile to become ennobled – a piece of really high level graft. The same sort of practice applied to the 740 jobs in the finance offices and many municipal jobs as well. Generally speaking, all the above constitute the *noblesse de robe*. There were, too, frequent assumptions of nobility. All one had to do was to acquire noble land, take up the title of the fief, and wait for recognition.

Within this second privileged order the *noblesse d'epée*, the 'nobility of the sword', who liked to think of themselves as blue-blooded, had kept apart from the 'nobility of the robe'. This separateness diminished during the eighteenth century. The 'nobility of the robe' had kept their wealth, which the 'nobility of the sword' had not always succeeded in doing; while frequent marriages between young nobles of high lineage and richly endowed daughters of the 'nobility of the robe' narrowed the gap. Fashionable life in Paris provided constant occasions for the two sides to mix. In the *parlements* the nobility of the robe defended their ancient privileges, and the others showed their gratitude. Both made common cause against reforming policies that threatened their rights. By the eve of the Revolution the widest gap was between court nobility and country nobility but the transition from one to another was blurred by an infinity of tiny gradations.

It is difficult to know how many nobles there were on the eve of the Revolution. Contemporaries varied in their estimates: Sieyès considered there were 110,000; the Marquis de Bouillé suggested 400,000. Perhaps the truth lies between these extremes. Historians now consider there were between 300,000 and 400,000 — between 1.1 and 1.5 per cent of the population.

Yet whatever their origin the various sections of the nobility were united in their attachment to their privileges. The latest creations were frequently the most determined defenders of noble privilege. The extent of these privileges was considerable. They can be divided into two types; honorific and useful. *Honorific* privileges included the right to wear a sword, hunting rights, the right to keep pigeons, the right to a seignorial pew in their parish church. *Useful* privileges included fiscal exemptions — from the *taille*, the poll tax and the *corvée des routes*, the road tax, although the nobility did pay the *capitation* and the *vingtième*; and exemption from the billeting of troops. They also had feudal privileges. Most nobles were *seigneurs*, lords of fiefs, and thus had seignorial rights which were levied on their tenants in kind and as money payments. Money dues were generally the lightest because of the rapid depreciation of money. Some were heavy, such as the rights of *lods et ventes*, levied when property changed hands. Yet the most productive from the point of view of the nobility were dues levied in kind, such as 'field-rent' (*champart*), which were immune to variations in the value of money. The seigneur also imposed the seignorial *corvée* — this represented a duty to provide labour or transport facilities; he also pocketed the dues from dispensing seignorial justice and drew profits from the *banalités*, seignorial monopolies such as mills and wine-presses. The nobility also enjoyed other privileges. By 1789 all the important offices of state were the exclusive preserve of the nobility. The most important ecclesiastical offices and benefices were in the hands of the nobility. And apart from lands held by the peasantry from the noble as lord of a fief the nobility also owned land either cultivated directly or leased out. The amount of actual noble property is not known in detail, but it seems that amounts varied from region to region, from between 9 and 44 per cent of the total. Noble landholding was strong in the west and north, and often around large towns — in the areas around Lille and Toulouse and in Brie. In central and eastern

France the amount was less. It would seem that on average the nobility owned 20 per cent of the land.

The nobility were allowed to cultivate certain of their lands without losing nobility (*dérogeance*[1]). They could even carry on certain profitable professions such as maritime and colonial commerce and working mines, iron and glass works, and some noble families had made a lot of money in industry; so much so that 'some had already achieved a place in an economic *nouveau régime*'. (Goubert) But this was the exception not the rule. Generally the nobility did not profit from the expansion of the economy in the second half of the eighteenth century. Often the nobility were adversely affected by the rise in the cost of living. They reacted, not only by hanging on to their privileges, but also by trying to enhance them. This 'aristocratic reaction' took various forms.

First, there was a tightening up of feudal dues. Those previously neglected were revived and levied, sometimes including twenty-nine years of arrears, falling within a thirty-year statutory period. Old land registers which listed these dues were brought up to date by valuers who specialized in this kind of work (*feudistes*) and thus gave a much clearer picture of farm dues and assisted a more energetic recovery of lapsed rights. An edict of 1786 laid down that the drawing up of new registers was to be paid for by the tenants: an aspect of the favour shown the nobility by the King. This had already been demonstrated by the favour shown large landowners in some areas in enclosure edicts and in the division of the common lands, from which the seigneur took one-third by the right of *triage*.

The attempt to reserve by legislation most public offices for the nobility was another aspect of the aristocratic reaction. There was no legal reason why commoners should not enter the upper ranks of the clergy — but they were not able to do so. An edict of 1781 closed direct access to the rank of army officer without first serving in the ranks to all those who could not prove four generations of nobility, except in certain sectors such as the engineer corps. This eliminated the newer nobility from the highest ranks. In the upper ranks of the administration the nobility were again dominant. In Louis XIV's government all *intendants*[2] were noble, with the sole exception of Necker, and most were from the old nobility. Here again the King was,

[1] Theoretically the removal of the rights of nobility because of involvement in some degrading activity such as trade.
[2] Royal provincial government officials on whom all power in a particular area was vested in the name of the King.

in effect, lending his support to the aristocratic reaction. The gains
made by the aristocracy at the end of the century in the face of general
historical evolution were remarkable. All their efforts were directed to
the formation of a closed caste, and the cessation of a centuries-old
process whereby the wealthy commoner was enabled to join their
ranks.

The third estate

The abbe Sieyès estimated that the *tiers état*, the third estate,
amounted to 96 per cent of the nation. But this was perhaps an
underestimate and the figure may have been nearer 98 per cent. But
within the third estate there were many different social categories,
some poor, some well-to-do, with widely opposed interests, and having
as their sole unifying bond the fact of being 'base commoners'. There
are reasons for suggesting that the poorest sections of the community
hardly belonged to this group. In a way they were outside the social
order and may be seen as forming a 'fourth estate'. The boundaries
between the bourgeoisie and the commonalty of town and country are
far from easy to outline. Originally the term 'bourgeoisie' was used to
describe those living in privileged towns, towns which had acquired the
droit de bourgeoisie. In the eighteenth century it was used to indicate
the richest section of the third estate which had made its money by
exercising a non-agricultural profession. Georges Lefebvre commented
that the bourgeois was a man 'who had broken away from the land
because his principal profession was sufficiently profitable'. The
industrial and commercial role of the bourgeoisie continued to grow
during the eighteenth century.

The *haute bourgeoisie* derived their wealth from industry, commerce
or finance. Large industrial businesses were few, but with the growth of
limited liability companies and limited partnerships there were entrepreneurs employing vast numbers of men. Decretot at Louviers was the
entrepreneur of the 'most important wool manufactory in the world',
according to Arthur Young. There were many others — Van Robais at
Abbeville, Oberkampf at Jouy, Réveillon in Paris and Dietrich at
Strasbourg. These men dominated the industrial bourgeoisie which
largely consisted of merchant manufacturers who supplied raw
materials to craftsmen working in their own homes and marketed the
finished product. Lyon provides a classic example of this type of
industrial set-up.

The greatest fortunes were made in finance and commerce. The great merchants, the ship owners of Bordeaux, Marseille, Nantes and Le Havre who carried on the flourishing 'islands trade', and even wholesale merchants in the large towns, were those who benefited most from the great expansion of business in the second half of the eighteenth century. The financial bourgeoisie made considerable profits from the services they rendered the government. This category includes the *fermiers généraux* (tax farmers) financial officials and even bankers, both French and foreign, who were concerned with the supply of state loans. The bourgeoisie was thus the great creditor of the French monarchy. The interest on the national debt stood at more than 200 million livres in 1789: this did not include the interest on debts incurred by towns, districts and the clergy. This interest kept the *rentiers* (holders of government bonds) going. This was another category of the bourgeoisie, estimated to be 10 per cent of their class. Theirs was an ideal bourgeois existence, since to live off one's investments was regarded as 'living as a bourgeois' (*vivre bourgeoisement*). The ostentatious display of the upper bourgeoisie (*la haute bourgeoisie*) seen in their town residences, their country houses and various extravagances, their culture and their concern for patronage, distinguished them from the middle bourgeoisie (*la bourgeoisie moyenne*) which included men of law, office workers, and members of the liberal professions.

If sectors of the bourgeoisie dominated the economy, others were involved in the administration of the country — these included holders of judicial posts which did not confer nobility, financial office-holders, inspectors of manufactures, inspectors of the royal domain and the royal forests, mayors, municipal officials and councillors in the towns and market towns and their numerous clerks. Whether they had bought and therefore owned their positions (*officiers*) or were civil servants by appointment who could therefore be dismissed, they formed the bulk of the public administration of their time. Among the liberal professions doctors were not held in great esteem and lawyers were not highly regarded either. The first rank among the liberal professions was really held by the attorneys of the *parlèments* (*procureurs des Parlements*) and by barristers. The latter were very numerous but in the large towns, and especially towns where a *parlement* was held, those who became well-known attained, through wealth and reputation, an exalted status. On the eve of the Revolution Mounier was an important figure in Grenoble; in Paris, Target was a member of the Académie Française. Because of their culture, their professional skill, their knowledge of procedure and their eloquence many became the first advisers and leaders of the third estate.

The bourgeoisie were an urban social group and founded their fortunes on urban professions, but they had always bought land. The ownership of land, and especially fiefs, since commoners could buy them, was held in respect. It was regarded as a more stable investment than the ownership of pecuniary wealth. Many bankers and business heads invested significant amounts of capital in land during and after their working life. In addition there was an important rural élite (farmers of tithe and of seignorial rights, collectors of *taille*) who swelled the ranks of the landed bourgeoisie. The amount of land held by the bourgeoisie is difficult to estimate, and varied from area to area. They did not hold much in the countryside proper, but tended to buy land nearer the towns. Over the whole of France the percentage of land owned probably amounted to 25—30 per cent. Much of it was of good quality and was put to good use, often with aggressive energy. The bourgeois, more than the noble, was determined to derive the maximum amount of profit from the lands he cultivated.

The lower fringe of the bourgeoisie, the *petite bourgeoisie*, was not easily distinguishable from the urban masses, because of the existence of the manufacturing and commercial guilds. These were legal bodies which ruled their members through collective regulations. Not every trade was ruled in this way — there were 'free' trades with rules less stringent than those imposed on members of a guild but they were becoming fewer in number. The statutes of the guilds were all-embracing and regulated apprenticeship, master-worker relationships, access to the mastership and relations between masters. Trade guilds (*communautés de métiers*) were chiefly concerned with maintaining the monopoly of masters of the same trade over that trade, and to reduce any elements of competition. Each trade therefore usually had an exclusive guild constantly struggling with the other guilds and these rivalries had produced interminable legal battles. It is indeed possible that there was more solidarity within one particular trade guild, between a master and his journeyman whom he often lodged and fed and with whom he shared a life of only a moderate standard, than between the masters of all the guilds, who formed a kind of petty bourgeoisie, on the one hand and the workers, who formed a kind of proletariat, on the other hand. There were some rich craftsmen and merchants, for example in the building, food and in the art professions. Conversely it must be remembered that there was solidarity between journeymen who frequently belonged to crude kinds of workers' defence organizations in opposition to the masters. These were the *compagnonnages*. Workers also knew how to use strikes in order to protect or improve working conditions. There were, then, conflicts between workers and masters. The government often intervened, firmly taking the side of the masters. Letters Patent of January 1749 forbade workers to leave their masters without their written approval: offenders could be fined as much as 100 livres. From 1781 this written approval had to be placed in a workers' hand-book (*livret*). Workers' combinations were forbidden as was membership of the *compagnonnage*. Outburst of violence from the workers were short-lived, arising from deterioration in their material condition and only rarely from class feelings. In Lyon this resulted largely from the divisive effect of craft structures on the mass of workers: 'The features of class struggle are still barely discernible' (Garden). Nevertheless when movements occurred they could be violent and well organized, as in Bordeaux where they took the form of monopoly control over the hiring of labour and a boycott of masters: 'the effectiveness of their action is borne out by the rise in wages' (Poussou). If in general the journeyman was in a position of ideological dependence on his master, with whom he mostly worked side by side, to whose authority he submitted and whose outlook he adopted, this dependence was not universal. In some industries, new both in scale and kind 'behind the journeyman of history the modern proletariat begins to take shape' (P. Léon) — witness the outbreaks in Beauvais led by Swiss, German and English agitators, the miners' revolt in 1788 in Rive de Gier and Montcenis, the troubles in Anzin, le Creusot and the Dauphiné ironworks.

Industrial workers in the countryside were outside the guild system; but the development of capitalism was threatening their independence. Those working in textiles and metal crafts usually received their raw materials from dealers who would later collect the finished product. They had a seeming independence and often employed one or two workers themselves. But they were tending to be exploited by the merchants and were becoming odd-job artisans, industrial workers in what was called *manufacture dispersée*, scattered industry. From a bargaining point of view they were weakened by their isolation. Unlike their urban counterparts they were incapable of banding together to enforce the satisfaction of their demands.

The peasantry formed by far the largest part of the third estate. According to contemporary estimates about 85 per cent of the population lived in the country at the end of the Ancien Régime. Not all of them were peasants, though nearly all had some connection with the land. The actual peasantry probably amounted to about two-thirds of the population, about 18 million people. They were almost wholly free, except in a few seignorial estates in east and central France. The King had abolished serfdom on his domains in 1779 and had condemned the practice as contrary to social justice.

Could a peasant own land? Seignorial right included the absolute ownership of all land of which a fief consisted, and especially peasant tenures which were very rarely fully autonomous. In theory the peasant only had the right to exploit land, or to an incomplete ownership; what the jurists of the Ancien Régime called 'beneficial property' (*domaine utile*). In practice peasant tenures were hereditary properties which could be transferred or bequeathed to the tenant's heir. But they were encumbered with quit rents and feudal dues.

How much land did the peasants actually own? If one accepts that the clergy owned 10 per cent of the land, the nobility 20 per cent (at least) and the bourgeoisie 25–30 per cent, the peasants were only left with between 40 and 45 per cent. The French peasants have been favourably compared with the serfs of Slavonic Central Europe and with the agricultural labourers of England – landless, but wage earning – and it has sometimes been claimed that the French peasants were a class of independent proprietors. But less than half of all the land, owned by 18 million souls, amounted to very little per family head. In addition the land was unequally distributed. Regional studies have pointed out that the number of really 'independent' peasants – peasants who did not need to work for others – was small: in the Limousin one family out of five; in the Gatinais one in ten; in Flanders one in twenty. Labrousse comments: 'The independent peasant, selling the produce of his property and living off its profits, was the exception.' The general picture was one of fragmentary holdings: holdings which were insufficient to live on, and which were being constantly divided at the death of the owner. This was what Arthur Young called 'the multiplication of wretchedness'. Because they had insufficient land of their own, the peasants were obliged to make up their income by other means – by tenant-farming, by labouring, by being *métayers*, share-croppers. These were the sole means of gaining a livelihood for the landless peasant. The proportion of landless peasants varied from region to region: 5 per cent of the total in the Gatinais; 15–20 per cent in the Cambrésis Plain; 40 per cent in some parts of lower Normandy and 75 per cent in the maritime plains of Flanders. But, comments Labrousse, 'Wage-earners of various sorts, either permanent, seasonal or occasional, seem to have been in the majority in the French countryside'. This situation had been worsened by the increase in population in the second half of the eighteenth century and this intensified the 'agrarian crisis' — the hunger for land — which typified French rural society on the eve of the Revolution.

Ancien Régime Society seems to have been fairly stable during the reign of Louis XV which, more or less, coincided with a period of prosperity. According to M. Luthy,

> The Ancien Régime in the total sense of the word was an economic and social as well as a political form of society, not only a means of awarding and distributing offices of authority, of administration, in the police or on the bench, and public jobs generally, but also and above all a system of awarding and distributing incomes; the Ancien Régime ended by being scarcely more than that.

The privileged orders, if they kept to the letter of the law, could not pursue any lucrative economic activity; their wealth was not, and was not meant to be, derived from their economic activity, but was a result of a grant from the King, from positions of authority, or from seignorial or spiritual functions which had been granted by the King in the past. Their revenues were, in the last analysis, derived from land rents and dues levied as temporal or spiritual lords. As the Physiocrats said, wealth was derived from land. The incomes of the privileged orders and of the monarch were derived from agricultural production but levied on the agricultural classes. The amount they took from agricultural production was the factor which determined the movement of the economy because it passed through their hands before entering into circulation. 'The social and economic function of royal society was to spend this "net product", and if possible to spend it wisely'. (Luthy).

But the stability of the Ancien Régime was faced with a twofold threat: in its internal functioning and in its essence. Internally because the privileged orders not only grabbed the entire end product but also lived parasitically on the rest of society by refusing to give up their fiscal privileges and to pay taxes; and there was always the danger that the producers (mostly peasants), if economic conditions were unfavourable and their basic needs for subsistence and family life were threatened, might start questioning the foundations of the system, and the whole business of payment of dues and taxes. In its essence, it was threatened by the growth of personal, realizable wealth. This favoured the rise of the capitalist bourgeoisie at the same time as it broke up the strength of the old orders. To enjoy to the full the benefits of established privileges it was no longer enough to be noble by birth or a cleric by vocation; to cut a figure a well-lined purse was necessary. A career at court or in the army was impossible without money. At the end of the eighteenth century the structure of the 'society of orders' was giving way to a different sort of social structure, to a 'horizontal', individualistic society – to a society of 'classes'.

2. The horizontal structure of society: the diversity of social conditions

The nobility of Perigord in their *cahier de doléances* for the Estates General of 1789 wrote, 'Our deputies will maintain with all the dignity of their noble descent, the inherent equality of the nobility, which can only be regarded as one class.' This was clear evidence of a desire to ignore the social reality; to maintain the fiction of a society resting solely on a rigid division into three orders. It perhaps indicates the response of the privileged to the menace to their unity. By the end of the eighteenth century wealth, prestige and culture were no longer distributed as they had once been. Economic fluctuations, the increasing importance of realizable wealth and the movement of ideas had increasingly complicated and fragmented the state of society. The juridical society of orders was being menaced by the pressure of new forces.

The countryside

There is a tendency to think of the huge rural population as being homogeneous or only slightly variegated, but in fact there was a vast diversity. Paul Bois has brought this out well in his study of the *département* of the Sarthe.

The privileged orders did not occupy the role one might have expected in this *département*. Certainly, each Sunday parish priests had their churches filled with their parishioners.

The strength of the faith may have been no stronger than in any other region but while in the nuclear villages of open field agriculture social contact took place daily between its inhabitants, here social life had more of a religious character. The climb to the village church was faithfully carried out, all the more so since it was the only time when the isolated life of the scattered hamlet could be exchanged for something approaching spiritual life.

During the rest of the week the parish priest was alone, and the faithful were isolated, especially those engaged in farming who would scarcely see anyone beyond their immediate family or one or two neighbours in the hamlet. The people seem to have liked their parish priest, but had little liking for the monks in the numerous religious houses of the area, whom they considered to be bad landlords and for whom the parish priests and their assistants seem to have felt only antipathy.

The nobility of this *département* did not occupy the position generally attributed to them. There was no upper nobility (*haute noblesse*), and half of what nobility there were lived in Le Mans and half on their estates. 'Only a fifth of those nobles having their principal landed and seignorial ties in the area actually lived in the countryside among the peasants – that is only two-fifths of all the nobles in the province. 261 parishes shared forty-seven heads of noble families. Whole cantons and groups of cantons had no nobles at all.' Here, at least, the nobility could not have played an important role in rural life and even when they were present they do not seem to have been obnoxious. Complaints against the nobility in the future *département* of the Sarthe do not feature greatly in the *cahiers de doléances*.

The small rural bourgeoisie (*la petite bourgeoisie rurale*) was to be found in nearly every parish. These were the men of law (lawyers, notaries, bailiffs, procurators of royal or seignorial courts) some of whom were *fermiers généraux* of noble or ecclesiastical estates, some doctors and a few people of independent means known as 'proprietors' or 'bourgeois'. But they were not a numerous group: two or three per village. There were merchants, more numerous and rather better off, especially those (and they were a majority) who employed workmen, such as cloth merchants. In every parish there were trades essential to agrarian life: blacksmiths, saddlers, wheelwrights, and trades supplying basic social needs: masons, carpenters, shoemakers. In some villages a majority of the population might be involved in these trades. In forested areas there were many involved in related trades – sawyers, cooper, turners, clog-makers and industries using fire (forges, glassworks and potteries) supported numerous artisans and their assistants. Everywhere there were linen weavers working on their own account. They bought the necessary raw materials, flax or hemp, had the preparatory work done by someone else, carried out the rest of the work themselves and marketed the cloth. The weaver would work in his cellar and might have one or two others working for him on one or two looms. Some might have three or four looms and were nearer to being manufacturers employing workers or merchant-manufacturers. But some had only one loom and worked with the help of their wives and their children. The weavers had a hard life and their condition deteriorated in the second half of the eighteenth century because the price of food and of raw materials increased much faster than did the price of manufactured articles. During the summer the weaver usually worked on the land; this source of income was vital to him. But despite this he was destined to a life of poverty. The inspector of manufactures of Le Mans wrote in 1780, 'There is no group of people worse off than the weavers. Scarcely a quarter can claim as their own the very cloth on their looms, poor though it is; hardly any know how to read and write.'

A group that was probably even poorer than the weavers was the forest workers – woodcutters, sawyers and charcoal burners. They were always moving about, only staying in one place for a few weeks in order to cut trees in one particular area. They lived in shacks, having only their wages as a means of support, victims of the smallest rise in the price of grain. Contemporaries regarded them as both wretched and unruly. They were feared by local authorities and even by neighbouring peasants.

Within the peasantry there were substantial differences in wealth. The peasants themselves were fully conscious of these distinctions. Bois comments, 'In electoral lists, tax rolls and on the registers of births, marriages and deaths before 1790 one never finds the term *cultivateur* (agriculturalist).' There was, however, a tripartite differentiation between *laboureurs* (or *fermiers*), wealthier, more independent peasants than *bordagers* (*closiers* in the south west) and *journaliers* who depended on wages to make a living, and if necessary *vignerons* might be added too. Only after the period of the Convention (1793–179?) did the term *cultivateur* appear in electoral lists and in registers of births, marriages and deaths. This is an indication that the drawing up of these documents was in the hands of townsmen contemptuous of the distinctions which the peasants regarded as important.

The *laboureurs* (husbandmen) were peasants who owned a plough and the means necessary to work it, and who had enough or nearly enough land to keep them in full use. This would be an area of about twenty hectares (about fifty acres). They were either proprietors or tenants or both together if they supplemented an inadequate property by farming other pieces of land. On the assumption that in order to support a family of five consisting of father, mother and three young children, a minimum area of five *hectares* was needed, then *laboureurs* were a favoured class. They were sellers of agricultural produce and therefore benefited from the upward movement of prices during the second half of the eighteenth century. They formed a kind of peasant bourgeoisie: and their reputation rested on their wealth, their available capital and their ability. They were employers of labour, rural bigwigs, and were sometimes described as the *coqs de paroisse*, cocks of the parish dunghill.

Bordagers and *closiers* were small cultivators, sometimes the owners of scattered patches of land, sometimes tenants and sometimes *métayers*. *Métayage* (share-cropping) was the most common form of cultivation, although not as common as has sometimes been claimed since the commonly used term *métairie* does not always mean that one area was farmed by the *métayage* system. *Métayage* was usually carried out on small areas of land and was not particularly productive: it was usually the *métayers* who bought or borrowed the seed corn, and were thus exposed to fluctuations in prices. Their condition seems to have deteriorated during the eighteenth century because of this and because of increases in costs and in taxes.

The fortunes of the owner-farmer depended on the size of his operation and on economic conditions generally. If his harvest gave him enough to live on and a surplus to sell, he would be able to profit from the continued rise in prices. But few peasants had a surplus to sell. Labrousse comments,

> The vast majority of families did not harvest enough to provide for their needs. Yield from the land was low. A third or more of the land lay fallow. A large proportion of the yield — a quarter or a fifth — was required for seed. In addition there were seignorial dues in kind to pay, and the tithe: perhaps 10 per cent of the amount harvested in all. From the rest the peasant had to feed his family, usually rather large, on account of the need for manual labour, and all, whether working or not, hearty bread-eaters. How many would be reduced to beggary in a bad year?

At the end of the century everything was going up — taxes, tithes, feudal dues, and if the harvest was bad these commitments were all the harder to meet in a time of falling profits. Complaints regarding these payments were more and more frequent.

At the very bottom of the peasant ladder were the wage-earners, the *salariés*. But these were of all different kinds. Some became wage-earners during times of bad harvest, some only worked as wage-earners when there was need for extra labour during the harvest season, some were permanent part-time wage-earners such as *métayers*, tenant farmers and even proprietors with too little land.

It was the possibility of being a wage-earner that provided the very small proprietor with the margin that guaranteed his subsistence.

Most of the peasant proprietors who appear in court rolls and
cadastres are wage-earners in disguise. The 'property' is simply a
makeweight. With a high rent, which doubled in the course of the
century, it contributed little towards subsistence. The appearance in a
given area of a large number of small properties is an indication of a
large number of wage-earners. (Labrousse)

But there were permanent fulltime wage-earners — *journaliers*, day-
workers. They might do various jobs — as innkeepers, artisans,
carriers — some, or even all, at the same time. There were in addition
permanent farm-workers, the *domestiques de ferme*. A plurality of jobs
was a common feature at the lower end of the scale.

The final picture of society is very different from ours. The fulltime
worker living solely from the sale of his labour was in a minority among
the diverse group of peasant wage-earners of that day. Within the family
a principal breadwinner was unusual. Usually the wife and children
supplemented family earnings; spinning and casual labour were universal, child labour was normal; children tended the flocks, which had
the advantage of keeping them out of the house; wives washed clothes
or worked by the hour. The picture drawn by Saint-Jacob is of a wide
variety of employments, more numerous and better paid for those who
lived near villages where something like urban life was developing.

The wage-earners in the countryside had therefore diverse occupations and this diversity probably prevented the development of 'class
consciousness'. Statistical information on them is lacking, but they
undoubtedly formed the majority of the rural population — possibly
three-fifths — and their number probably increased in the eighteenth
century because of the rise in population and the general decline in the
condition of the small landowner.

All these wage-earners were sellers of labour and buyers of food and
were therefore exposed to fluctuations in prices. Wages undoubtedly
increased during the century, particularly after the 1730s. This rise has
been estimated at around 20 per cent. But prices rose quicker during
the same period — food prices rose, for example, by about 50 per cent.
The purchasing power of these people was therefore reduced, although
by less for those who received some of their payment in kind or were
fed by their employer. But the family as a whole was not fed in this
way and the wage-earner was only fed if he worked, and work rarely
lasted the whole year — the average length of work was 200 days for an
agricultural wage-earner. He would therefore be unemployed for nearly

half of the year. He set great store by his rights to common land and pasturage where he could keep his sheep or cattle and provide his family with milk. But the big landowners wanted to round off their property by enclosures, and the lord of the manor kept a greedy eye on the common. At the end of the century there were many battles over collective rights which, with the aid of the courts, could only end in victory for the wealthy and privileged.

The condition of these wage-earners was undoubtedly wretched. The line between wage-earners and beggars was a very narrow one, and it would seem that what they could gain from begging was an integral part of their incomes, except in good years. In times of bad harvests they were thus unemployed and without income just when food prices were rapidly rising. This led to bands of beggars in the countryside, knocking on the doors of the more well-to-do, obtaining by threat what they could not obtain through private charity or public relief.

In a recent work J. P. Gutton has analysed these manifestations of poverty and vagrancy. His evidence comes from the Lyonnais, but the implications are general. 'Both in town and country the poor had nothing to fall back on; they had just enough possessions to live a hand to mouth existence, and the common people seemed, even in a normal year, to be entangled in debt', at the mercy of the slightest deterioration in the cost of living. Everything tended to swell this army of beggars and vagabonds. Most of them were uprooted countryfolk, but the vagrant horde wandered from country to town and back again, a source of dismay and alarm, a sort of reserve force of popular feeling whose troops were readily available for any sort of riot. They terrorized the countryside and contributed largely to pre-revolutionary unrest. In the 1780s their numbers, already large as a result of the rigid social and economic structure of the Ancien Régime, were swollen by population increase and economic crisis. In the country round Paris in 1788–9 the armed forces were hard put to hold them down and keep the roads open. It was the same in Languedoc where brigands and bandits multiplied. There was nothing new about this, but it was much on the increase after 1780.

As the most conspicuous symptom of public unrest the vagrant horde was a decisive factor in its aggravation, which is why at the end of a decade of turbulence it reached its climax in the summer of 1789, and the deputies to the National Assembly, stung to action by the Great Fear, tried to settle the problem by the decisions of the night of 4 August.

The towns

Extremes of affluence and poverty were more marked in towns, but there were of course great variations depending on local activities, as a few examples drawn from medium sized towns, of less than 50,000 inhabitants, will show.

Montauban had between 25,000 and 28,000 inhabitants. It was a thriving industrial town, with an active woollen industry in the hands of 250 to 300 families, mostly protestants. They were excluded from holding public office by their religion and had thus been able to devote their attention to business: fearing renewed persecution they had not been tempted to purchase land, but on the contrary had invested sums of up to 600,000 livres in their businesses. These merchant manufacturers were the cream of Montauban society. Living in luxurious town houses they led a colourful social life with concerts, theatres, picnics and shooting parties; keen art lovers, their commissions supported a minor school of painting. The only men above the protestant upper classes of Montauban were the *intendant*, the King's representative, who was a member of the nobility, and the Bishop, who enjoyed an income of 70,000 livres. Apart from these two no public official or cleric could rival them as far as wealth was concerned. The popular classes were either engaged in industrial work and were thus dependent on the merchant-manufacturers, or were involved in other local commercial enterprises, or were gardeners or employed in other forms of manual labour, activities which were also to be found in the countryside. Some of the masters were fairly well-to-do. A thousand paid the *capitation*, although only small amounts. But the workers in the guilds had a wretched existence. It is impossible to estimate the number of poor, because they did not appear on tax rolls, but certainly they were numerous.

Rennes was not an industrial and commercial town to any great extent yet had more inhabitants than Montauban (approximately 32,000). There were 600 clergy and the Church as a whole was rich and owned half of all the house property in Rennes. But the nobility of the sword was not particularly important. Rennes was an administrative town, it was the seat of the *parlement* of Brittany and the élite of Rennes consisted of lawyers and important officials. The richest were financial officials (the *receveur des domaines*, collector of domain revenues, paid 600 livres in capitation, a fairly considerable sum), and then came the members of council of the *parlement*. The highest social status belonged to the nobility of the robe and above all to the men of law and attorneys in the *parlement*. Below these social groups were governmental officials and officials of the Estates of Brittany, members of the liberal professions and persons of independent means. They formed a kind of middling bourgeoisie of rather varied character. The commercial bourgeoisie counted for little, partly because they were not very well-to-do and partly because they were dependent for a living on the upper bourgeoisie, the clergy and the nobility. Beneath this middling bourgeoisie were the artisans and craftsmen of the guilds who were frequently poor. Beneath them were the small independent trades often exercised by women — laundry women, embroiderers and knitters, stocking-frame workers, menders, vegetable sellers and milk sellers. All these, together with various journeymen and labourers, formed a category which was characterized by poverty, and which tended to live in crowded conditions in the old areas and suburbs of the town. Again it is impossible to put a number to those whose poverty meant they did not appear on the tax rolls, but according to Henri Sée 'it would not be rash to believe that the town contained a mendicant population of several thousand'.

Toulouse was a town of some 50,000 inhabitants and drew its wealth more from its administrative, commercial and residential activities than from its industries. There were great contrasts in society — at one extreme there was a rich aristocratic group, and at the other a mass of poor. In one part of the town only two out of five heads of families paid taxes equivalent to three days work in 1790 (three livres) and thus qualified to be active citizens. 54 per cent of the third estate belonged to a kind of proletariat. Probably only about half of the population of Toulouse had an income of over 300 livres, and thus the other half would be near poverty. The popular classes consisted of journeymen, apprentices, shop assistants, domestic servants and other small trades folk.

A little less than a fifth of the population consisted of guild masters who owned their equipment. Their incomes varied from 300 to 4,000 livres, but most had less than 1,000 livres. The tradespeople accounted for another fifth of the population. Their incomes varied too and ran from 300 to 4,000 livres, but most (two-thirds) had an income of over 1,000 livres. The richest were the more important merchants and some of the innkeepers. Those trading in food were not so wealthy — small innkeepers, publicans, pork-butchers, cookshop keepers had an average income of less than 500 livres.

The bourgeoisie of the liberal professions were rather better off, although apothecaries, doctors, bailiffs, clerks of courts, and even most of the barristers were scarcely more wealthy than most of the tradespeople. The average income of the liberal professions was 3,000 livres; but certain important office holders had 5,000 livres and were thus on the borders of the 'high society' of Toulouse.

This social élite consisted of the aristocracy — nobles of the sword and the robe, approximately half of each; out of 204 nobles on the *capitation* lists of 1789, 112 were attached to the *parlement*. By 1789 all the *parlementaires* of Toulouse were of noble birth. There was frequent intermarriage between the two nobilities. For instance the First President, Cambon, had married the daughter of the Marquis Riquet of Bonrepos who had the greatest fortune of any Toulousain — 2 million livres in 1760. The incomes of the *parlementaires* were from 3,000 to 6,000 livres a year, and 20,000 for the First President. A nobleman's average income would be about 8,000 livres. The nobles of the sword and the robe led similar existences. The noble of the sword was usually a country gentleman on his domain for eight months of the year, and derived three-fifths of his income from the yield of the harvest. The noble of the robe did not mind releasing himself from some of the duties of a *parlementaire* and might well pass the summer in the countryside. Both invested some of their capital in bonds issued by the town or by the provincial estates.

The money market of Toulouse was controlled by the nobility. They were the leading figures in the winter social life of the city, a provincial, emasculated version of life in Paris (that dreadful place where young folk went to the bad), but even so no lack of theatres, parties, banquets, balls and even gambling. A touch of bourgeois morality — no debts and no extravagance. The family fortune was well looked after and living was not on too grand a scale. Retinue and servants were kept to a minimum and wages, although fair, were paid six months in arrears.

In this town dominated by the aristocracy the divisions between different social groups were wide. The average income of a noble was two or three times that of even a well-to-do merchant, fundholder (*rentier*) or barrister; it was sixteen times greater than the income of an artisan, and sixty times greater than that of his own farm foreman. The economic power of the aristocracy was overwhelming. At the end of their day they controlled 53 per cent of all personal wealth, 68 to 85 per cent of all government stock, 71 per cent of rural property, 92 per cent of all shares. It follows that bourgeois fortunes were rather mediocre. Unlike Bordeaux, in Lyon or Nîmes there were no wealthy

Girondins or Federalists capable of standing up financially or politically speaking against a combination of royalists and Montagnards. In Toulouse the nobility were unbelievably rich.

The case of **Bordeaux** is no less interesting and in striking contrast with Toulouse. The population had risen steadily (more than 4 per cent annually) from 55,000 in 1715 to 110,000 in 1790. This twofold increase, in which a socially very mixed immigration played an important part, reflected a more varied social structure. As elsewhere the gap between patrician and plebian was very wide, but in many ways the picture of Bordelais society presents more variety than that in other cities. The main cause was the importance of business.

As in Toulouse, the nobility, members of the *parlement* and those with a 'vineyard-based wealth', were the richest. Of thirty-five noble marriage contracts all involved incomes of more than 13,000 livres; 75 per cent of them 51,000 livres in contrast to 21 per cent of merchant marriages. But the *négociants*, the wholesale merchants, were gaining ground: in mid-century seventeen merchant marriage contracts involved over 25,000 livres, in contrast to twenty-two nobles'; between 1782 and 1784 the number of merchants had risen to forty-three, against thirty-seven nobles. Overall the wealth of Bordeaux surpassed that of all other cities and even challenged comparison with Paris.

The size and growth of this wealth explain why one is more struck by the way social differences shaded into each other than by their contrasts. On one side there is the great number of intermediate strata, tradespeople, the professions, private citizens, a few master-craftsmen; on the other there is the difficulty of distinguishing various social groups of which the artisan's world (consisting of about 45 per cent of the population) seems to be the meeting point. This last alternated ceaselessly between affluence, sometimes even wealth, and indigence. Some even became landowners: at the end of the century even journeymen were known to buy land and build on it. Elsewhere insecurity and impecuniousness were their lot and we pass by imperceptible degrees from master craftsmen, some of whom (especially shoemakers and tailors) were far from well-to-do, down to the proletariat of minor crafts and thence to the beggars and the underworld. Looked at from another angle the distribution of the working population is very traditional: nothing modern goes on; coopers and carpenters abound. Changes in the city's economy have not kept pace with social developments.

Lyon and its suburbs had 110,000 inhabitants at the beginning of the eighteenth century and nearly 150,000 on the eve of the Revolution. It was the second city of the kingdom and the largest industrial city. The pre-eminence of the silk trade gave it a unique character. The numbers engaged in this trade doubled in fifty years. Life was hard for silk workers, less from poverty than from insecurity, less from bad pay than from the uncertainty of employment. In normal times the silk worker ate meat every day, bought tobacco, wore a periwig; there was some poverty but only at occasional periods of economic stress. Lack of money saved was the characteristic of the silk worker's budget and this was the reason for dramatic changes in his way of life at the arrival of the least crisis. Nevertheless many of them appear to have been reasonably prosperous: between 1750 and 1789 in 11 per cent of marriage contracts the dowry exceeded 2,000 livres.

In 1789 the silk industry employed 40 per cent of the work force of Lyon. But there were other fairly considerable activities: clothing and other textiles accounted for 16 per cent, the hat trade 9 per cent, building 9 per cent, shoemaking and foodstuffs 7 per cent. The silk industry was characterized by numerous workshops, all very small and with few employees, who had to endure a long apprenticeship and detailed code of behaviour. Nowhere but in the silk industry were there more masters than men; for the position of journeyman was an entirely transitory one between apprentice and master. Every journeyman was a future master. By contrast master builders were only a fifth of all members of their craft.

There remained a wide gap between the earnings of masters and men, which widened in the course of the century. Nor were the humbler class any better off than elsewhere. Most of them were 'new citizens'; three-quarters of the day labourers were born outside Lyon, and 90 per cent of them contributed less than 1,000 livres to their marriage contract. Finally, as elsewhere, merchants and tradespeople accounted for over half the marriage contracts involving over 10,000 livres, but only 28 per cent of those over 100,000. As in Bordeaux and Toulouse, where really big money was involved the world of trade was no match for the world of the nobleman. Such was the paradox of Lyonnais wealth, the pre-eminence of the nobleman in the business capital of France.

Paris showed the widest diversity of social divisions. The standard of living varied enormously between the more plebeian areas and the aristocratic quarter of the Marais: between the faubourg St. Antoine and the faubourg St. Germain, and the court of Versailles. The picture of the court at Versailles swarming with its 15,000 court officials and an equal number in search of royal favours is well known. In the eyes of the public the court symbolized the nation's wealth cornered by a group of sterile non-producers. In 1785 the royal treasury had been milked by the beneficiaries of 137 million of letters patent; *fermiers généraux* and courtiers, acting as go betweens in obtaining contracts or favours from the King or the royal offices, regularly pocketed their payola. Life at court was expensive and the incomes of court nobility, enormous though many of them were, were not sufficient to enable them to lead it indefinitely. Ruin was faced with nonchalance and it was considered good form to be heavily in debt.

The wealth of the nobility of the robe could rival the wealth of the nobility of the sword. The former tended to be less frivolous and more cultivated, patrons of artists and men of letters and not spendthrifts.

This is all well known, but a complete statistical study of the character of the Parisian society has yet to be undertaken. A beginning has been made by A. Daumard and F. Furet who have drawn up a statistical analysis of various aspects of Parisian society in the eighteenth century (*Structures et relations sociales à Paris au XVIIIe siècle*) based on an analysis of 2,500 marriage contracts drawn up by Parisian lawyers in 1749. By studying the matrimonial contributions mentioned in these contracts they have been able to obtain 'a picture of Parisian society from a cross section of a generation about to begin its adult life in the year 1749'.

The least well-off are badly represented. Although for obvious reasons the dregs of Parisian society escape analysis, further up the socio-professional scale one can distinguish various social groups.

At the bottom came the industrial and commercial wage-earners. For most of them (74 per cent) marital contributions were between 500 and 5,000 livres and for the rest under 500 livres, a sum which would only pay for a bride's trousseau and a few pieces of furniture. The poorest were wage-earners paid daily, and others who were paid a low rate working in various Parisian trades; then there were the shop assistants, clerks and the better-off guild journeymen.

Minor craftsmen (jobbing tailors, workers at home) and domestic servants are categorized with journeymen, with contributions of 500 to 5,000 livres. The figure of 5,000 livres was, however, comfortably exceeded by masters and tradesmen, many of whom produced very large sums, sometimes as much as 50,000 livres. These were the well-to-do members of Parisian crafts and commerce. Affluence began with mastery of a craft or the possession of a shop.

Those who paid a contribution of 50,000 livres and above can be defined as the bourgeois of Paris. This group included those living off investments, members of the liberal professions, doctors, lawyers, people employed in the royal administration, and above all office holders who had purchased their office. The latter often had considerable fortunes, many of several hundred thousand or even a million livres. They were the very rich commoners.

The summit of the Parisian social hierarchy was occupied by the nobility. Contributions in over three-quarters of their contracts came to more than 50,000 livres. Only a few nobles with less than this sum managed to maintain an aristocratic way of life off revenue from capital; but the nobility of the robe and those occupying military posts all had fortunes of from 50,000 to 1,000,000 livres and sometimes more. This study has provided statistical confirmation of the old view of aristocratic wealth, and its place in the social structure of Paris and other major cities in the eighteenth century.

3. Conclusion

Social conditions and wealth varied considerably under the Ancien Régime but some general features of contemporary French society of the time may be pointed out.

The life of the masses, of whom the vast majority lived in the countryside, was one of uncertainty. They constantly hovered on the brink of poverty. Everything about their life was uncertain. The quality of the harvests was always problematic, for a backward agriculture was always at the mercy of the weather, and therefore food supplies were always uncertain. Employment was another uncertainty. An agrarian crisis would throw out of work many agricultural workers, but unemployment often spread into the industrial sector. The growth of the population had intensified these problems by increasing the competition for labour. The standard of living could therefore change for the worse at any moment. When it did and times were hard popular agitation would probably occur as a result, and discontents would be kept on the boil. The common people blamed, and often attacked, anything which seemed to keep them in misery — tithes, seignorial rights, and taxes. But this was the actual limit of their aims; they did not question the actual social order. They may have shared some of the ideas of the bourgeoisie, but not necessarily their aims. For example they resented the idea of any blow against their collective rights in the countryside or against corporate organizations in towns which were often their sole guard against destitution.

Although the bourgeoisie was not a united body it was the essential driving force of the economy. It disapproved of all regulations and controls that inhibited the full functioning of its productive forces; it was in favour of economic liberty and economic individualism. It was especially opposed to privileges and to other barriers in the way of its own social betterment. Bourgeois discontents were not caused by an uncertain standard of living but by frustrated social ambitions. The aristocracy had closed its ranks. The response of the bourgeoisie to this was to call for equality of rights. Thanks to the progress of education it was capable of taking in the doctrines of the 'intellectuals' whose philosophy provided them with ideological weapons: a rather bourgeois philosophy which the most timid could subscribe to and which could attract the more enlightened of the aristocracy.

The aristocracy too were restive. Rich and privileged, they had their own ideology and the means to fulfil it. Their aim was revenge against royal despotism, the system initiated by Louis XIV who had freed himself from dependence on the nobles and turned the tables on them by setting up a new ruling caste of newly ennobled peers; their means were mobilized in the *parlement* by their legal pundits. By neutralizing royal power and forcing the King to summon the States General the aristocracy succeeded, in the summer of 1788, in destroying royal absolutism. But the crisis unleashed forces they could not control which compelled the aristocratic revolution to give way before a bourgeois and popular one.

documentation

Problems of classifying and categorizing society

If I have identified a labouring proletariat in Orléans (*un prolétariat manuel*) this is because the documents justify it: they indicate the existence of trade journeymen, of day wage-earners and of domestic servants.

If I said that there was a 'popular' section of society this is the result of comparison based on two means of classification, firstly private income and secondly the ownership of the means of production. But this 'popular' section also included people who might be regarded as 'bourgeois' because they lived off investments of various kinds, and did not work, but the significant thing to note is that these particular people were poor and could not be included in a 'middling' social category.

There are equally wide disparities in the other class: At the top came refiners, merchants, large landowners. At the bottom came the artisans, shop-keepers, small independent vine-growers. Lower still were stall-holders in street markets and barrow men. All had something in common: they sought customers, but not employers; profits, not wages; and even though their equipment was simple they had a certain independence.

Some were rich but most of them were poor: this can be seen by checking against the first method of classification. Some were truly owners of the means of production and were employers of labour; others worked alone and with their hands. Those who could not be considered in a 'middling' category have been placed in this 'popular' category.

The question of the wage-earners is not an easy one either. Some owned their houses, or owned small plots of ground. There was a real distinction between manual workers and shop assistants, clerks, bagmen. The latter tried to live as bourgeois and would have been indignant if regarded as workers or proletarians. Yet they were poor, and sometimes even poorer than a manual worker. They have been placed in the 'popular' category. Those lower down than the proletariat: tramps (*clochards*) and beggars (*mendiants*) are not being considered here.

If I had been speaking of the nineteenth or twentieth century I might have labelled my 'popular' category *petite bourgeoisie*, or even something less than that, *très petite bourgeoisie*, but this would be anachronistic for 1791. Nowadays the petty bourgeois is better off, less ignorant, even more 'bourgeois' and certainly less hostile to the rich than were the popular masses of 1791.

My popular category belongs to what contemporaries, and in particular Robespierre, called 'le peuple', which they distinguished from the 'populace' — 'la canaille', the rabble. But Robespierre included an entrepreneur, Duplay, a printer, Nicolas, a café owner, Chrétien, as his 'peuple' — his popular category, whereas they might be placed in a 'middling' category. And Robespierre also included trade journeymen.

I have, however, formed a popular category rather more limited than Robespierre's 'peuple'. But its composition was varied. The documents, which I have examined in detail, indicate this great social complexity — the kind of complexity to be found during all historical periods — and which becomes more complex still when one takes into account ideas and outlooks. The same goes for the structure of the countryside.

(From a letter written by Georges Lefebvre in April 1957.)

Statistical history

On concluding this study of social history, based on the use of statistics, it seems very important to try to sum up the advantages and inadequacies of this method, before deciding in general what light such a localized study can throw on the contradictions inherent in French society at the end of the eighteenth century and the part they played in the drive to revolution.

The social historian is faced with an enormous number of documents. In our case they were fiscal papers scrupulously entered up and well preserved, together with legal documents; in all a mass of paper quite beyond the researcher's power to analyse without statistical methods and a computer. This type of history has not arisen fortuitously but as the result of new information techniques without which social history remains purely fictional. This study of the inequality of wealth in a large city at the time of the Revolution is the first of its kind and we believe it will be of great value.

We must not overstate the importance of this contribution. We are aware (as Tirat has written) that quantitative social history, or statistical history, cannot do justice to the complexity of a social structure without taking account of psychology, religious and social behaviour, mentality generally. But to round off a statistical history in that way the statistical work has to be done first! But apart from a few recent articles no research worker has produced a work on the scale of the present one.

We are well aware of the limitations of this approach. It will be said that we are bewitched by figures, that we have indulged in calculation not description, but the line we have taken was in full realization of the sort of criticism we should encounter. . . .

For most modern historians history must be reckoned as a humane science. But if man as a free individual may escape objective study, men, by contrast, as members of groups and as social beings conform to the laws of these groups and may be scientifically studied only by statistical methods. So it is with sociology, psychology, demography and economics, in short all the humane sciences. If history, the study of man's past, is excepted, it is to relegate it to what it has long been, a collection of hallowed traditions without any scientific basis. Even if statistical history is inadequate and needs supplementing with biographies and literary descriptions, as we willingly concede, it still remains a fundamental necessity. Nothing constructive can be achieved without it. At a time when the new philosophy of structuralism is proclaiming the death of mankind and the end of history it makes sense for the historian to rethink his methods and look for hidden 'structures': in this case those of the half feudal, half capitalist society at the end of the Ancien Régime and on the eve of the Revolution.

J. SENTOU, *Structures et groupes sociaux a Toulouse sous la Révolution. Essai d'histoire statistique* (Toulouse, 1969)

The two peoples of the bocage
(*Bocage:* mixed woodland and pasture)

The west of Upper Maine and a fairly large part of Lower Maine was an area where 'real' peasants were found: men attached to the land with their backs turned on the rest of the world. The land was quite fertile. It was not vastly over-populated, the peasants lived off what they grew and on the whole the economic conditions of the eighteenth century had benefited them. Corn, cattle, flax and clover seed were all sold from this part of the country. Prices rose. So did farm rents, and although there was some feeling against this, the burden was not excessive, and did not swallow up everything. There was often a bit of money over, and as it would be invested in land the size of land-holdings actually owned would increase. The movement was slow but sure and because of it there was always a mood of optimism – a hope that some day real independence might arrive, the sort of independence only partially present with lease-farming. All of these people were peasants. There was nothing in the way of outside influence to alter traditional habits, and traditional methods of working. The *seigneur*, the lord of the manor, was held in respect; but he was distant and was rarely seen. As for the clergy, the peasants drew a definite distinction between the parish priests — *their* parish priests who brought almost the only intellectual contribution to their lives, usually on Sundays for these men were alone six days out of seven — and the rest, the monastic and chapter clergy who farmed the tithe and occupied the land without any real entitlement. The peasant felt a mounting anger and resentment against these people. He also distrusted the bourgeois — the townsman who was so different from himself, who did not belong to the countryside and only came there to quarrel with him over land, and to collect his rent.

When occasion warranted the peasants could show an absolutely united front against the outsider. The first group they wanted to rid themselves of was the landed tithe-levying clergy; the second was the bourgeois — greedy for land and ready to take over the lands of the first group. The first elections of the Revolutionary period revealed quite clearly the desire of the peasants to have no encroachment from and even no contact with strangers.

In the *bocage* of the east there were traces of a similar outlook, but with a difference. Here the land was less fertile and in some areas unable to support its large population. Here economic conditions were much less favourable for the peasants: the rise in prices had not benefited them because they had little surplus to sell. They had few savings and were thus unable to buy land and had no hope of being better off or of being independent. They were resigned to their lot; they did not resist the people who occupied the land and monopolized wealth. The nobility was no more tiresome there than anywhere else, and the clergy was probably less so. There were fewer monastic settlements than elsewhere. Here the peasantry were less vigorous than in the west, not so tough-minded, more amenable. Socially they were more diversified, since, in order to live, all the poorer folk had to turn to another occupation, namely weaving.

Working away, out of sight in cellars, another race of peasants was evolving with a different way of life. In spite of their cellar work these men were less isolated than the others because of their necessary contacts with the markets, which were sometimes far off. Through this contact the influence of the towns penetrated the countryside. And here the men from the towns took on a different aspect: they were not competitors for the land but men responsible for the disposal of the goods they had manufactured. Here too the common enemy was different: it was more likely to be the inquisitorial royal administration, and all the threats to their existence that implied. Thus, to the little power of opposition to the Ancien Régime found in the west, was added the resistance of this trading petty bourgeoisie.

Because of this the eastern *bocage* was more in tune with the rest of the French countryside. Except in the western *bocage* the more populated country areas were more prepared to accept the influence of the towns. This was especially true if they too had trades such as weaving in addition to other more usual rural activities.

When the Revolution came the eastern *bocage* was, to some extent, more ready to place its future in the hands of the townsmen, and to let itself be guided by them.

P. BOIS, *Paysans de l'Ouest* (Paris, Mouton) p. 572–4.

A different type of peasant: the vine-grower

Between the towns and the vine-growers there was a kind of natural affinity, a mental and material accord. The vine-grower was not isolated, his work involved a cooperative effort. Physically and socially he had an 'intermediate' position between town and countryside. To use the expression of Vidal de la Blache, he was more of a villager than a peasant. He did not usually live on his piece of land: he simply had his place of work, and kept his implements there. His was not an isolated existence, as the existence of the *métayers* tended to be, he was used to living with others. Perhaps he was even more than a 'villager' – perhaps a 'semi-townsman'. The vine-growing communities of today in Burgundy, Lower Languedoc and Roussillon had ancient origins. The vine-grower dealt with many people in his business. In many instances he was both producer and merchant. Sometimes he was a transporter too: vine-growers from Burgundy delivered as far as Paris. Whether he was half townsman or not, this tradesman, who belonged to the land, and who was fully conscious of his superiority over other men who worked the land but with whom he would drink and gossip, was really representative of the towns.

Besides, his material interests were bound up with the towns. The towns purchased his wines and his *eau de vie*. Whereas the peasant ate, the townsman drank. But the government and the municipal authorities intervened between producer and consumer with their levies, and thus increased the price of the product. But government and municipalities stood between grower and drinker, levying customs on bulk and bottle at every stage of the journey, and uniting both in implacable resistance to this tax on consumption which fell so much more heavily on the town dweller. The grain monopolists came in for the same hatred – a proletarian reaction to threatened subsistence. Revolutionary Paris did not end at the suburbs, it extended into the neighbouring vine-producing areas, as far as the edges of Normandy and right into Champagne: areas already inflamed by the crisis in vine-growing of 1789–90. Vine-producing areas were like worker-satellites of the working areas of the towns, large 'rural' suburbs whose economic outlook was urban in character: springboards of urban influence, ready to receive and transmit the message of the towns throughout the district.

E. LABROUSSE, *La Crise de l'économie française a la fin de l'Ancien Régime et au début de la Révolution* (Paris, 1943) pp. 598–600.

Manufacturing in Lyon

'Everyone knows that Lyon owes its growth, its splendour and opulent wealth, which place it among the leading commercial towns of Europe, to its manufacturing' but 'the slightest adverse conditions cause this apparently solid great fashion centre to shudder'.[1]

During the reign of Louis XV Lyon seemed to regain the height of economic activity it had known under Henri II. The number of looms increased. There were more than 11,000 in 1777, an average of 12,000 in 1784 and possibly 15,000 in 1788. The quantity of silk processed increased – in 1766 1,146,000 pounds (livres) of foreign fibres, 800,000 pounds of French fibres came to Lyon and two-thirds of these were used in the town. The value of the production increased too: from 46,000,000 livres in 1752 to an average of 60,000,000 per annum between 1770 and 1784. The same pattern emerges from examining the numbers employed: 25,000 merchants, workers and journeymen were counted in 1777. Roland de la Platière, inspector of manufacturers, estimated the figure to be 26,500 in 1786; and another source counted 28,600 and among these were nearly 10,000 women working at warping, reeling and twisting thread.

So many were employed in this industry that social life was permeated by it. There were 400 master-merchants with capital; 6,000

[1] *Mémoires du comédien Bénard, dit Fleury, 1750–1822* (R.D.L., 1836, III) p. 91.

master-workers employing journeymen, apprentices and many other assistants in their small workshops.

The lives of all these people were closely regulated: subordinate staff could never become masters; the length of apprenticeship of a weaver was laid down — five years from the age of fourteen with one master; to be a journeyman the apprentice had to undergo an examination by preparing a piece of particular cloth in which he specialized, and had to pay a fee. After a further two years in different places and another test the journeyman received letters of mastership and he could set up his own workshop. Only those born in Lyon could enter the professional guild.

The constant increase in population kept labour cheap, and despite the rising cost of living the employers refused to increase wages for fear of the effects on sales. 'We all know the cost of living affects the cost of labour but what is more important is that we owe our domination of the European market to cheap labour'.[1] The low wages paid to the journeymen guaranteed they would be controllable. 'For manufacturing in Lyon to be prosperous the workers must never make a lot of money, they should have only enough to feed and clothe themselves well. If certain of the population are well-off industry becomes less active, and idleness and a host of other vices which it brings, are the result.'[2]

From: L. TRENARD, *Lyon, de l'Encyclopédie au Préromantisme* (Paris 1958) I, p. 22

[1,2] E. Mayet, *Mémoire sur les fabriques de Lyon* (1786) pp. 37, 60—61.

Table II.1 Details of average income from estates of twenty noble families in the Toulouse diocese in mid-eighteenth century

Source of income		Total in livres	Percentage of gross revenue
Corn land		3 577	62
Woodland, pasture, vineyards		1 434	25
Mills, smithies, kilns		285	5
Seigneurial dues		452	8
	Gross income	5 748	100
Expenses:			
Wages		262	5
Taxes		836	15
	Net income	4 650	80

Table II.2 Rent from land

Marquis de Gardouch (781 arpents)*			Comte de Caraman (170 arpents)*		
Period of lease	Length in years	Annual rent	Period of lease	Length in years	Annual rent
1747–56	9	11 000 livres	1722–24	3	2 450 livres
1756–65	9	16 000	1725–31	6	2 450
1773–79	6	26 298	1742–48	6	3 500
1780–86	6	26 169	1748–54	6	3 800
1792–93	1	26 844	1761–67	6	4 000
			1777–83	6	6 680

Source: R. FORSTER, *The Nobility of Toulouse*, Baltimore, The John Hopkins Press.

*An *arpent* equals roughly 1½ acres.

Table II.3 Income of a noble family in the diocese of Toulouse at the end of the Ancien Régime

(Madame Adélaïde Lévis, marquise de Mirepoix)

INCOME FROM PROPERTY		
1. A house in Toulouse: rue du Temple		1 200 livres
2. Land in the Agenais and the seneschalsy of	23 535	
Carcassonne	Total	24 735
INVESTMENT AND REVENUES IN PERPETUITY		
1. 114 000 livres invested with the Etats de Languedoc	5 700	
2. 30 000 livres invested with the Seneschalsy of		
Toulouse	1 500	
3. 12 000 livres invested with the archbishopric		
of Auch	600	
4. Investment in local taxes, Paris	1 045	
5. Investment in India Company	80	
	Total	8 925
SETTLED ANNUITY PAYMENTS		
1. 50 000 livres with Baynagnet (Carcassonne) at 4%	2 000	
2. 33 000 livres with O'Kelley (Toulouse) at 4%	1 320	
3. 7 000 livres with de Riquet (Toulouse) at 5%	350	
4. 7 000 livres with d'Ormesson (Paris) at 5%	350	
5. 20 000 livres with Gignoux cadet (Valence) at 5%	1 000	
6. 25 000 livres with billets à Mme Vieuville (Paris)		
at 5%	1 250	
	Total	6 270
	Gross income	39 930
INTEREST DUE ON LOANS AND ANNUITIES		
1. One-third of widow Gerly's pension	666	
2. Interest on Guillaume's 12 000 livres	600	
3. Interest on Lasalle's 6 000 livres	300	
4. Life pension to Madeleine Bribal, through my		
husband's will of 21 June 1779	50	
	Total	1 616
	Net income	38 314 livres

Source: R. FORSTER, *The Nobility of Toulouse.*

Fig. II.1 The craftsmen of Lyon in the nineteenth century: the
widening gap between the earnings of masters and men in the
course of the century

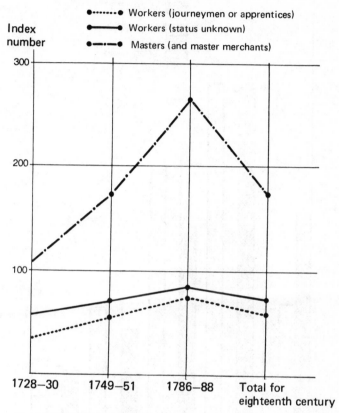

Source: M. Garden, *Lyon et les Lyonnais au XVIIIe siècle* (Paris, Les Belles
Lettres, 1970).

Fig. II.2   Differences in wealth among silkworkers in the eighteenth century (from marriage contracts)

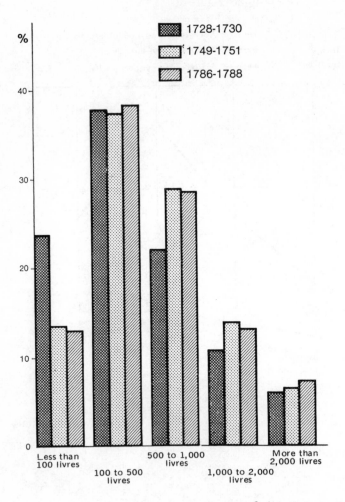

Source: M. Garden, *Lyon et les Lyonnais au XVIIIe siècle* (Paris, Les Belles Lettres, 1970).

Fig. II.3 Preponderance in wealth of nobility over merchants in Lyon
(marriage contracts, 1780–89)

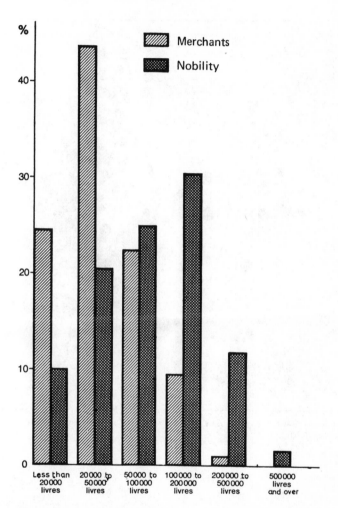

Source: M. Garden, *Lyon et les Lyonnais au XVIIIe siécle* (Paris, Les Belles
Lettres, 1970).

Fig. II.4   Migration: native parishes of newcomers to Lyon, from the
Lyonnais, Forez and Beaujolais provinces, 1786–8

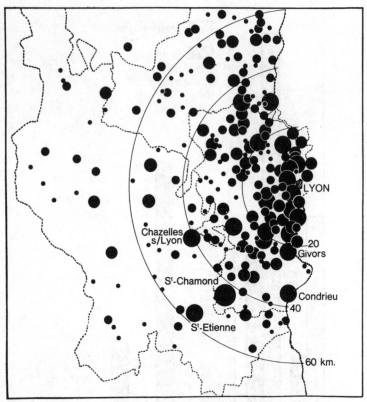

Source: M. Garden, *Lyon et les Lyonnais au XVIIIe siècle* (Paris, Less Belles
Lettres, 1970).

Fig. II.5 Toulouse: social inequality at time of death

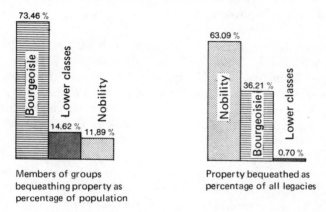

Members of groups
bequeathing property as
percentage of population

Property bequeathed as
percentage of all legacies

Source: J. Sentou, *Fortunes et groupes sociaux à Toulouse*, op. cit.

Some aspects of bourgeois happiness

The exaltation of bourgeois 'virtues' is linked with the idea of the golden mean. The bourgeois is seen as occupying a satisfactory intermediate position between the debasement of poverty and the corruption of greatness. The bourgeoisie was the only social class not isolated from the others. A bourgeois could be more completely a man than a man of the masses or a courtier. The face of the former was distorted by poverty, illness, ignorance and bitterness. The latter were either vicious or futile. But the bourgeois had neither of these defects: he occupied an intermediate position between these two extremes.

Some kinds of happiness were beyond his reach. The only love he experienced was conjugal devotion; passion would appal him. He was no hero; he lacked heart, but he was sure of himself. For him there was no disturbing contrast between dream and life, instinct and conscience; there was no distinction between the possible and the real.

In his private life he did not attain true greatness. There he was only happy. But he played an important role in the nation at large through the effectiveness of his work. His role in the commercial world gave him a kind of greatness he did not have in his private life. Here he represented the face of the modern world. Here his greatness was not mere ostentation, as was the greatness of nobility, but it was an active, beneficial greatness. He was not only working for his own happiness, but was making a positive contribution towards the happiness of others.

The *abbé* Coyer developed this theme in his *Noblesse Commerçante* (*The Commercial Nobility*) where he tried to persuade the nobility that commerce was not unworthy of their attentions. Whilst at one time they had protected the King with their swords, now their duty was to make the nation wealthy by participating in a glorious commercial enterprise.

This therefore enhanced the prestige of the bourgeois. By attending to his own business he was, at the same time, also contributing to the greatness of the state and the happiness of his fellow citizens. He was the equivalent of the knight of his times. He was strong, and his strength was extensive. If they were sufficiently enlightened others could appreciate this. Magistrates and soldiers could only defend the lords of the land and the security of the King, but the bourgeois acted in the interests of all humanity. While the gentleman was involved in the rivalries between nations, the role of the bourgeois was to bring all men of all nations together in understanding. Through the special conditions of commercial exchange, the bourgeois could achieve universal friendship.

Because of the conduct of the bourgeois the conception of what constituted 'honour' changed. Whereas previously it had meant the pursuit of prestigious aims, now it meant respect for genuine principles. This was less something new than a return to the conception of honour held before aristocratic society, with its pride and futility, had de-natured the idea. The virtues of the bourgeois, making him a man of 'honour', were the opposite of the characteristics of the nobility. The bourgeois was obedient, hard-working, concerned with his well-being, and with securing harmony between nations. This should have contributed to both the greatness of kings and the happiness of men. . . .

This was the commercial bourgeois. But there was another side to him. There was also the bourgeois who was essentially a family man. The characteristics of this bourgeois are to be found in Lordelot's treatise of 1706: *Les Devoirs de la vie domestique par un père de famille*. Religious feeling and a fear of God lead to the respect for one's father and are thus at the very basis of the peace and harmony of family life. Religious feeling also causes the husband to be kind, the wife to be dutiful, the children obedient and the servants faithful. Conjugal comforts are important for the bourgeois. They are a peaceful haven, a refuge from the stormy world of business and its demands. . . .

This bourgeois is no revolutionary and although proclaiming his belief in natural equality yet considers social inequality to be a pre-ordained feature of life. He is thus socially conservative. He considers that the poor may hope for improvement, but have no right to demand anything else from society. Yet since gifts for the poor are a feature of his religious duties, he fulfils them. For the bourgeois this is pure charity: a gift freely made. This contributes to his virtues, but for the noble this gift is a reparation, in expiation of past misdeeds.

But the bourgeois described by Lordelot in 1706 changed during the eighteenth century. He became less and less of a Christian, and came to regard himself more and more as master of the world. He was no longer content to be merely content and happy among his fellows, but wished to be recognized as the cornerstone of the state. This was a kind of bourgeois 'patriotism'. By the end of the century he dreams of being at the head of the social order: a position he believes he deserves because of his work and his virtues.

He considers his own happiness to be based in reality, unlike the frivolity of the aristocracy and the misery of the lower orders of society. Bourgeois happiness is a judicious balance of joy and virtue: virtue derived from the rectitude of his personal life and the useful role he played in the life of the state.

R. MAUZI, *L'idée du bonheur dans la littérature et la pensée française au XVIIIe siècle* (Paris, Colin, 1960). From Chapter VII, 'Le bonheur bourgeois'.

The end of the Ancien Régime
The abolition of the feudal system (Decree of August 11 1789)

1. The National Assembly abolishes the feudal system in its entirety, and decrees that both feudal and censuel rights ... and personal servitude ... are abolished without indemnity, and all others declared redeemable ... Those of the said dues which are not suppressed shall continue to be rendered until reimbursement has been made.

2. The exclusive right to own dovecots is abolished; pigeons shall be penned at periods fixed by communities; and at such times they shall be treated as game and anyone may kill them on his own land.

3. The exclusive right of hunting and open warrens is also abolished, and all proprietors have the right to destroy or cause to be destroyed on their own land every kind of game. ...

4. All seignorial courts of justice are abolished without compensation; but officials of such courts shall continue in office until the National Assembly has set up a new judicial organization.

5. Tithes of every kind are abolished ... subject to the provision in some other way for defraying the expenses of divine worship, the maintenance of ministers of religion, the relief of the poor, the upkeep

of churches and presbyteries, and for all establishments ... for the maintenance of which they are responsible. Until such provision is made the National Assembly orders that collection of the said tithes shall continue. ...

6. All perpetual ground rents, in kind or in money ... shall be redeemable.

7. Neither judicial nor municipal functions are to be open to purchase nor the subject of fees. Justice shall be rendered gratuitously. ...

8. The supplementary fees of *curés* are abolished. ...

9. Pecuniary privileges in tax matters are abolished. All citizens shall pay alike on all property. ...

10. ... All special privileges enjoyed by provinces, principalities, regions, cantons, cities and communities are abolished and are merged into the common rights of all Frenchmen.

11. All citizens may be admitted to all employments and functions ecclesiastical, civil or military without distinction of birth.

The complete abolition of feudal rights (Decree of July 27 1793)

1. All *ci-devant* (former) seignorial dues, feudal rights ... including those unaffected by the decree of 25 August are abolished without compensation.

2. The previous article does not apply to rents or rights of a proprietorial rather than feudal character.

6. (States that all documents and title deeds recording such rights shall be burnt.)

Abolition of guilds and corporations of masters (Decree of 2–17 March 1791)

1. All rights known as *droits d'aides*, taxes levied on the stocking or transportation or sale of drink, or playing cards, or in respect of marks or seals that manufacturers have to affix to cloth or other goods are abolished.

2. (Abolishes all special trade or professional privileges, charges for membership of guilds, etc.)

7. After 1 April it shall be open to anyone to take up any business, profession, art or craft they desire; they shall, however, provide themselves with a licence and pay the fees hereinafter laid down and conform to such police regulations as shall be fixed.

Licences need not be held by public officials, farm workers, apprentices or wage earners, or holders of stalls in public markets.

Freedom of agriculture (Decree of September—October 1791)

I.1. The land of France is in its totality as free as the persons who inhabit it; hence no territorial property may be alienated to anybody except for rents or dues the conditions of which are permitted by law. . . .

I.2. Proprietors are free to cultivate their land as they wish, to retain as much of their produce as they want, or to sell the produce of their property within the kingdom or without. . . .

II.1. The duration and conditions of leases shall be subject to individual agreements.

IV.1. Proprietors are free to keep herds of whatever size or variety they consider suitable for the exploitation of their land. . . .

IV.4. The right to instal or remove fencing belongs to proprietors and cannot be contested.

The ban on combinations (Decree of 14 June 1791, the 'le Chapelier' law)

1. The abolition of every kind of combination of citizens of the same way of life or profession is a fundamental principle of the French constitution; their restoration in any form or for any reason is forbidden.

2. Citizens of the same way of life or profession, entrepreneurs, shopkeepers, workers and journeymen may not when gathered together name any president . . . secretaries . . . or draft regulations concerning their alleged common interests.

4. If contrary to the principles of liberty and the constitution citizens engaged in the same professions, arts and crafts deliberate or agree amongst themselves with the aim of fixing the price of their service or labour such deliberations and agreements are declared unconstitutional . . . and of nil effect. . . . Their instigators . . . shall be . . . fined 500 livres and suspended for one year from all rights of active citizenship. . . .

6. If the said deliberations . . . result in threats against entrepreneurs, artisans, workers or foreign day-labourers working there, or against those who accept lower wages, all . . . instigators . . . shall be punished with a fine of 1,000 livres and three months imprisonment.

8. All such assemblies . . . shall be considered as seditious assemblies and as such shall be dispersed by those entrusted with the maintenance of public order . . . and shall be punished. . . .

Freedom of work (Law of 12 April 1803)

6. All combinations of employers of labour aiming at an unjust or detrimental lowering of wages, followed by an attempt at or initiative to carry out such intention shall be punishable by a fine of at least 300 francs or at most 3,000 francs; or if necessary by a maximum one month's imprisonment.

7. All combinations of workers simultaneously to stop work or forbid work in certain workshops, interfere with work or its duration and generally to hold up, prevent or bid up the price of labour shall be punished. . . .

8. If any act described in the preceding article is accompanied by assault, violence or riotous assemblage the instigators and their accomplices shall be punished. . . .

11. No employer of labour may take on an apprentice without a *congé d'acquit* (formal notice of discharge). . . .

12. No employer may hire a worker unless he can show a *livret* endorsed with a certificate of discharge from his previous employer.

III Towards an industrial society

The vast political upheaval of the Revolution reflected a social struggle in which all levels of Ancien Régime society were involved. By attempting to break down royal 'despotism', the aristocracy opened the door to revolution. Indeed for this reason some historians have argued that the Revolution began in 1787; that the actions of the aristocracy were the first phase; that there was an 'aristocratic revolution'. But the aristocracy was very quickly overtaken, bypassed and finally outlawed by subsequent developments. The bourgeoisie became the driving force behind the Revolution. At first the impulse came from the professional, intellectual and legal bourgeoisie who effected the 'revolution of the jurists' (1789–91). Then came the upper and middle bourgeoisie with Girondins until their expulsion in 1793; then the *petit bourgeois* Parisian Montagnards and Jacobins.

There was no spontaneous action from the masses (except during the *grande peur* in the countryside 1789 and the *sans-culotte* movement). In general they represented a tool of revolutionary violence manipulated by the various bourgeois factions. The bourgeoisie found their protector and master in Napoleon. Napoleon claimed to stand above factions, to base his power on all levels of society or rather on everybody, whatever their social origins, who offered themselves for his service. These were what he called 'decent folk'.

With the fall of the First Empire and the victory of the ancient monarchies and traditional society, the way was open to a restoration, which looked as if it could take the shape of social counter-revolution. Those defeated by the Revolution thought that 1815 would be the time of revenge: but they were to be proved wrong. Pressure from the outside world, the military situation and the restoration of the monarchy made 'revenge' seem possible. But against this stood public opinion and changed economic conditions. The future lay not with the landed wealth of the traditional aristocratic society of the past but with the liberal economic bourgeoisie profiting from the beginnings of the industrial revolution and already risen because of the economic prosperity of the eighteenth century.

1. The losers: nobility and clergy
The privileged orders had lost in the fight with the third estate: privilege had been replaced by the equality of all Frenchmen before the

law. The Revolution had, above all, achieved civic equality and this had not been reversed by the reactionary mood of the First Empire with its new court and civil-service nobility and the creation of a Concordat which described roman catholicism as no more than the religion of 'the majority of Frenchmen'. The social hierarchy was now based on wealth.

The destruction of privilege meant a loss of wealth for the nobility, because of the abolition of seignorial dues, and for the clergy first through the abolition of tithe and then through the loss of its lands, since the property of the clergy was now forfeited to the nation, as was that of nobles who had emigrated. The losses were not total. Not all nobles emigrated. Some who did managed to preserve their property with the aid of their relatives, and those clergy who remained were paid by the state and received substantial compensation in that way. Yet the first two orders of pre-revolutionary France, apart from no longer existing in law as 'orders', had lost a good deal of their wealth.

The spectacle of a clergy split over the Civil Constitution (12 July 1790) and trying to interfere in politics had lost it a lot of respect and authority. The faithful were shocked at the conflict between clergy who had taken the oath of allegiance and those who had not, patriots were shocked that non-jurors could stoop to plotting with counter-revolutionaries; while for opponents of the Revolution the attitude of the oath-takers seemed disgracefully time-serving. Recruitment into the clergy slowed down considerably during the Revolution and despite Napoleon's Concordat with the Papacy, which removed obstacles to joining the priesthood, recruitment only picked up slowly. The profession had lost much of its prestige.

But the nobility emerged from the Revolution with its prestige even more diminished. The emigrés had dissociated themselves from the nation: patriots considered treasonable their fleeing to join forces with the enemies of revolutionary France. Although Napoleon's amnesty to the emigrés and the passage of time had subdued passions, the prestige of the nobility had suffered a further blow. Before the Revolution they epitomized the virtues of war, but during the Revolution they had been surpassed in valour by their social inferiors. The so-called 'nobility of the sword' had lost their raison d'être.

The old privileged orders were quick to seize the opportunity offered by Napoleon's defeat of pursuing a policy of revenge. The restoration of the monarchy, the election in 1816 of a chamber dominated by the provinical nobility seemed to present an ideal opportunity for a new start. The restored nobility had their plans. They had awaited the restoration for many years and wanted it to be much

more than a return to the Ancien Régime. They yearned for the
establishment of their own romantic version of medieval monarchy.
Non-despotic, and paternal as was 'good Henry IV'; dependent upon a
hierarchy of privileged bodies headed by a privileged nobility and a
church restored to its old rights and properties. They wanted a social as
well as a political revolution. Society should be based on natural
inequality, because this was how God had created it, on authority and
heredity; for them society was not contractual – men had duties, not
rights. To this end, all who did not agree with this view should be
eliminated from power, and the aristocracy should dominate. This was
attempted by various means and with varying degrees of success,
throughout the fifteen years of the restoration period.

The nobility had first to be given a legal existence, and this was
achieved by article 71 of the Charter which stated: 'Members of the
ancient nobility shall resume their titles; members of the new nobility
shall retain their titles. The King may create nobles as he wills, but he
may only grant them rank and honours. They shall in no way be exempt from the duties and burdens of society.' The restoration nobility
were thus a nobility without privileges, and without legal means of
enforcing their hierarchical position. The old nobility were rather short
of titles conferred by royal warrant or letters patent, and most of those
who had reached manhood in 1815 bore none, since in 1789 they had
been children; so they gave themselves what titles they wished, apart
from the title of Duke which only the King could confer. Some nobles
registered their new titles by securing letters patent of recognition, but
most did not bother – giving themselves 'courtesy' titles which were
juridically unsound. During this period the use of the *particule* 'de'
before the surname acquired a significance it had never known under
the Ancien Régime.

The wealth of the nobility had always been derived from the land.
The abolition of seignorial dues led them now to pay particular
attention to the retention of their land and the regaining of lost land.
The question of national lands (*biens nationaux*) was therefore of great
importance. Would the lands of the emigrés which had been sold be
restored to them? Those who had lost them through loyalty to the King
in exile thought they would be restored. But Louis XVIII was aware
that by doing this he would arouse massive hostility from those who
had bought them. As soon as he returned to France he announced that
this transfer of property was irrevocable. But some kind of compensation was another matter. The government could not afford a total
re-imbursement and so in 1825 provided compensation in the form of

3 per cent government stocks which provided an annual total of 30 million francs, and represented a capital value of a billion francs. A fall in stock exchange values reduced the value of the *rentes* to 620 million francs. This was still a considerable sum which, in time, might have allowed the nobility to re-purchase their lost domains. But it seems that this was rarely done. Although the amount of land held by the nobility after 1815 was not as great as the amount held before that date, it was still considerable, and particularly in some regions such as the *département* of the Eure, where

> most of the nobility had preserved their wealth and influence ... In each village the château was the political and social centre and the various activities of the *commune* went on around it. The charity dispensed by the lady of the manor and her daughters was the only form of poor relief in the countryside. Local tradition still lived on in the great seignorial château employing entire families of servants and housing the poor and needy, who paid, if they were able-bodied, for a night's shelter and a meal, by doing odd jobs. The noble was often the mayor of the *commune*. In this way he maintained the kind of political control known by his predecessors. (J. Vidalenc)

The aristocracy therefore had a fair degree of social power — because of their titles, their wealth and also their social influence. In the political sphere they were very powerful. The electoral system was heavily weighted in their favour since the franchise was restricted to those who paid a certain amount in taxation. There were 90,000 electors and only 16,000 eligible to stand for election to the Chamber of Deputies. So the electorate was small and was therefore more 'manageable', more open to the pressures of the administration and especially so because elections often took several days. The landed aristocracy played a dominant role in these elections, and was heavily represented in the Chamber of Deputies. In 1816, 176 out of 381 deputies were nobles and seventy-three of these were returned emigrés. In the Chamber of 1821 the proportion of nobles had risen to 58 per cent. Throughout the Restoration period the aristocracy managed to retain political power with the aid of their allies and their hangers on — politicians who had betrayed the Empire in 1814 and 1815 and lawyers and middle-class supporters attached by self-interest or conviction.

They infiltrated the administration as well. At the top, because clearly the government needed reliable hands to wield its formidable power — lower down, for other than political reasons: deprived of royal liberality to support their social pretensions they turned to the state, pushing for all sorts of government jobs that the pre-revolutionary aristocracy would have considered beneath their dignity – police officers, magistrates, tax collectors, even postmasters. Bertier de Sauvigny, the main authority on the restoration period, comments: 'For the first and last time in modern French history prestige from birth and title was linked with political and administrative power.' They seem to have given honest service to the restored monarchy. There were never so few political and financial scandals as at this time. It is easy to see what extensive local powers were in the hands of a social group which combined wealth, consequence and the right to speak in the name of the state; often, too, the right to judge. The magistrature was dominated by the legitimists, the supporters of Bourbon restoration, who were not always nobles. This was revealed by the purge of officials after the Revolution of 1830: Louis Philippe's government dismissed seventy-four *procureurs généraux*[1] and their deputies and 254 *procureurs du roi*[1] and their deputies, but did not revoke the principle that the judges were immovable. However a hundred refused to swear the oath of fidelity and resigned. Others continued to make no secret of their legitimist sympathies.

The landed aristocracy had thus attained ascendancy in the political, administrative and judicial spheres. They attempted to create spiritual support for their domination through the power of the clergy, since under the Restoration, Roman catholicism was the state religion. The Church was quite prepared to form an alliance with the nobility, for it too looked to the government for material backing. Some ecclesiastics expected more: the Archbishop of Toulouse listed what he considered were the legitimate demands of the Church: adjustment of the civil code to suit canon law; restoration to the Church of the keeping of registers of births, marriages and deaths; restoration of synods and provincial church councils: restoration of religious holidays suppressed by the Concordat; restoration of religious courts, of the religious orders and of the financial independence of the clergy; and suppression of the Organic Articles. This was, in effect, a demand for a return to the Church of the Ancien Régime.

The clergy order of the Restoration was similar to and yet different from that of the Ancien Régime. The upper clergy mostly consisted of members of the aristocracy. Seventy out of ninety bishops appointed between 1815 and 1830 were nobles. But these bishops were unlike the

---

[1] Government appointed representatives of the Crown in Court, and subject to dismissal, unlike judges.

episcopate on the eve of the Revolution since they were not recruited from the upper nobility. The smaller provincial nobility were represented and some commoners too. On the whole the clergy were more dignified and more conscientious in carrying out their duties than the clergy of the Ancien Régime. They were, also, dedicated to the task of leading back to the fold a flock that had largely gone astray. In order to achieve this the upper clergy used three means: the influence of the parish priest, education and propaganda.

The condition of the lower clergy called for immediate attention. Recruitment had almost come to a standstill during the Revolution, and had made only slow progress after the Concordat with the Papacy. Under the Empire, the average was 500 ordinations per year. Most of the 36,000 clergy were therefore rather elderly (more than two-fifths were over sixty), had been trained under the Ancien Régime, had been maltreated by the Revolution and were discouraged by the indifference to organized religion of most of the population. But a vigorous effort to remedy this was undertaken with the encouragement of the state, which provided some finance for ecclesiastical institutions (legislation of 10 June 1814); allowed the opening by the bishops of one school in each *département* independent of university control (legislation of 5 October 1814); allowed the ownership of real estate by ecclesiastical institutions (legislation 1817) and above all allowed an increase in expenditure on religion, which had doubled by 1830 and had led to substantial improvement in clergy salaries. Clerical recruitment made remarkable progress (1,000 ordinations in 1815; 1,500 in 1820; 2,000 in 1828 and in 1830 a peak never to be obtained again of 2,357). With this influx and the death of many of the older priests the clergy experienced a revival which lasted until the middle of the nineteenth century. But it is difficult to say how effective the clergy were. The new recruits were frequently drawn from rural areas and the level of seminary instruction was not high. Well received by their parishioners, but not greatly needed, they frequently complained of a decline in religion which they attributed to 'unhappy days' (*le malheur des temps*) by which they meant the 'revolutionary ideology' and for which they only saw one cure: return to the pre-revolutionary *status quo* and a renewal of the throne—altar alliance. Thus they ended in becoming enthusiastic supporters of counter-revolution. Left high and dry by the Revolution of 1830 and the wave of anti-clericalism which followed it, the clergy retreated into silence and waited for divine intervention in the shape of a legitimist restoration.

Religious action through education, to be effective, involved abolishing the state monopoly exercised through the universities: or such was the view of some catholics. But the bishops, brought up to the doctrines of the Ancien Régime, were alarmed by the idea of replacing university monopoly by general freedom of education, which seemed a most dangerous plan. They preferred church control of the universities. They succeeded in 1822 in effecting the appointment of Bishop Frayssinous as Grand Master of the University, and in 1824 he took charge of a ministry of ecclesiastical affairs and of education. Clerics were placed in charge of lycées, now called 'royal schools', and he nominated their chaplains too. He packed the teaching and administrative staffs of communal colleges with priests and changed private boarding schools into church colleges. But above all it was in the 'little seminaries' that the clergy exerted their influence most effectively. These 'littles seminaries' and particularly those run by Jesuits, whose teaching abilities were much respected, were highly successful. They turned simple secondary teaching institutions into places where the sons of nobles and the catholic middle classes could acquire some culture and a religious education as well as a preparation for a proper seminary. Such were the ways by which it was hoped to guide the ruling classes back to the Church.

Various forms of propaganda were tried. Religious societies started by the famous devotional society, the *Congrégation*, which had been founded in 1801 and dissolved under the Empire, reappeared and reached all sections of society: the poorest through the *Société des Bonnes Oeuvres* (Society for Good Works), the young through the *Société des Bonnes Études* (Society for Good Study), the educated through the *Société Catholique des Bons Livres* (Catholic Society for Good Books) which could distribute 800,000 copies of works in a year, and the public at large through the *Association de la Défense de la Religion Catholique* (Association for the Defence of the Catholic Religion) and an independent society founded in Lyon in 1822, the *Société pour la Propagation de la Foi* (Society for the Propagation of the Faith). But the most spectacular instruments of propaganda were the *Missions*. The *Société des Missionnaires de France* was authorized by an Order of 15 December 1816 and preached its first mission at Nantes on 5 May 1816. It was successful and as a result the idea developed of a large evangelistic camaign throughout France, with peaceful demonstrations involving the public at large, often encouraged by the civil and military authorities. The missionaries were not afraid of intervening in politics. For example they organized ceremonies of atonement for the crimes of the Revolution. These actions provoked reactions and played some part in the spreading of the idea that the clergy supported the most extreme forms of royal reaction.

The Revolution of 1830 was therefore a severe blow to the catholic clergy as well as to the Bourbon monarchy. The church never enjoyed so close a relationship with the government as in this period of throne-altar alliance. Louis Philippe was ill-disposed toward the clergy during the early part of his reign, and if there was an easing of his suspicious attitude towards the end of his reign this was because he saw them as a bastion of social order. For the same reason the conservatives in the Second Republic sought clerical support, most notably through the issuing of the *Loi Falloux* of 15 March 1850; and Napoleon III loaded it with favours during the Second Empire. But the role of the clergy had changed. It became no more than a tool of the government in power, used to maintain Catholic loyalty and acceptance of the established order.

After 1830 clerical influence waned and the so-called religious revival of the years 1835—1840, shown in particular by the success of Lacordaire's lectures at Nôtre Dame de Paris, were more indicative of intellectual anxiety and a need for religiosity than a need for faith in the traditional sense of the word, or a return of the educated young to Roman catholicism. The number of candidates for ordination, on the other hand, declined each year and by 1841 they had reached the level of 1817—18. And it cannot be said that the clergy made up for lack of quantity by increased quality. They seem to have lost a lot of their influence over the population — over peasants who varied from hostility to religion on the one hand and, on the other, superstitious attachment to 'old-fashioned' religious practices such as fasts or pilgrimages rather than to the sacraments. The increasing numbers of industrial workers in the towns do not seem to have been greatly influenced by the clergy either. This may well have been because the bishops' views of poverty were out of tune with the situation and feelings of the workers. They condemned poverty but did not condem social injustice. To them poverty was simply a moral problem, and as upholders of the social order they could see no remedy other than charity.

But the decline of the aristocracy after 1830 was much more striking than that of the clergy. Lhomme comments, 'One must be surprised that this class allowed itself to be put to one side so easily. At one moment it was at the head of French society. A moment afterwards it had lost its position. History has few examples of so sudden and complete a transformation. No resistance, no movements of any kind, merely acceptance of the fait accompli and resignation to its fate.'

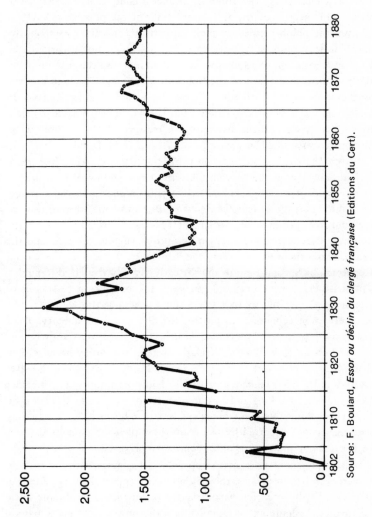

Fig. III.1 The secular clergy (ordinations)

Source: F. Boulard, *Essor ou déclin du clergé française* (Editions du Cert).

But their submissiveness appears less remarkable when one remembers that the aristocracy did not owe their position in restoration France to their own efforts: they had been too gravely hit by the Revolution to be able to do that. They owed their position to force, and in particular to the force of France's conquerors in 1815. The shock and surprise of the rest of the bulk of the population in 1815 allowed the nobility to assert their supremacy for a few years; but the bases of this supremacy were insecure and could not withstand the Parisian Revolution of 1830 especially when there was no reaction from the provinces in defence of the Bourbon monarchy. The failure of the Duchesse de Berry's attempt to raise the west in legitimist revolt in 1832 only confirmed the position. The aristocracy were unable to regain their lost power: their attempts to reassert their position when circumstances seemed auspicious, in 1850 and 1873, failed.

After 1830 the aristocracy only had local power. Their sphere of influence was now the canton. Here the large landowner of legitimist views could often command sufficient votes, under universal suffrage, to gain the position of *conseiller général*. But an *arrondissement* was too big and the position of parliamentary deputy usually escaped the nobility. Certain regions were an exception: such as the west and the south. From these regions came the 'legitimist' deputies of the Second Republic, the Second Empire and the early years of the Third Republic. The aristocracy were only able to swell the opposition to successive régimes in France but by themselves could never overthrow them.

There were economic reasons for the decline of the nobility. Their economic power rested on landed wealth. But this power was dwindling in an absolute as well as in a relative sense. Absolutely because they made hardly any effort to improve their lands. Relatively, because after 1830 wealth from landed property had lost its importance, incomes from industry, banking and business generally were making themselves felt. The nobility were not much interested in business. Although they were no longer debarred by law from these plebeian pursuits the idea that it was not an occupation for gentlemen persisted.

Although some aristocrats appear in the nineteenth century as directors in big businesses, they by no means appear in every variety of business: hardly at all for instance in the turbulent and profitable world of finance. Lecouteulx de Canteleu was the only one to participate in the foundation of the Banque de France; and on its governing body only a few Napoleonic titles appear. The great names occur much later on. The more 'aristocratic' banks were only founded towards the end of the nineteenth century: the *Crédit de France* in 1879, the *Banque*

Romaine in 1881 and above all the *Union Général* whose financial crash made sensational news. But the aristocracy were interested from an early date in insurance, metallurgy in Alsace and Lorraine and mining in central France and in the south. And they were beginning to involve themselves in business, if only through marriage. Marriages with bourgeois, Jewish and American heiresses were fashionable at the end of the century.

In general this reflected developments of pre-revolutionary trends. Under the Ancien Régime the nobility could engage in metallurgy and mining without *dérogeance;* there were prosperous insurance companies before 1789 in which several nobles invested their money, although discreetly. Marriages of convenience were known, often with wealthy members of the administrative bourgeoisie. In the nineteenth century great fortunes were made in business, and it was among bourgeois families that the aristocracy sought wives; but not careers. They founded no industrial or financial dynasties. In the eyes of the aristocracy it would seem that intrusion into the world of business was only a temporary necessity or even an accident.

This attitude was not confined to aristocrats. It was imitated by other social groups which looked towards them and regarded them as a kind of model to follow. They passed on their prejudices – their scorn for politics (after their failure in 1830) which they came to regard as a degrading activity and also their contempt for business, and their failure to adapt to the capitalist character of big business.

2. The gainers: peasants and bourgeoisie
The peasants

After the Revolution, as before it, France remained a predominantly agricultural country and was to remain so for a long time. Agricultural output was worth three times industrial output in 1830, and was still worth twice as much at the beginning of the Second Empire. The outputs were of about equal value only at the very end of the nineteenth century. Analysis of inheritance annuities confirms this: in 1826, 66 per cent of the values of these were made up of landed property; movable wealth only equalled landed wealth in 1896. It has already been shown that in the middle of the nineteenth century the agrarian population represented slightly more than half of the total population.

To what extent was the condition of the peasantry – by far the largest section of society – changed by the Revolution? The agrarian reforms of the Revolution are well-known: abolition of the 'feudal' régime; increase of property owners through the sale of national lands and division of the common lands; extension of property rights through abolition of collective rights and by the declaration of freedom of cultivation and trade. How effective were they? Freedom from seignorial dues and also from the tithe were urgent peasant demands and obviously gave great satisfaction to those who benefited. But not all the peasants improved their position. Only property owners profited in full from the abolition of money payments; share-croppers and tenant-farmers had to pay higher rents to landowners as a result of measures passed by the Constituent and Legislative Assemblies; as for wage-earners, they gained nothing.

But did the sale of national lands allow the landless to obtain some land and those who owned a little to own more? This is the crucial question for an understanding of the social effects of the Revolution in the countryside. A total survey of the sales of national lands does not exist, but it is possible to give some regional indications. Some national lands were never sold. Those which had not been disposed of were restored to their original owners during the Empire and the Restoration period. The peasants, furthermore, did not buy all those lands sold. Some were bought back by emigrés through third parties. Several bourgeois bought them: in some districts they bought most of the lands offered for sale and for this reason the bourgeoisie are often said to have been those who profited most; but there were regional variations which do not allow this generalization to be made with total certainty. Certainly all church property disappeared, and a fair section of aristocratic property, to the advantage of the bourgeoisie and the peasantry. But which peasants benefited? Sale was by auction, which favoured the wealthy, but the poor were sometimes able to group together and buy a block of land, even sometimes forcibly to displace other bidders. Occasionally they were able to buy land which speculators had bought *en bloc* and resold in small parcels. Some small peasants and even wage-earners who had a little money saved up may therefore have been able to acquire some land, particularly with the rapid depreciation in value of the *assignats*, since land had to be purchased with the new paper currency created by the Constituent Assembly. But did the very poorest inhabitants of the countryside disappear? The answer is no: for this to happen national land would have had to be not sold, but shared out. This was never the intention of the Revolutionary assemblies, largely for political and financial reasons.

The Revolution may even, unintentionally, have worsened the

condition of some of the peasants by a wide extension of the rights of private property. By ending collective rights in the countryside and proclaiming liberty of cultivation the Revolution had left the wage-earner with his wage as his only resource, and made life harder for the very small property owner. Lefebvre comments, 'The Revolution, by darkening the prospects of the poor peasant, paved the way for his leaving the countryside; all that remained was to build the factory: workers would not be lacking.'

There were a great many small property owners. This can be seen by examining the statistics of the assessments of land made for taxation purposes. The information they provide, however, is limited: a distinction between property with or without buildings was only made in 1884. Assessment is based on value of land not on its extent; the total of people in each taxation category was not given until 1858 although it is possible to give an estimate using the 1858 figures as comparison. Yet despite their lack of precision, these statistics are valuable. The figures of 1826 give the following information (total values are estimates):

Table III.1 Taxable values of land in 1825

Assessment category	Number	%	Estimated total value	%
20 francs and below	8 024 987	77.94	40 365 685	16.99
21 francs to 30 francs	663 237	6.44	16 050 335	6.75
31 francs to 50 francs	642 345	6.24	24 865 175	10.46
51 francs to 100 francs	527 991	5.13	36 589 776	15.41
101 francs to 300 francs	335 505	3.26	52 952 754	22.29
301 francs to 500 francs	56 602	0.55	21 680 830	9.14
501 francs to 1 000 francs	32 579	0.31	22 671 075	9.54
1 001 francs and above	13 447	0.13	22 362 630	9.42
TOTAL	10 296 693	100.00	237 538 260	100.00

The number of assessments is not the same as the number of landowners, since many held land in several *communes* and were therefore counted several times. Those who administered the taxes said that there were sixty landowners for every 100 assessments, which gives a total figure of 6,200,000 landowners. It seems likely that these multiple assessments were to be found evenly distributed between all categories, making comparison between them valid.

Fig. III.2   Substantial properties in 1826: proportions of properties
assessed at over 500 francs, by départements

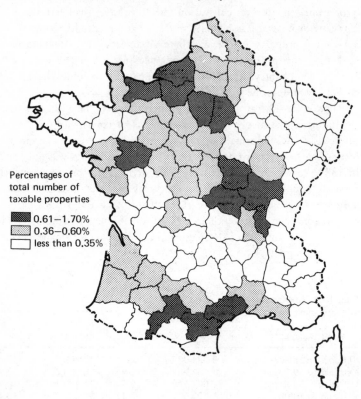

Percentages of
total number of
taxable properties

■ 0.61–1.70%
▨ 0.36–0.60%
□ less than 0.35%

The very small assessments were the most numerous. Assessments
of less than twenty francs probably correspond to small properties of
possibly less than two *hectares* and definitely less than five. These small
patches of land represent 75 per cent of the total *number* of landed
properties. But they represent less than 20 per cent of the total *value*.
But on the other hand the higher assessments (of more than 300
francs), which only account for 1 per cent of the total number, account
for 28 per cent of the total value of the assessment. In other words
fewer than 60,000 landowners held more than a quarter of the land.
The division of land was much less equal than is sometimes imagined.

These larger landed estates were concentrated in certain regions (see the map opposite). They were above all in the northern area of France, except in Brittany: in Normandy, Picardy, the Ile de France, and in the Loire region. They were also to be found in the valley of the Saône, the Nivernais, and in southern France — in Languedoc and throughout the Garonne basin. But they were far less common in the east, in Brittany, the Massif Central and the Alps. Large properties were to be found in the plains and where the land was rich, as in the alluvial soils of the Paris basin, and valley.

The democracy of small independent landowners to which the Montagnards aspired did not exist in 1826. But would that part of the Civil Code which established equality of inheritance establish a more equitable distribution of property? Was this a 'machine for mincing up property' as has sometimes been said? The number of assessed properties increased from 10 million in 1826 to 11.5 million in 1842 and 13 million in 1858: an increase of 27 per cent. This may have been partly due to the law of inheritance, but its effects were not uniform and it seems to have had most impact on the smaller and very small assessments also on the very large ones. The number of middling assessments only increased very slightly. These probably corresponded to middle-sized properties whose owners made special efforts to avoid subdivision through inheritance.

The statistics of 1884 allow one to be more precise since they give information not only on the amount of the assessments but also on their actual extent, and in addition they give more information on the character of the land — whether it was built on or not. (Fig. III.3).

It will be seen that when plotted by *size* the curve rises fairly evenly, but with a larger proportion of assessments of over twenty hectares, but when the *number* of assessments is plotted a vast preponderance of small ones can be seen, those of less than one hectare representing three-fifths of the total, those less than five nine-tenths of the total. On the other hand the large assessments are few but represent a high proportion of the land: 16 per cent for assessments of more than 200 hectares, 25 per cent for those of more than 100. Taken as a whole they show a significant differentiation: 50 per cent of French agricultural land consisted of properties of less than twenty hectares, that is some 13,700,000 assessments; the remaining 50 per cent consisted of some 400,000 properties of over twenty hectares. In other words 3 per cent of all proprietors were sitting on as much land as the other 97 per cent. The dominant factor in the pattern of land-ownership was its concentration in a few hands.

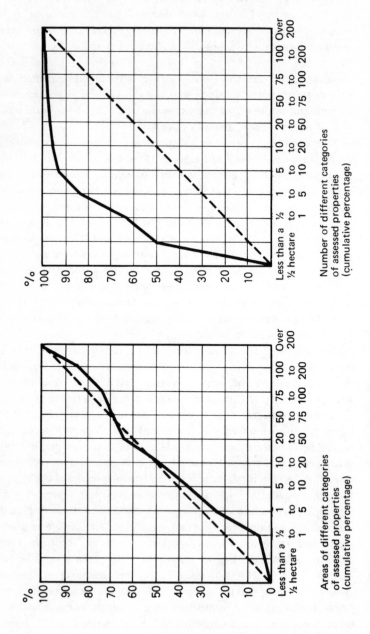

Fig. III.3 Figures for assessments for land tax in 1884 *(unbuilt-on land)*

Table III.2 Working agrarian population, 1862–82

	1862	1882
Owner-cultivators		
Farming only their own land	1 812 573	2 150 696
Farming their own land but also working as:		
tenant farmers	648 836	500 144
share croppers	203 860	147 128
day labourers	1 134 490	727 374
Non-owners		
Tenant farmers	386 533	468 184
Share-croppers	201 527	194 448
Wage-earners		
Managers	10 215	17 966
Labourers	869 254	753 313
Domestic servants	2 095 777	1 954 251
TOTAL	7 363 065	6 913 504

One need not, however, conclude from this that almost all the peasantry on these small plots of land were condemned to poverty. This would be confusing ownership and cultivation and would neglect the fact that large landowners did not generally farm their own lands, and thus those without land, or with insufficient for their needs, could cultivate the land of others. The statistics of ownership therefore do not give the whole answer. Statistics showing who actually cultivated the land are also needed. But these are not so reliable, and only came into existence in the second half of the nineteenth century with the agrarian inquiries of 1862 and 1882. The information they give on the working agrarian population (men and women) is listed in Table III.2

Although the figures given are probably not very accurate the proportions of one group to another and the variations between 1862 and 1882 are worthy of note. One peasant family in two was without land and four-fifths of these were mere wageearners; the other fifth were either farmers or sharecroppers. Among those who owned land, about half had enough to support their families; the other half were owners of small plots of land forced to make up their income by renting other plots of land, or more commonly by seeking part-time agricultural employment. Those without enough land were thus able to make up for the deficit by cultivating the land of others for their own benefit or for wages. There were about 2 million independent landowners and a further 1,500,000 cultivators who were not wage-earners. But in the countryside those dependent on wages were in the majority. There were 3 million day-labourers and farm servants and a million small landowners obliged to seek day-labour to make ends meet.

The period between these surveys, from 1862 to 1882 is, admittedly, a short one but it enables one to have some idea of the changes taking place in the countryside. Throughout the nineteenth century the first tendency to be noted may be summed up in the term 'deproletarization' – an increase in the numbers of those cultivating their own land and a drop in the number of farm-servants and day-labourers. The number of small landowners dropped whereas the number of those cultivating sufficient land for their own needs increased by 50 per cent. Similarly the drop in the numbers of day-labourers and farm-servants was compensated by an increase of one-third in the number of tenant farmers. Perhaps some of the small landowners were able to increase the size of their holdings and become independent landowners, and a similar number had left the countryside for the town. Among the farm-servants possibly some had become tenant farmers and probably some day-labourers too had left the land. In the long term the character of the countryside was changing: seemingly by the departure of the poor and the improvement in the lot of the better-off, or the more efficient.

The material condition of the peasantry was affected by changes in their legal status, the development of land-ownership patterns, but also by economic circumstances. Agriculture made some progress during the first half of the nineteenth century. The changes which took place are difficult to pinpoint exactly. Among the main changes there seems to have been an increase in the amount of land cultivated. In some areas more land was brought into cultivation. In the *département* of the Eure, for example, one-fifth of all waste land was brought into cultivation between 1800 and 1837. And after the 1830s the amount of land allowed to lie fallow was reduced. Between 1840 and 1862 the amount of fallow land fell from 6,700,000 hectares to 5,150,000. Some of this reclaimed land became leys which both enriched the soil and provided a much needed source of food for livestock. A cycle of agrarian improvement was thus set in motion. An increase in livestock (20 per cent increase of sheep between 1812 and 1852 and 30 per cent of cattle between 1830 and 1850) led to an increase in farm manure which in turn led to better soil conditions and finally more abundant harvests.

Where farm machinery was concerned progress was slower. There was little change in the first half of the nineteenth century. Modern ploughs were not widely used outside eastern and northern France and the Paris basin. The sickle was used more than the scythe; mechanical reapers, seed-drills and harvesters only appeared during the Second Empire. The 'steam revolution' had not greatly affected agriculture and the threshing machine was the only agricultural machine powered by steam. There were other reasons too. Many peasants had too little capital to afford modern equipment. Some even lacked the inclination.

Contemporaries testify to the peasants' passion for land; to their great desire to round off their properties. As a result these much desired plots reached prices greater than their yield could justify and the purchaser might run into debt. The precise amount of peasant debt is unknown because they often used promissory notes, of which there are no records, rather than mortgages. The peasants thus preferred to spend their capital on land rather than equipment, fertilizers or better quality seed. Productivity was therefore sacrificed for ownership. This is quite understandable: in a period of slow technical progress there was no social advantage to be gained by super productivity; it was impossible in fact to distinguish oneself by getting much better results than one's neighbours. One could however gain prestige and enhance one's social status by acquiring property.

French agriculture in the nineteenth century retained many of the features of the eighteenth, which served a still largely subsistence economy. Cereal crops were therefore of paramount importance. Yet other crops were being substituted for cereal crops. There was less rye; in Brittany buckwheat was tending to disappear. The potato now held an important place among food crops. Although production increased this was not sufficient to protect consumers from occasional harvest failures. There were still crises caused by high food prices in 1816–17, 1828–9, 1837–9, 1846–7 and even in 1853–5. This type of crisis continued until 1867.

Agriculture also produced primary materials for industry. Hemp, flax, oil-seeds and plants yielding dye-stuffs were grown over wide areas. More than 50,000 hectares in the Rhone valleys were used for growing mulberry trees to provide food for silk worms and towards the middle of the century 25,000 tonnes (one metric ton equals 1,000 kg.) of cocoons were being produced, but although these forms of agriculture provided a useful source of revenue for some peasants for a time, this was soon to disappear with foreign competition.

Peasant isolation was being eroded by improvements in main and minor roads, and soon by the introduction of the railways. These improvements in transport led to the appearance of a more commercial agriculture replacing the age-old subsistence agriculture. The peasant might well now take the increased yield of his cultivation to market. In some cases he might begin to specialize and take part in what might be termed an 'exchange economy'. Those peasants with something to sell soon saw that their future depended upon price fluctuations. A larger number probably had something extra to sell because of the abolition of seignorial dues (in particular tithe) and increased agricultural productivity. But the general rise in prices came to an end in 1817 and the general trend until 1851 was for prices to fall. The lower prices being obtained threatened to reduce the profits of the cultivator and the income from land rents received by landlords. As a result these interested parties turned towards the state and demanded protection against imported foreign cereals which they held responsible for the drop in prices. And they received satisfaction by the law of 16 July 1819 when, for the first time in its history, France imposed restrictions on grain imports. But the fall in prices persisted and this led to the law of 4 July 1821 which established a sliding scale of customs' dues and even prohibited imports when prices fell to a specified level. This law remained in force until 1861 but it was ineffectual. The value of agricultural produce increased between 1817 and 1851 despite the decline in prices. This was because of the growth of agricultural output.

But in 1851 there was a change of enormous importance. Agricultural production continued to increase, but prices began to rise and continued to do so until 1873. The farmer who sold the surplus of his agricultural produce thus had a double advantage: from the rise in production and the rise in prices. In some areas such as the Beauce, the profit doubled in thirty years for the owner-cultivator and more than doubled for the tenant-farmer. The owner who did not cultivate his land, and those with investments in the land, also benefited from this situation but their profits were more modest: ground rents only increased by two-thirds.

But what about the wage-earner who had only his labour to sell? During the first half of the nineteenth century agricultural wages seem to have varied very little. They rose during the period of the Empire, perhaps because of a shortage of labour, and although they did not fall under the Restoration and the July Monarchy any rise seems to have been slight — probably around 10 per cent. The cost of living seems to have decreased, so possibly the position of the agricultural wage-earner improved. But some of his pre-Revolution additional sources of revenue disappeared: by 1851 there was much less rural domestic weaving than there had been, and common rights such as the rights of common pasture were disappearing too. Between 1851 and 1881 wages increased by more than 50 per cent, but there was no corresponding increase in purchasing power because of the rise in prices. It seems, nevertheless, that the real earnings of agricultural wage-earners increased by at least one-third between 1851 and 1873. The agricultural wage-earner was, on the one hand, conscious of the improvement of his lot, but on the other hand he was also conscious that the improvement in the lot of his employers was much greater.

Fig. III.4 Number of recruits able to read and write, 1830–33

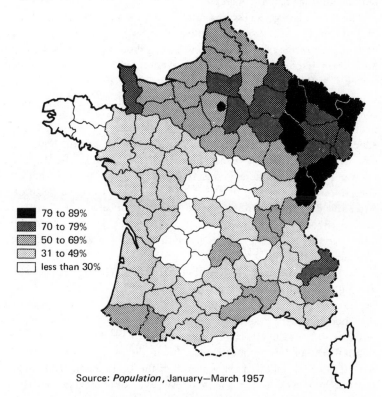

79 to 89%
70 to 79%
50 to 69%
31 to 49%
less than 30%

Source: *Population*, January–March 1957

   To what extent did better material conditions affect the peasants' intellectual level or their outlook? One tends to think of them as leading a life of unremitting toil and isolation, far from schools or any sort of intellectual life. One may obtain a fairly precise idea of the level of their education from the annual statements undertaken for the Ministry of War after 1827 to ascertain the educational level of conscripts. In 1832 half of the conscripts were illiterate, 46 per cent knew how to read and write and 4 per cent to read only. But there were distinct geographical variations. A line drawn from the bay of Mont Saint-Michel to the Lake of Geneva separates a surprisingly highly-educated north-east from a relatively ignorant south. The origins of this difference are unknown, but the phenomenon was an old one and had already been noted at the end of the seventeenth century. Possibly the relatively different speeds of economic development may provide some explanation, or possibly the existence of dialects in the south which only resembled French to a greater or lesser degree.

The differences grew less as a result of educational legislation. A law of 1833 made obligatory the running of at least a primary school for boys in each *commune* (although several neighbouring *communes* could pool their resources and form one school); it also provided for a teachers' training college in each *département*. A law of 1850 made it compulsory, with possible exemptions in exceptional cases, for every *commune* with more than 800 inhabitants (reduced to 500 in 1867) to maintain a primary school for girls. A law of 1881 made primary education free, and a law of 1882 made it compulsory for boys and girls from six to thirteen years. The statistics produced by the Ministry of War show how illiteracy was reduced. In 1835, 50 per cent of conscripts were illiterate; in 1850, 39 per cent; in 1861, 32 per cent. After this date the decline was more rapid: 22 per cent in 1868, 18 per cent in 1876, 15 per cent in 1882. The effects of the laws of 1881 and 1882 were being felt on the eve of the first world war when the rate of illiteracy had fallen to 3 per cent.

For a long time peasants played no part in French political life. This was not only because of the low level of their education but also because of the restricted nature of the franchise. When universal manhood suffrage was declared under the Second Republic, many peasants did not know what to do with their vote. This worried some political sectors, but without reason, for in the elections of 23 and 24 April 1848 they followed the guidance of the local notables and, under the watchful eyes of the parish priests and local mayors, generally returned candidates acceptable to the moderate republicans. But with the elections to the presidency of the Republic the *notables* were divided: some supported Cavaignac; others supported Louis Napoleon, followed by the majority of peasants, many no doubt influenced by the 'Napoleonic legend'. This unanimity of peasant opinion was of short duration and there was a split when the deputies for the Legislative Assembly were elected on 13 May 1849. Some were afraid of those advocating land division and supported the conservative, even reactionary candidates. Others supported the 'reds' — the socialists, who were successful in sixteen *départements* some of which were the most rural in France, including the départements of Saône-et-Loire, Allier, Corrèze, Haute-Loire, Dordogne and Basses Alpes. Government officials in their reports considered that these candidates owed their success to massive peasant support. This polarization of attitudes into extremes resulted from a deep peasant unrest caused first in 1847 by food shortage, then by the fall in produce prices. The peasantry was therefore in some ways a disruptive element among the electorate. The bourgeoisie had misunderstood and feared the peasants ever since the agrarian troubles of 1789, and earlier; now, over-reacting to the size of the socialist vote, they became really frightened.

These fears were calmed during the period of the Second Empire. The 'reds' were more or less put out of political business by the constraints of an authoritarian régime, and later discontents lessened because of increased economic prosperity. In 1860 a prefect commented, 'The main pre-occupation of the peasants was with the amount they could produce.' They kept eyes on the movement of grain prices and generally gave their votes to government candidates. They were developing into that massive conservative force which the bourgeoisie were going to depend on when, with the increasing organization of the working classes, revolution seemed to threaten. Yet the reality of the situation was rather more complex. Most of the peasants were certainly loyal to the Empire, but not all. The 'democratic' candidates, labelled 'reds' by the government in the 1869 elections, gained a significant amount of support from the peasants in some areas. They were undeniably successful in *départements* which may be considered typically 'rural' — in the Landes, the Côte-d'or, the Jura, the Loiret and the Yonne apart from the area of the Rhône Valley, Languedoc and the Mediterranean south where they had often enjoyed such success. A leftist tradition had, therefore, already established itself in certain rural areas.

Within seventy-five years peasant society had undergone significant changes. From being inward-looking and socially and culturally self-sufficient, with its outlook confined to the neighbourhood, it had become, thanks to the progress of transport and universal male suffrage, much more susceptible to outside influences. But the rate of change inevitably varied from region to region. Some areas barely changed at all and the tempo of their life was largely what it had always been. But in others, such as Aquitaine, said to be 'drained' by 1840, the props of a traditional economy had been eroded and prosperity had declined. In others the character of agriculture had changed and had become more specialized and more capitalist in character. The result was that there was not one society of peasants in the second half of the nineteenth century: it had become a mosaic of agricultural zones whose level of economic development differed — as did the degree of social and political development in these zones too.

The bourgeoisie

The Revolution established economic liberty, thus opening the way to capitalism and to business concentration. The abolition of internal customs duties and the ensuing freedom of the home market, the adoption of a unified system of weights and measures and the subsequent enlargement of this market to areas annexed during the revolutionary and imperial period, presented the bourgeoisie with a splendid new field of action. But if the Revolution, which was made by and in the interests of the bourgeoisie, opened up immense possibilities for their enrichment, it was not equally favourable to all of them. Financial difficulties, and in particular inflation, dealt a blow to those living off fixed incomes such as state or local loans, or annuities. Luxury industries dependent upon the patronage of the nobles had been wiped out by their emigration. The continental blockade had inflicted heavy loss on the merchants of the Atlantic and Mediterranean ports, and those industrialists who had been protected from external competition through Napoleonic legislation and the Continental System were to be adversely affected by the re-introduction of English competition after the defeat of Napoleon. Evidently a significant section of the bourgeoisie foundered in the stormy atmosphere of the revolutionary and imperial period.

But the storm which shipwrecked some blew others to success: better-equipped, luckier or less scrupulous, a class of bourgeois *nouveaux riches* rose rapidly in the social scale. financiers and financial adventurers amassed private fortunes by skilfully speculating on both specie and the paper money introduced by the Constituent Assembly (the *assignats*). These fortunes were protected from political risks by providing loans to hard-pressed governments, by bribing politicians and even by making grants to emigration agencies.

There was, in addition, speculation in the purchase of national lands with individual speculators grouping together, buying large estates, breaking them up and selling small plots at highly inflated prices. Admittedly this enabled some peasants to gain plots of land which would otherwise have been impossible, but the real gainers were the speculators.

If they were sufficiently skilful many were able to profit from times of economic difficulty: cornering food cereals in times of dearth, dealing on the black market providing goods otherwise unobtainable as a result of official requisitioning, and smuggling on the frontiers at the time of the continental blockade. War provided one of the main and certainly one of the most rapid means of self-enrichment. There was systematic looting by Napoleon's generals in conquered countries, especially Spain. But much more common were the scandals associated with army suppliers. This had existed under the Ancien Régime but during the early stages of the Revolution financial weakness and economic and administrative dislocation provided many of these suppliers with a splendid opportunity. The Montagnards, during the period of 'Terror' controlled the situation much more effectively than had the Girondins, but the Thermidorians and their successors lacked the means to do this, and even Napoleon who detested them could not feed or equip his troops without contractors. At least he had no illusions about them: 'they make me pay for every soldier killed'.

This then, was a new bourgeoisie which had got rich quickly. It was tougher and less scrupulous than its predecessors and took a more cynical view of public life. It had managed to survive the different régimes of the revolutionary and imperial generation and in addition had drawn from its experience during these years a degree of political scepticism unknown to the bourgeoisie of the eighteenth century.

There was one section of the bourgeoisie which had not been greatly affected by revolution. These were the landowners. Those who had owned land before the Revolution gained both from the opportunity to buy more land and the increased profits gained from the sale of foodstuffs because of the rise in prices in the opening years of the nineteenth century, and, as a result, many were able to acquire more property. Many of the *nouveaux riches*, in addition, had taken the precaution of investing some of their newly-made wealth in land in order to protect themselves from the uncertainties of business and to gain the social status they so much desired. The category of landed proprietors was the largest of the bourgeois categories. This is revealed for example by examining the electoral lists which, after 1831, showed all those paying more than 200 francs in direct taxation. The landowners dominated the electorate and especially in areas, numerous in those days, where industrial development was slight. In the south-west landowners accounted for more than 50 per cent of the electorate in eleven out of thirteen electoral areas examined by Armengaud, and accounted for as many as 70 per cent in four of them.

In the *département* of the Eure men living off their revenues or deriving sufficient from their lands to pay the minimum amount of taxation necessary to vote (the *cens*) were by far the most numerous section of the bourgeoisie. There was a constant interest in land which gave the bourgeoisie a rather archaic character, and reinforced their intention to be the guide and mouthpiece of the peasantry. In addition income from land provided growing industry with some of the capital which it needed. By force of number, power, positions and ambitions the landed bourgeoisie was the very backbone of French society in the first half of the nineteenth century but it was not the most dynamic group and it was not the group which was politically dominant. This, according to Lhomme, was because 'the most important source of revenue – the land – was giving way to profits from industry, finance and commerce. Land was no longer the wealth factor determining the social hierarchy.' Economic power was passing into the hands of another social category, although still a part of the bourgeoisie. This was the *grande bourgeoisie* defined by Lhomme in the following way. 'The *grande bourgeoise* is made up of people who (1) work, who (2) are engaged in activities which are especially remunerative and (3) who have large incomes at their disposal.' The first two criteria distinguish them from the landed aristocracy, the third from the middle and lower classes.

According to Lhomme the *grande bourgeoisie* was a distinct social class because it was conscious of its strength and its ambitions to acquire political power and hold on to it. But the *grande bourgeoisie* was not a homogeneous social class. Lhomme distinguishes three main groups. At the top there were those involved in banking and industry. Following this group came those involved in big business, holders of ministerial office, and men of law closely attached to the business world. The status of this second group was high but not quite so high as that of the first group. And then, at a somewhat lower level, came the more important civil servants, and the wealthier lawyers. Members of the university teaching profession and Parisian journalists might be added to this list provided they supported the ambitions of the *grande bourgeoisie*, and in general sang for their supper. The interests of the *grande bourgeoisie* were well served by the 1830 Revolution and without hesitation they grabbed the chance of power it offered them. Throughout the reign of Louis-Philippe their triumph was complete.

Marx took a rather different view however. In *The Class Struggles in France* he comments:

It was not the French bourgeoisie that ruled under Louis Philippe but *one faction* of its bankers, stock-exchange kings, railway kings, owners of coal and iron mines and forests, a part of the landed proprietors associated with them — the so-called *finance aristocracy*. It sat on the throne, it dictated laws in the Chambers, it distributed public offices, from cabinet portfolios to tobacco bureau posts. The *industrial bourgeoisie* proper formed part of the official opposition, that is, it was represented only as a minority in the Chambers. Its opposition was expressed all the more resolutely, the more un-alloyed the autocracy of the finance aristocracy became.[1]

If the opposition between financiers and industrialists was not as clear-cut as Marx claimed, this may have been because there were important links between them. The Delessert, Seillière and Périer families, for example, were financiers and industrialists at the same time. There were matrimonial alliances between the two groups. Generally it seems agreed that the bankers were the 'aristocracy of the bourgeoisie', as Stendhal called them during the July Monarchy.

The first half of the nineteenth century was a period when ready money was scarce and ill-deployed, that is, either privately hoarded or publicly spent on war debts, armaments or prestige enterprises. In such conditions power lay in the hands of the few who had large capital sums at their disposal. Marx commented, 'Owing to its financial straits, the July monarchy was dependent from the beginning on the grande bourgeoisie.' Or, more correctly, on the big Parisian banks. Public loans passed through their hands, and since the loans were very large so were the profits. The Baron Rothschild, who had been on good terms with the Bourbons, almost fell during the Revolution of July 1830 but he soon put himself, and his credits, at the disposal of Louis-Philippe and re-established his position to such an extent that he had a near-total monopoly in the placing of state loans, and was undoubtedly at the head of the banking world. But other families were involved too — Jewish families such as the d'Eichtal and Fould families; protestants, frequently of Swiss origin, such as the Delessert, Mallet, Hottinguer, Vernes and Pillet-Will families; and old-established wealthy bourgeois families from the provinces, such as the Périer and Davillier families; and self-made men like Laffitte.

These men of high finance who lived off the stock market and other financial affairs were not, at this time, closely involved with industry. They were investing capital in insurance companies which had developed rapidly during the early years of the Restoration, in

[1] Karl Marx, *The Class Struggles in France 1848—1850*, Moscow, Foreign Languages Publishing House, pp 44—5.

insurance against fires, which had been favourably received in town and countryside, against storm, accident and also in life assurance. The first life assurance company, the *Compagnie d'assurances générales sur la vie*, had been founded in 1819 by the Neuflize and Mallet banks; and the *Union-Vie* Company was founded in 1829. However, the progress in life assurance was slow. The big bankers were also involved in trade. Some were involved in financing the importation of food products and raw materials for the textile industry. The Rothschilds imported tea, the Delessert and Hottinguer families imported cereals and cotton, the Seillière family imported wool. Under the July Monarchy bankers started to take an interest in railway construction, especially when the government took on the responsibility for expenses concerned with compulsory purchase of needed land and necessary sub-structure construction. The Rothschild, Fould, Pillet-Will and Hottinguer families were involved in the setting up of many railway companies. For the first time the banks had taken part in a national industrial enterprise.

Although it is true that the bankers did not greatly concern themselves with the financing of industry this was because employers did not call for capital from bankers. Industrial enterprises were basically family affairs making use of capital acquired in trade or by exploiting landed property, or self-generated if the firm was an old-established one. Industry developed through being self-financed, by the systematic reinvestment of profits. This had two main results; firstly industrial products were often expensive; and secondly entre-preneurs were less concerned with productivity than with profit. This explains their protectionist outlook and their Malthusian behaviour.

There were many forms of industrial enterprise. The oldest sectors – textiles and small-scale metallurgy – often maintained their dispersed character. The majority of work was more often put out rather than done in a factory. This was particularly so in the weaving of linen, hemp and silk. But in Alsace the manufacture of cotton was carried on in large factories. The big cotton entrepreneurs of Alsace looked down on their smaller Norman counterparts. There was already industrial 'concentration' in other sectors – in metallurgy and mining, in chemical and glass industries. But although by the middle of the century concentration was a trend it was not yet a dominant one. The building industry still maintained a 'dispersed' character. But this was especially true of the textile industry – the leading industry from the point of view of both numbers employed and the scale of output. According to the census of 1851 large-scale industry, broadly defined as consisting of enterprises employing ten or more employees, employed

1.5 million; but 3 million people were still employed in small-scale workshops.

Industrial development and an increase in the number of industrial firms led to a fear of competition among employers. Protagonists of free enterprise, they believed in refusing workers the right of forming associations to compel wage increases, and in keeping out any possibility of government intervention or any regulation of working conditions. But they were not prepared to accept much in the way of competition. Employers' associations were formed as a result of the realization of the need to organize the defence of their interests. These had appeared in 1830 and continued to grow in number under the July Monarchy with the tacit approval of the authorities. A union of textile manufacturers was started at Lyon in 1830 by the silk manufacturers; committees were founded for linen in 1837 and cotton in 1839. A committee of manufacturers of home produced sugar was formed among sugar beet producers in Lille in 1832, in order to fight against competition from cane sugar. Forge masters formed a 'committee for the defence of metallurgical interests' in 1840. This was the origin of the famous Comitè des Forges founded in 1864, allowed official recognition in 1884 by the law of associations. The first 'Committee of Coal-mining' was founded in 1840. Founded primarily to protect themselves from competition, the committees tolerated or encouraged all kinds of agreements, cartels and arrangements for keeping up price levels or dividing up markets. The same results were obtained by simple agreements between leading firms such as that fixed by the two big glass producers Baccarat and Saint Louis which lasted for a quarter of a century (1830–57).

This readiness to use any means in defence of its interests is the most striking aspect of the behaviour of the big industrial and commercial bourgeoisie. This social group only contributed to general economic progress and the growth of output if such behaviour furthered its own interests. If it did not then it would not hesitate to be obstructive. Lhomme speaks of a culpable inertia: 'reluctance to change from wood to coal in iron-making is a prime example of lack of perspicacity and vision. Certainly they made occasional innovations but not with any regularity.' Tocqueville had earlier noted the bitterness with which they defended their interests and their inability to see beyond their own immediate advantage. Since they dominated power in the state, the government could not be expected to act contrary to their interests and in accordance with those of the public.

Things were to change around mid-century with the arrival of

Napoleon III. Not that a change of régime and ruler were enough to effect a radical shift in the social equilibrium; but the event coincided with a change in economic conditions which the Emperor himself was planning to make use of. He had no precise plan but a few definite intentions, foremost among which was to achieve the material well-being of the French people. 'Having been an eye-witness of the rapid industrialization of England and glimpsed some of the means by which this staggering transformation had been effected, he saw, from his exile, a vision of France as a huge and powerful country, wealthy and full of natural resources, badly administered and backward. He envisaged as his opening gambit the creation in France of a modern economy' (Blanchard). No doubt the chance of bringing prosperity to the French arose out of the change in the economic climate, but it is to Napoleon's credit that he did not neglect the opportunity presented. He grasped it firmly and pursued an ambitious, interventionist economic and social policy which aimed at breaking out of the 'restricted liberalism' of the policies of Louis Philippe.

A reversal of previous economic trends took place between 1850 and 1851. It took the form of a world-wide, long-term rise in prices which lasted for almost twenty-five years. This had several causes, amongst which was the beginnings of the working of the gold mines in California, Australia and New Zealand. The amount produced between 1850 and 1870 more or less equalled the total amount produced since the discovery of America. The whole of the economic life of the period was dominated by this slow, moderate rise in prices (which amounted to around 30 per cent between 1851 and 1873). Profits rose quicker than prices, and this had a stimulating influence on all production. To judge from the evidence of proved wills, the amassing of private fortunes seems to have increased during the same period. Between 1829—31 and 1849—51 they had increased by 30 per cent; but for a similar time span, from 1849—51 to 1869—71, they increased by 50 per cent.

A third factor was *Saint-Simonisme* and the *Saint-Simonistes*. Saint-Simon and his followers offered theory, methods, and personnel in the service of economic development. Saint-Simon had emphasized production and the material and moral well-being of the workers; Saint-Simon's followers emphasized production to the exclusion of all else and regarded the entrepreneurs, the 'industrial class', as being the great dynamic element in society. They saw humanity's golden age as lying not in the past but in the future. They believed in progress and managed to achieve it. Enfantin and the Péreire brothers concentrated on banking, Michael Chevalier taught at the Collège de France and became one of Napoleon III's economic advisors and Talabot was involved in the railways. These men and others gave economic development a new momentum.

As a result of their influence the provision of credit became a 'motivating industry'. The new large scale enterprises needed more than family capital to finance them. The new capitalism was financial and speculative. The means used for providing capital was to mobilize previously unproductive savings already growing because of increased prosperity. This was first achieved by an institution encouraged by the Pereire brothers — both *Saint-Simonistes* — the *Crédit Mobilier*, founded in 1852. This institution aimed to facilitate industrial investment by putting capital needed by large companies at their disposal. The capital was gathered together by the *Crédit Mobilier* from investors in return for redeemable stock. The capital was then lent to companies which, it was hoped, would lead to a kind of grouping of companies, the most solvent of which would guarantee the less well established firms. In 1855 the banking rivals of the Péreires created an association which later (in 1864) became the *Société Générale*. This was a deposit bank which also financed industrial enterprises. The *Crédit Industriel et Commercial* was created in 1859 and the *Crédit Lyonnais* in 1863, by which time a new banking network had thus been established. But under the Second Empire the older banking institutions changed too and began using methods similar to those of their new rivals: financial credits to industrial enterprises, acquiring share interests in companies and issuing shares to attract capital. Many different methods got under way but the effect was to open greater possibilities of credit to entrepreneurs.

Among these entrepreneurs metallurgists and especially the 'iron kings' — the Talabots, Schneiders and Wendels — rose to the top of the most dynamic section of the bourgeoisie: the industrial bourgeoisie. Demand from railways, army and navy orders, and construction industries led to larger markets for their products. The leading textile industries profited from the rise in the standard of living. Scientific discoveries and technical progress benefited pioneers in the chemical industries (the Kuhlmanns, Guimets, Deutsches, Desmarais). The industrial bourgeoisie not only profited to the full from the favourable economic conditions but also developed their power more fully by centralizing their enterprises, or concentrating them in a more limited area; financial concentration, effected by taking over firms hit by seasonal economic setbacks; technical concentration through work being done in factories rather than in small, scattered workshops, or 'put-out' to individual workers; and geographical concentration by grouping enterprises in towns or near mines. This 'concentration' was particularly marked in the metallurgical industries (the Wendel establishments employed more than 9,000 workers at the end of the Second Empire, the Schneider factories employed 2,500 in 1845, 6,000 in 1860 and 10,000 in 1870) and in the railways (forty-two companies in 1851, six in 1860). The situation in the textile industry was rather different, because of the strength of its craft and family character and the force of tradition and routine, although even here some progress towards 'concentration' was being made. During the 1850s and, especially, the 1860s the bases of the old artisanal structure of the textile industry were crumbling and were soon to give way to the modern factory system of production.

Many of the big industrialists went further, concentrating many different kinds of economic functions in their hands. The investment world was dominated by very few men indeed. In 1862 George Duchêne, an associate of Proudhon, estimated that 183 men controlled capital, and even within this number there was an élite some thirty strong including the Péreires and the Rothschilds. The Péreires directed nineteen companies and 3,500 million francs. These 183 controlled more than 20,000 million francs in shares and bonds — a real 'industrial empire'.

But this concentration of economic power in the hands of a few was viewed with great disfavour,and denounced not only by socialists but also by many of the bourgeoisie itself. These were people still attached to the sort of 'liberalism' which had existed under the July Monarchy: small manufacturers and merchants whose material interests were threatened, or intellectuals who were opposed to recent developments as a matter of principle. The ranks of the bourgeoisie were threatened by a schism whose seriousness was intensified by the fact that though the *grande bourgeoisie* had been powerfully boosted by prosperity, the smaller fry had also benefited. The patent records bear witness to the increase in the number of new undertakings, while the number of public officials and technicians grew increasingly. If the *grande bourgeoisie* hoped to turn its domination of politics and finance into a monopoly they risked a confrontation with those whose hopes of power sharing they wished to frustrate.

From this time onwards the *grande bourgeoisie* seemed to be growing into a kind of caste. Historians have noted close relationships between families which tended to reinforce the unity and exclusiveness

Fig. III.5 Growth of industrial property taxpayers recorded in original and supplementary lists, 1827–1913

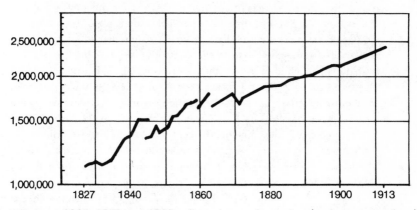

The breaks at **1845, 1859** and **1863** reflect changes in tax law (various exemptions)

Source: *Annuaire statistique,* 1961.

already existing among big capitalists. Marriages were a frequent expression of this and were concluded, if not between members of the same occupation or trade, at least between those of a similar degree of wealth: in short between those of the same economic élite. Yet it was possible, at least before 1870, to rise into this élite from below. The Parisian gold and silversmith Christofle, many of the heads of the chemical industries and the Normandy textile industrialist Pouyer-Quartier are just a few examples of men who had all risen in this way from more humble beginnings, and many of them were to pursue notable political careers too.

So long as it left the door open to candidates for social promotion the *grande bourgeoisie* succeeded without much difficulty in having its superiority recognized by other bourgeois groups, the more pushing members of which might hope to be admitted to its ranks. Conscious of its power, envied by some, admired by all, its very superiority caused its values and standards of behaviour to be accepted as typically bourgeois.

Family life provided the clearest manifestations of bourgeois behaviour. Marriage was all important; fear of a bad match haunted the paterfamilias. The partners should be of equal economic standing, or with the expectation of being so. They should also be of similar educational standard. The wife was expected to be able to play the piano (just as the husband should be versed in Latin), and her husband, though probably not himself a believer, would expect her to have had a religious upbringing – a sure guarantee of moral behaviour and a stable home life. Once married the bourgeois was master, his power over his nearest and dearest was absolute. The Civil Code took no cognizance of woman. Even more than under the ancien régime her life was spent as an eternal minor, moving from the control of her father to that of her husband. The child was not mentioned in the Civil Code; he only interested the lawyers as a future proprietor. The family was primarily an acquisitive group, and sentiment came second to self-interest. Some writers have made out that love of children was an endearing characteristic of the nineteenth century bourgeois, so unlike the eighteenth century aristocrat who was content to leave them to be brought up by servants. Régine Pernoud contrasts their attitude, not to children ('they took good care of them as they did of any other property') but to childhood in general, quoting from debates in the Chamber on child labour (in 1840 and 1841). Hardness of heart, hypocrisy and monstrous smugness characterize this mouthpiece of the bourgeois business world.

For the bourgeoisie the only possible basis of society was private property, the source of profit and guarantee of security. Hence bourgeois virtues were those which were rewarded by the accumulation of wealth: wordly wisdom, hard-headedness, carefulness, order, thrift, application to work. The worst vices were those which were bad for business: dishonesty, theft, fraud, deceit. Debauchery was to be condemned if it led to the financial ruin of a family and so to loss of social status. It was pardonable if practised in moderation. But in the pursuit of personal enrichment all means were regarded as justifiable, even at the expense of the wage-earner – fines for bad workmanship, stoppages and deductions from wages for the slightest reason. This reflected the need for the bourgeoisie to exploit the lower classes in order to get rich; and this situation could only exist if the lower classes accepted or were resigned to their fate.

Yet despite their admitted selfishness the bourgeois are sometimes said to have been lovers of peace and liberty. Certainly they disliked war: Louis-Philippe, the 'bourgeois monarch', pursued a peaceful foreign policy; the Rothschilds feared the establishment of the Second Empire because of the possibility of war. Yet naturally behind this love of peace was a knowledge that peace was economically beneficial and that war might be economically destructive. But the liberty they were said to have loved was limited to the bourgeois themselves. It was liberty for the employer, but not for the employee. They had no objections to monopoly – a monopoly of the economy through protectionism; of wealth through its concentration in their hands; and of education, since secondary education was only for the sons of bourgeois.

The most characteristic trait of the bourgeois was their conviction of righteousness. Bourgeois thinkers had no difficulty in convincing themselves that they were justified in occupying the best seats, and they found their justification in history. History, as interpreted by Guizot, showed that the bourgeoisie, which in medieval France had founded the *communes* and in eighteenth century England had secured the paramountcy of Parliament, was worthy of its commanding position. For Guizot the whole of French history culminated in the Charter of 1814. Only Tocqueville, an aristocrat, saw that the triumph of the bourgeoisie was not the end of the story.

3. The growth of a 'proletariat'

By doing away with guilds and introducing freedom of work, the Revolution abolished many of the restrictions on the economy of the Ancien Régime. But the industrial revolution was slow in coming, especially when compared with England. France experienced an industrial evolution rather than an industrial revolution. Mechanization of industry with steam power only took place gradually during the first half of the nineteenth century. At the beginning of the nineteenth century a quarter of all industrial energy came from water power compared with 2 per cent in Britain. And the transport revolution only took place after the industrial revolution, in 1850, and not simultaneously as in Britain.

The rise of a modern economy was thus slower and more arduous in France than in some other countries, in particular Britain, and for much of the nineteenth century old and new economic forms existed side by side. On the one hand there were factories, on the other artisan-type establishments with a master and a few workers and work being 'put-out', just as it had been in the eighteenth century. Even in 1848 only a quarter of all workers were employed in factories. The new industrial proletariat was, as yet, in a minority, submerged by the more traditional artisans and journeymen working older machinery. Together with the artisans and journeymen the lower factory workers constituted the 'popular classes'; they were not yet the working classes.

The more traditional 'artisan' type worker was different from the newer factory-worker. He was usually qualified in his job after undergoing a period of apprenticeship. He might be a printer, cabinet-maker, carpenter, tailor, hat-maker — all trades of the crafts-man. The newer worker had to learn his job on the spot. The artisan was often educated and attached importance to education for himself and his children. He placed his confidence in schools and was concerned that they should be free of external influence and in particular of clerical influence. He led an irreproachable family life, his conduct was austere and he did not waste his time on drinking but spent it with his family. The number of children would not be excessive, so that each had the opportunity of a decent life and a chance to improve their standard of living. He would read, reflect upon and discuss important issues of the day.[1] These artisans rather than the newer workers were the militants among the popular classes and were to remain so until the early years of the Third Republic.

But the new factory workers came from a different milieu, usually the countryside. They were not landowners who had left their land or even those with insufficient land, because the latter usually stayed in the countryside hoping to add to their land. But the new workers were former agricultural wage-earners, or workers formerly employed in cottage industries who had found themselves out of work because of the ruthless competition of the factories. They had come to the towns in search of work or a less miserable wage. In some areas they did not immediately seek work in factories. The Lorraine peasant who left his native village to work in the great iron-working centres seems to have shunned the mine and the foundry, and preferred to work as a delivery man, a grocer's or a butcher's assistant, as a navvy or a roadworker: it was his children who got sucked into the Wendel organization. But in the Loire area, the miners of Rive-de-Gier taking part in an inquiry in 1848 said 'the countryfolk leave their lands untilled and pour into this neighbourhood . . . . they prefer our sort of work because it does not require as long an apprenticeship as do other industries.' Although this rural emigration may have solved some of the problems of the rural poor it caused great housing problems in the towns. Their living conditions were terrible. Many contemporaries remarked about this. Villermé wrote about the cotton, silk and wool workers, Guépin about the workers of Nantes, and Blanqui about the French working classes. 'The most noticeable characteristic of all these houses is a degree of filth which makes them real breeding-grounds of infection. . .' Their living conditions caused these workers great suffering.

---

[1] Cobblers' shops were well known centres of discussion while customers waited for their shoes to be mended.

But these workers had to suffer more besides. Their lives became dominated by the routine of the machine. Work became monotonous. The varied, relatively unorganized work of the fields was a thing of the past. Independence had been exchanged for a degrading life as an industrial worker. The peasant had been drawn from his traditional surroundings and was now exposed to isolation, demoralization, instability and an unruly social environment. There were many results of this process of demoralization. It led many to drink excessively in an attempt to forget the monotony and misery of their present condition.

Industrialists, above all in the textile industry, discovered that physical strength was not needed for certain simple tasks such as refastening broken threads, and even for starting up and watching over some of the machines. This led to the employment of female and child labour. Women were much cheaper to employ: they were paid between half and one-third less than men and children received absurdly low wages. By 1847 out of 1,054,000 employed in establishments with more than ten workers, 670,000 were men, 254,000 were women and 130,000 were children. The effect of this kind of work on the health of children was disastrous. Villermé commented,

> This is not piece-work but torture inflicted on children of six to eight years. Badly dressed, and badly fed, they have to set out at five in the morning on the long journey from their houses to the workshops, and face the same journey home in the evening. As a result there is an excessive rate of infant mortality.

There were not infrequent cases of children being ill-treated in factories. The rope's end figured as a working tool in some Normandy factories. Their only apprenticeship was a precocious introduction to the sexual promiscuity of factory life.

Women did not enjoy a much better fate. The factory buildings were often unhealthy. The air might be polluted with dust or be humid. Long hours would be spent working standing up. Nervous shock might well be sustained as a result of working machines. All this gravely affected the health of the women workers. In 'mixed' factories they were exposed to the desires and demands of foremen and bosses. In 1855 the procurator of the Appeal Court of Alsace said that the factories were 'dens of shameless debauchery'. In order to earn a little extra some women might leave the factory early and engage in prostitution during what was called 'the fifth quarter of the day'. In this industrial iron age the manufacturing 'proletariat' paid dearly the costs of economic development. In the *département* of the Loire the average expectancy of life in the middle of the nineteenth century was fifty-nine years for farmers but forty-seven for lace workers and only thirty-seven for coalminers. They were deeply demoralized. Many were alcoholics, others were in such financial distress that they were prepared to deny their children an education in order that they might go to the factory and bring in money, however little it might be.

But the picture was not the same everywhere. There were geographical differences. Large-scale industry was not to be found throughout France. Brittany and most of the south had none. It was more or less concentrated in the north, where artisans had been unable to withstand factory competition, and where there were large urban manufacturing communities, in Lorraine important for its metallurgy, Alsace important for its textiles, central France (Lyon, the Saint-Etienne and Creusot basins, and the Montluçon–Commentry area), and the lower Seine area. Large-scale industry had not made much headway in Paris where small workshops and skilled craftsmen and artisans still predominated. Larger enterprises were set up, by preference, in the suburbs.

There were sociological differences too. Duveau considers there were four main 'types' in the middle of the nineteenth century. Firstly there was the rural worker who can be put in the same category as the worker of a 'putting out' industry if he lived in the countryside. The rural worker would be less imprisoned by his work; his environment would be more healthy but he would be remote, crude and primitive in his reactions. Secondly there was the urban worker living in a fairly important town without large firms, where there would be little basic difference between trades, and where wages and standards of living would not show marked differences. Life would be simple and peaceful. Thirdly there was the worker in a small town suddenly taken over by a large factory such as the Le Creusot works. This factory would overshadow everything and the owner everyone. Fourthly there was the worker in one of the very large towns such as Lyon or Paris with a relatively free intellectual atmosphere. But there was a basic unity between them all – a unity of similar hopes and grievances which cut across individual factories, workshops or forges.

There were chronological differences in their condition too – the character of the French working classes changed during the nineteenth century for economic and political reasons. The period 1815 to 1848 was not a favourable period for them. On the political front government was dominated either by the property-owning nobility who took no interest in working-class problems, or by bourgeois business men who were much tougher, and firmly opposed by conviction as well as self-interest to any measure that took account of the human element in work. This they regarded as something to be bought and sold like any other merchandise and subject to the laws of a laisser faire economy. On the economic front there was a long-term fall in gold prices and a collapse in industrial prices, starting with the crisis of 1817—18 and lasting until 1851. This threatened the profit of the entrepreneurs which led them to try and cut their costs, which could most easily be done by depressing wages.

The development of wages was not the same in all professions. In the older professions not greatly affected by mechanization, like building, wages remained more or less steady. There was expansion in the mining industry and here the tendency was for wages to rise. But in the mechanized industries, in metallurgy and particularly textiles, there was a general fall in wages. Often this was a sharp fall: and wages for men in textiles fell by 40 per cent between 1810 and 1850. On average there was a general tendency for wages to fall. But the condition of the workers did not depend only on wages. It depended on the availability of work, on the cost of living and on the length of the working day. There are no statistics on unemployment, largely because this was not the sort of question which greatly interested governments. The rise in population and the movement of people from countryside to town seem to have led to an increase in the supply of labour which outstripped the rise in demand, if indeed demand rose at all. All of which probably helped employers to keep wages down.

The cost of living for the workers was linked to the cost of food (on which three-quarters of their budget would be spent) and especially to the price of bread. According to Villermé meat was eaten and wine drunk on pay day or the day after and thus only twice per month. There was a sizeable fall in bread prices between 1817 and 1827 but after 1827 there was a tendency for them to rise until 1847. 10 to 20 per cent of the workers' budget was spent on rent and rents were rising faster than food prices. Thus in the first half of the century the cost of living must have risen by about 10 per cent. As money wages were falling, their purchasing power — or real wages — were falling more rapidly. Such was the overall movement between 1817 and 1850; but there were in fact periods of more intense wage depression which coincided with the 'food crises' of 1817, 1828—32, 1838—40 and 1847. When these crises occurred the worker had to deal not only with a sizeable rise in bread prices (from 50 to 100 per cent) but also with a sudden fall in the size of money wages received and an increase in unemployment, because the agrarian crisis spread into industry. These were crises of the 'old type'. They led to an evaporation in the spending power of the working class who now spent most of their money on food and had little or no money for the purchase of other articles. Because of the decline in demand for these articles those working in their manufacture were soon put out of work. This type of crisis had been common under the ancien régime but was largely over by 1860. After 1860 the previously common phenomenon of a coincidence of a decline in nominal wages with a rapid rise in the price of essential food stuffs and the consequent explosions of poverty were over.

The length of the working day tended to increase for technical and economic reasons. Steam power was continuous, and was tending to replace water power which was inclined to be erratic. By using artificial light, such as gas, the working day could also be prolonged. The entrepreneur needed to use his machines as much as possible so that the capital he had invested in them did not remain long unproductive, and in order to combat the keen competition of his rivals. These factors do not seem to have affected the older industries which were not, as yet, fully mechanized. Here the length of the working day seems to have settled down to twelve hours. But these same factors mattered very much in large-scale industry and there was a noticeable increase in the length of the working day. This was sometimes admitted even by the factory owners themselves. The working day was from twelve to twelve and a half hours in the textile factories of Reims, thirteen in the north and in Saint-Quentin and at least thirteen and a half hours in the Upper Rhone area.

A series of factors, some of more importance than others, was therefore causing a deterioration in working-class standards of living, at least in big industry. The workers had no support outside their own ranks. Far from being protected by the state, they were subjected to highly restrictive legislation. They were forbidden to form associations, even temporary ones; if they went on strike the ringleader would be arrested, tried, and imprisoned. Employers often received the support of the armed forces in order to make them return to work. They were treated as suspicious characters, obliged to carry a *livret* (workers' handbook) numbered and initialled by the mayor or the police and which had to be endorsed if the worker changed his place of residence; if he did not have it he risked being considered a vagabond. This *livret* was kept by his employer who would put in it details of any money advances that might have been made to him. The worker could not change jobs without producing his *livret*. Article 12 of the law of

1803 stated: 'nobody may take on a worker unless he carries with him a *livret*, carrying with it a certificate from his last employer stating that the worker had discharged his obligations'. Although the *livret* regulation was not always strictly observed, it could be a heavy legal burden on the worker.

Working-class activity was confined to a narrow sphere at the beginning of the nineteenth century. The old practice of *compagnonnage* still existed; although illegal it was unofficially tolerated. This system helped affiliated members to gain a job. They went on the *tour de France*, spending a length of time exercising a particular trade in one place, and then moving on to another. This also provided something of a crude welfare service. It would allocate funds to sick members or to members out of work. But few people belonged and the kinds of trades practised were traditional ones. It consisted of only young unmarried men and as a force tended to be weakened because of internal squabbles and even fighting. There were some attempts to reform it by Agricol Perdiguier but the movement seems to have been in decline by the end of the July Monarchy.

There were other sorts of workers' associations. These were the societies of mutual aid (*sociétés de secours mutuel*). The Restoration had allowed the foundation of some of these. They were only authorized after an official inquiry, their meetings had to be presided over by a police superintendent or a mayor, and the number of members was limited – usually to less than 100. Their funds could only be used to help out the old, sick and disabled. This movement started in Paris, where there were 132 professional societies at the end of 1823. The movement then spread to the provinces, particularly in Lyon, and made definite progress during the July Monarchy. By 1848 there were probably over 2,000 of them. These workers' mutual aid societies consisted largely of the more skilled workers, and thus only a tiny section of the proletariat, and there was little in the way of contact between different societies.

But some of these societies were more than the charitable institutions they were supposed to have been. They were active in defending workers' rights and were prepared to run the risk of striking. One of the most powerful of these was the *Société de devoir mutuel* (Society of Mutual Duty) founded by weavers in Lyon in 1828. It was a secret society divided into various groups in order to conform to article 291 of the Penal Code which required authorization for any society of over twenty people. Some others were organized in Marseille, and Roanne during the Restoration. The number increased under the July

Monarchy in Paris and the provinces and were strengthening their organizations between 1840 and 1848. Their avowed primary concern was with wages and working conditions and sometimes they were able to impose minimum wages for a particular profession. These may be seen as the faint beginnings of collective wage agreements.

The first mass working-class movement in France was the 'Lyon insurrection' of 1831, triggered off by a wage rate dispute. Some factory owners refused to recognize agreements freely negotiated by the prefect Bouvier du Molart between workers and factory owners. This insurrection of thousands of workers, shouting 'Live working or die fighting', paralysed Lyon for several days. But workers did not know what to do with their victory. They returned to their homes but then found themselves exposed to government reprisals. Lyon was occupied by the military. The wage agreements were cancelled and ten thousand workers were labelled 'undesirable' and thrown out of the town. This was a spontaneous movement confined to Lyon alone and completely unsupported by workers of other towns. The movement consisted of traditional and new workers alike. The insurrection proved that the proletariat was not afraid to take action to back up its demands but had no definite programme apart from the wage question.

There was no working-class ideology at this time. Ideologically the working classes were still dependent on the bourgeoisie. Some people were beginning to ask questions about man and machines, to point to the contrast between the rapid growth of material wealth and the wretched condition of those who produced it; they felt that if this was the dire product of a 'liberal' direction of the economy, the structure of that economy should be changed. But these social reformers, *Saint-Simonians*, followers of Proudhon and Fourier, were bourgeois intellectuals who had only a slight impact on the workers. They looked to all society to effect these changes, not solely the workers. They sought social change but wanted it to be accomplished peacefully as a result of spontaneous innovations influenced by particular successful examples.

Nevertheless there were more working-class upheavals under the July Monarchy, sometimes with political repercussions. There were strikes throughout France in 1833–4. In Paris the aim of the strikers was a ten hour working day and a rise in wages. In Lyon the aim was a new scale of wages. In Paris after 1840 there was more agitation and more strikes and a threat of general strike action. But the government now took up the cudgels for the employers and strengthened the Penal Code. By the law of 10 April 1834 'the provisions of article 291 of the penal code are applicable to associations of more than twenty people even if they are divided into groups of less than twenty and they do not meet every day or on appointed days'. This law did not destroy all workers' societies but it changed the conditions in which they had to work and replaced informal tolerance by a more arbitrary attitude. Even if the government permitted the foundation of such societies, that permission could always be revoked, and in fact was only extended to those that seemed least offensive. The most active workers were thus forced into forming or joining secret societies. This prefigured the coming together of the republican and the worker movements. The first evidence of this was the second Lyon insurrection of April 1834 and the episode of the rue Transnonain in Paris. This alliance was to come out into the open with the fall of the July Monarchy in 1848. The workers hoped for and expected much from the revolution of 1848. The provisional government did do something to meet their demands by legislation. But the impulse lasted a few weeks only. By June 1848 the workers were bitterly disappointed.

'Splendid in conception, wretched in execution', Such was the contrast in 1815–51 between the ideological power of socialism and the feebleness of working-class action. But after the middle of the nineteenth century there was a change. The economy expanded and there was a change in government. Between 1851 and 1871 the working-class movement increased in scope and importance. Above all the entrepreneurs profited from the years of economic prosperity between 1851 and 1873. Profits and production both rose and industrial profits seem to have increased fourfold during this period. But the workers also benefited. Factory owners were now more prepared to give way to workers' demands for higher wages.

Money wages rose: in the building industries wages increased by 40 per cent between 1851 and 1873, in metal industries by 50 per cent, in mining by 60 per cent and in textile industries by 78 per cent. The rise was probably greater in large towns where workers' pressure was more significant than in small towns which were probably less industrialized. Again the rise was probably higher in big industry than in the more traditional artisan industries. The average rise in money wages was between 40 and 45 per cent. This was an enormous improvement over the past when money wages had, at best, been stagnant. Admittedly real wages were more significant from the point of view of the standard of living. Nevertheless the worker attached great importance to the amount of money he actually earned and undoubtedly welcomed this rise.

But what were the costs of this rise in wages? Had it been paid for with a longer working day? The decree of the provisional government of 2 March 1848 was partly the result of pressure from the workers. It fixed the working day at a maximum of ten hours in Paris and eleven in the provinces. But this concession was withdrawn in the decree of 9 September 1848 which established a maximum of twelve hours work in industry, and even this was often ignored. During the Second Empire the general length of the working day was twelve hours in the provinces and eleven in Paris. Obviously there were certain exceptions in some trades and in some workshops, but the tendency for a systematic increase in the working day, which had characterized the first half of the century, had disappeared.

Were workers subjected to more rigorous discipline than in the past? Some workers lost something. For example the practice of staying away from work on Mondays, which had been current in many large towns, was no longer allowed. Yet if working conditions had deteriorated one would expect a decline in the health of the workers. But according to demographic records this does not appear to have taken place. G. Duveau, in his researches on the working classes under the Second Empire, states that the health of factory workers had noticeably improved.

But there was a price to pay for this rise in wages, and this was the rise in the cost of living. The rise was very rapid between 1851 and 1855–6 and although it lessened until 1866–7 it speeded up again after that date. By 1860 the rise in the cost of living seems to have absorbed the rise in money wages and the purchasing power of the workers was much as it had been before. But after this date the rise in wages overtook the rise in the cost of living, increasing purchasing power by 20–30 per cent. Real wages continued to increase until 1914. This new trend was a remarkable phenomenon which led to a lasting improvement in working-class living standards. The amount of meat consumed rose; the amount of bread consumed fell. The amount of meat consumed in Paris in 1867–9 was already almost as great as the highest figures for the nineteenth century.

The workers had therefore benefited from improved conditions, but others had benefited much more. The rich, the employers, had made enormous gains from increased profits and production. What they had gained made the improvement in the workers' condition look quite negligible. The gap between rich and poor was increasing. How did the improvement in working-class living standards and this increasing cleavage between rich and poor affect the development of the working-class movement under the Second Empire? To begin with, under the authoritarian period of the Empire, the workers found themselves subjected to government oppression; in the second phase, after about 1860, things changed and a workers' offensive began to take shape.

Immediately after Louis Napoleon's coup d'état workers' organizations were sought out and repressed and a decree of 2 August 1848 which had permitted non-political associations was repealed. The legislation of the July Monarch (article 291 of the Penal Code and the law of 1834) was restored. Mutual aid societies, if authorized, were closely controlled and a decree of 26 March 1852 laid down that their presidents should be nominated by the prefect. Combinations of societies were still forbidden, and the workers still had to carry their *livrets*. A law of 14 July 1851 forbade masters to write down money advances given to workers but the number of professions for whom the *livret* was compulsory was increased to include miners, road-workers and those working for an employer in their own homes. Faced with this situation, workers adopted a stance of apparent acceptance, though there were continued strikes of a rather defensive character, to maintain earlier gains. The disillusion of 1848 seemed to be widespread, except among a few active militants.

But from 1860 onwards the character of politics changed as did the attitude of the government towards the workers. The Italian war had alienated some supporters. The Chevalier—Cobden commercial treaty with England alienated more. Now it seemed that the government was seeking some kind of reconciliation with the popular classes and was even seeking the support of the workers. An early indication of the government's good will towards the workers was the concession of an unofficial subsidy for a delegation of two hundred workers to visit the Great Exhibition in London. The delegates were greatly impressed with the efficacy of the Trade Union movement and, on their return, demanded the rights of association and coalition for French workers. The government also faced the problem of combination because of a printers' strike in Paris. These strikers were condemned by the courts but pardoned by the Emperor. Some toleration had already been granted for combinations but it was of an unnofficial kind. But workers' associations were tolerated implicitly after the publication in the *Moniteur* of 31 March 1868 of the report of Forcade de la Roquette which said that trade unions would, in fact, be tolerated.

Fortified by the indulgence of the state, or at least by its non-intervention, the workers hardened in their attitude towards the employers and sought satisfaction of their demands. After the legislation of 1864 strikes once again became a feature of French economic life: the lace-makers of Saint-Etienne went on strike, so did the coachmen of Paris, hat-makers, bronze workers and miners in the north. There was a further bout of strikes involving bloodshed in 1869–70 in the mines of the Loire region, the foundries of Aubin where troops fired on strikers in October 1869, and in Le Creusot where Eugène Schneider forced the miners to capitulate. Circumstances were therefore favourable for a revival of the old mutual aid societies. The success of the strike movement obviously helped this revival. Sometimes these were now called *chambres syndicales* (trade union chambers). Many of these were founded towards the end of the Second Empire, especially in those older trades with a well-founded artisanal tradition – building, leather, hat, book and mechanical trades. Some of these joined together to form *chambres fédérales* (federal chambers) – the beginnings of regional organizations in centres such as Paris, Lyon and Marseille. There were even *fédérations de métiers* (trade federations) bringing together workers of one trade at the national level. But by 1870 only the hatmakers had done this.

These association movements culminated in the founding in 1864 of the First International, the result of French initiative, at an international meeting at St Martins's Hall in London. An international body at the top was thus formed before national groups existed. This was followed by the formation of a French section between 1865 and 1868 through the efforts of men such as Tolain, Richard, Benoît, Malon and Varlin. By 1870 there were possibly several tens of thousands of members. The militants of this International were to attempt to divert French trade unionism from its current role of negotiator towards revolutionary action. The offensive of the workers between 1860 and 1870 was not only directed towards economic targets. They also had political ambitions. The more advanced of them sometimes spoke of the political autonomy of the working classes. In the elections of 1863 two workers stood as candidates in Paris on the basis that the interests of the workers could best be served by working-class deputies. The *Manifeste des Soixante* of 17 February 1863, drawn up by Tolain, declared the need for autonomous action by the workers. In the following year this theme was taken up by Proudhon in his *Capacité politique des classes ouvrières* (*The Political Capabilities of the Working Classes*).

After the fall of the Empire the Commune was set up. Twenty-four workers were elected onto its general council. This, in addition to the part played by the members of the International and Marx's interpretation of the revolutionary commune in his *Civil War in France*, created the myth that the power of the workers had created a working-class state. Nevertheless, despite what the Commune might or might not have been, it was an attempt at government of the people by the people, and revealed, if only for a few weeks, that the workers of Paris were capable of establishing a new kind of power.

4. Conclusion

From 1815 to 1870 France experienced three types of régime — monarchy, republic and empire — but throughout them all the *grande bourgeoisie,* conscious of its interests and strength from the beginning of the century, maintained and consolidated its supremacy. Although at the end of this period it pretended to fear an aristocratic and clerical resurgence, it did so only to stoke up the hatred of privilege and attachment to the principles of 1789 in the population generally, sentiments which it could exploit electorally in its own interests.

But the *grande bourgeoisie* did fear the growing power of the working classes which it had so ruthlessly exploited. The working classes were slowly becoming more conscious of their power as a class. Yet this was a slow progress and had few really positive manifestations before the Paris Commune. In reality the greatest danger to the *grande bourgeoisie* came from within the bourgeoisie itself. Economic development had led to internal disagreements. Many petty bourgeois felt threatened by the tendency towards industrial and financial concentration. They were the heirs to the egalitarian and Jacobin traditions of the Revolution. They were to be the adherents of radicalism, whose ideology suited their interests, and they were even to find allies in the peasantry. They had definite political aims of their own and were quite prepared to demand what they considered to be their rightful share of political power.

documentation

Table III.3 Fragmentation of property through inheritance

Assessed value of properties by categories

	1826		1842		1858		Indices 1858 (1828 = 100)
	Number	%	Number	%	Number	%	
20 F and below	8 024 987	77.94	8 873 951	77.09	10 446 757	79.63	130
21 F to 30	663 237	6.44	791 711	6.88	821 852	6.26	124
31 F to 50	642 345	6.42	744 911	6.47	758 876	5.78	118
51 F to 100	527 991	5.13	607 956	5.28	609 562	4.65	115
101 F to 300	335 505	3.26	375 860	3.26	368 631	2.81	110
301 F to 500	56 602	0.55	64 244	0.56	59 842	0.46	106
501 F to 1000	32 579	0.31	36 862	0.32	37 333	0.29	114
1 001 F and above	13 447	0.13	16 346	0.14	15 870	0.12	118
TOTAL	10 296 693	100.00	11 511 841	100.00	13 118 723	100.00	127

Taxable property (unbuilt on) in the registers of 1884

Type	Number of units	Taxable area (ha)	Percentage of all units	Percentage of total area
Less than 50 acres	6 597 843	1 147 804	46.90	2.31
50 acres to 1 hectare	1 987 480	1 426 785	14.12	2.88
1 to 5 hectares	3 735 173	8 647 714	26.54	17.50
5 to 10 hectares	892 887	6 254 142	6.36	12.67
10 to 20 hectares	476 843	6 629 491	3.38	13.42
20 to 50 hectares	261 829	7 866 769	1.84	15.95
50 to 75 hectares	50 230	3 044 065	0.36	6.17
75 to 100 hectares	23 273	2 015 752	0.16	4.08
100 to 200 hectares	31 567	4 338 240	0.22	8.79
Over 200 hectares	17 676	8 017 542	0.12	16.23
TOTAL	14 074 801	49 388 304	100.00	100.00

Legislation concerning associations

a. *Article 291 of the Penal Code of 1810*

No association of more than twenty persons intending to meet every day or on specific days in order to concern itself with religious, literary, political or other matters, may be formed without governmental approval, and then only if such a society respects the terms on which the government decides to give that approval.

b. *Law of 10 April 1834*

Article 1 The provisions of Article 291 of the Penal Code are applicable to associations of more than twenty people even if such associations are divided into sections of a number less than twenty, and even if they do not meet every day or on specific days. Governmental authorization may at any time be withdrawn.

Article 2 Anyone belonging to an unauthorised association will be subject to a period of imprisonment of between two months and one year and to a fine of between fifty and one thousand francs. Should the offence be repeated the penalties are liable to be doubled. Anyone condemned for such an offence may also be placed under the supervision of the relevant police authorities for a period not exceeding double the maximum laid down for the first offence. Article 463 of the Penal Code may be applied at any time.

Article 3 Accomplices will be punishable. These are defined as anyone who may have knowingly lent or hired their houses or apartments to an unauthorized association.

c. *Decree of 26 March 1852 concerning mutual aid societies*

Article 1 A Mutual Aid Society will be set up through the initiative of the parish priest and the mayor of each *commune* provided such a society will have a useful function.

Article 2 These societies will consist of participating and honorary members. The latter will pay fixed subscriptions or will make a donation to the funds of the association, but will not enjoy the privileges of the association.

Article 3 The president of each society will be nominated by the President of the Republic.

Article 6 The societies' aim will be to ensure temporary aid for sick, wounded or disabled members and to provide a financial contribution towards their funeral expenses.

d. The right of coalition
Law of 25 May 1864: Article 1
Articles 414, 415 and 416 of the Penal Code are repealed and are replaced by the following Articles:

(*i*) *Article 414* Anyone attempting by violent or fraudulent means to cause or continue an organized stoppage of work aiming at obtaining a rise or fall in wages, or anyone interfering with the freedom of work, will be subject to a period of imprisonment of between six days and three years and a fine of between sixteen francs and 3,000 francs, or to one of these penalties.

(*ii*) *Article 415* If these offences have been committed as a result of a preconcerted plan, those found guilty may be placed under the supervision of the relevant police authorities for a period of between two and five years.

(*iii*) *Article 416* Any worker or head of an establishment who makes a deliberate attempt to interfere with the freedom of work by means of fines, prohibitions, proscriptions, suspensions, will be punishable by a period of imprisonment of between six days and three months and a fine of between sixteen francs and 3000 francs, or by one of these penalties only.

Article 2 Articles 414, 415 and 416 above-mentioned are also applicable to farmers or tenant farmers, harvest workers and rural labourers.

Report to the Emperor on the petition of workers' delegations to the Universal Exhibition of 1867 (31 March 1868):

The desires of the workers on the question of trade-union chambers (*chambres syndicales*) have recently received satisfaction through state legislation. After the Universal Exhibition the rules applying to employers' unions were also extended to workers' unions. These laws and rules have their origins in the legislation of the Constituent Assembly which abolished the old trade guilds and their inherent privileges. This legislation contained severe penalties which were necessary to get rid of the abuses which had existed under the Ancien Régime and which interfered with the liberty of commerce and industry. But as time passed the government saw fit to be less severe in the application of the legislation with regard to gatherings of reputable manufacturers and merchants.

Today the law only recognizes those trade-union chambers whose function it is to regulate the discipline of certain special professions such as stockbrokers, and bill-brokers. The law only allows the chambers of commerce and consultative chambers of arts and manufactures to represent industrial and commercial interests on an official level. But for a few years it has been the custom for independent trade-union chambers to be formed in certain Parisian trades. Chambers have been established for a long time — in the wine trade, in those industries connected with house building and the construction of public works, and in the manufacture and sale of cloth — the numbers of these has greatly increased in recent years and at the present time there are probably over eighty of them in Paris.

Fig. III.6 Increase in average hourly pay

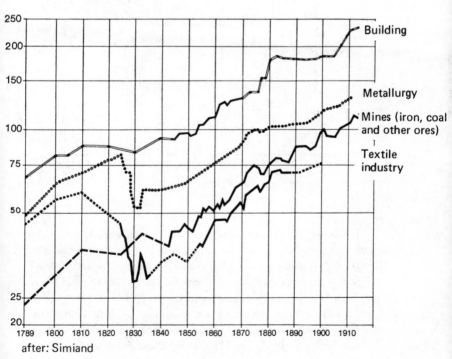

after: Simiand

Fig. III.7 Transfer of wealth by inheritance *Bequests and settlements per individual deceased*

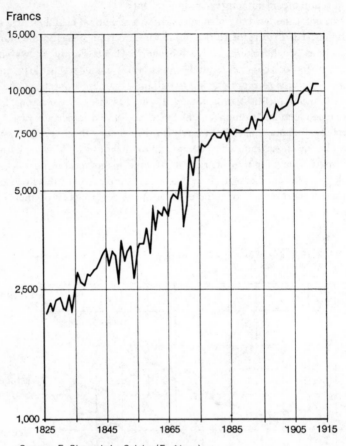

Source: F. Simand, *Le Salaire* (F. Alcan)

The desire of the workers to form similar assemblies to the employers is worthy of consideration, based as it is on principles of justice and equality. And in accordance with the wishes of Your Majesty, workers of several professions have been able to meet freely and discuss the position of their trade unions.

The workers' trade-union chambers will be subject to the same rules as the employers' chambers and as a result the administration will not have to intervene in the matter. These chambers will not be forbidden unless they contravene the principles behind the law of 17 June 1791 by interfering with the freedom of commerce and industry, or if they become political meetings unauthorized by the law. Obviously workers will realize that it is in their interests to maintain the purely professional character of their assembles.

The Minister
of Agriculture, Commerce and Public Works.
FORCADE
(*Moniteur Universel,*31 March 1868)

Chronology of the workers' movement 1800–1870

1803 Law of 22 germinal Year XII establishing the workers' *livrets*

1806 Re-establishment of the Conciliation Boards (*Conseils de Prud'hommes*). Only employers and workshop-masters are represented.

1810 Promulgation of the Penal Code. Articles 414, 415 and 416 forbid combinations.

1817–19 Founding of professional associations of the hat-makers and fullers of Lyon and the street cleaners of Paris. General strike of hat trade workers.

1822 Strike of the carpenters of Paris.

1823 Founding of the Society of the Union of Workers on the Tour of France (the *Compagnonnage* movement)

1825 Economic Crisis.

1826 First French railway line from Saint-Etienne to Lyon. Numerous strikes.

1830 Opposition to government conservatism.
    The 'Ordinances' of July 26.
    Employers support workers' part in the Revolution of 1830.
    The 'Three glorious days' of 29, 30 and 31 July.
    Louis-Philippe, Duke of Orleans, becomes King of France
    Many strikes during the autumn.

1831 Formation of the Philanthropic Society of Tailors.
    21–3 November: three days of insurrection in Lyon.
    5 December: royal troops occupy Lyon.

1832	June: trial and acquittal of those accused over the troubles in Lyon.
	Republican insurrection in Paris.
1833	Formation of the Society of the Fraternal Union of Weavers. Strike by the tailors, printers and shoemakers of Paris, and the porcelain manufacturers of Limoges.
	September: Carpenters' workers strike in Paris.
	November: Three workers' leaflets distributed in Paris among workers of tailoring trade, printers and shoemakers.
	The 'Republican Association for the defence of freedom of the press and personal freedom' intervenes on behalf of the strikers.
1834	February: members of mutual aid societies of Lyon decide to strike. 14,000 looms stop working.
	Plans drawn up for laws against associations.
	April: Trial of strikers of Lyon.
	Insurrection breaks out 11 April. It is put down in Lyon but breaks out in Paris, 13 April. Massacre of several workers, 14 April (incident of the rue Trasnonain).
	Law against associations is voted.
1839–40	Economic Crisis. Unemployment. Workers agitate.
1839	13 May: Republican insurrection led by Blanqui and the Society of the Seasons. Relentless persecution of secret societies.
1842	Railways law marks beginning of large-scale railway developments.
1847	Grave economic crisis.
1848	24 February: Revolution in Paris. Proclamation of the Provision Government of which Blanqui and Albert were members.
	25 February: Proclamation of the right of association, of universal suffrage and the right to work.
	27 February: Setting up of poor relief schemes (sometimes called national workshops, *ateliers nationaux*) to give work to the unemployed.
	28 February: Setting up of the Luxembourg Commission to deal with the 'organization of work'.
	4 March: Decree instituting a fixed working day, ten hours in Paris and eleven in the provinces and abolishing bargaining over the length of the working day.

23 April: Elections (universal suffrage) for the Constituent Assembly. Supplementary elections in May.

16 May: Suppression of the Luxembourg Commission.

13 June: Parisian crowd invades the Assembly.

21 June: *ateliers nationaux* abolished.

23–6 June: The June days – 'civil war' in Paris. Insurrection ferociously put down under the direction of Cavaignac.

4 November: Vote of the new constitution. By majority vote the right of work and the right of education were not included.

10 December: Louis Napoleon Bonaparte elected President.

1849   May: the montagnards – left-wing deputies – successful in supplementary elections.

Electoral law removing the right to vote from 3 million citizens.

August–September: Meetings of the delegates of forty-three associations to found the Union of Workers' Associations.

Foundation of the Fraternal Association of Socialist Teachers by Pauline Roland and Lefrançois.

1850   News of the discovery of gold in California.

Improvement in the economic situation.

1851   Coup d'état of 2 December.

1852–7   Authoritarian period of the Empire. Economic prosperity, 'golden age' of speculation, railways and banking.

1857   Financial crash on the Stock Exchange, economic crisis, strikes.

Five republicans elected on to the Legislative Assembly. (*Corps Législatif*)

1860   Michel Chevalier concludes the free trade treaty with England on behalf of Napoleon III (Chevalier–Cobden treaty).

1863   Founding of the *Crédit Lyonnais* (Bank).

Workers' coalitions and strikes. Miners from Anzin gain a reduction of working hours.

1863–4   Workers' discussions on the question of elections. Manifesto of the Sixty drawn up by Tolain which proclaimed the necessity of autonomous action by the working classes.

1864   Founding of the *Société Generale* (Bank) and the *Comité des Forges* (Association of Foundries).

Binders' strike. Beginnings of the *Caisse du Sou* (Penny Fund), for loans to strikers.

Law on the right of coalition and the right to strike.

Formation of numerous workers' trade-union chambers with the tolerance of the administration.

1865   Setting up of the French branch of the International Federation in the Place de la Corderie.

1866   Economic crisis.

Strike by the miners of Anzin.

1867   Law on joint stock companies.

Universal Exhibition in Paris. The elected workers' commission submits a report to the minister.

1868   Strike in the building trades in Paris.

First proceedings of the Paris International.

Women's workers' society founded in Lyon (the *ovalistes*).

1869   Many strikes. *Caisse du Sou* widens its sphere of action.

Bloody incidents at La Ricamerie and Aubin.

Federal chamber of workers' societies of Paris (in the Place de la Corderie).

Liberal and Republican opposition obtain a majority in the Legislative Assembly.

1870   Strike at Le Creusot.

Federal chambers of workers' societies founded in Rouen, Marseille and Lyon.

Second and third proceedings of the International.

IV From the Commune to the 'Belle Epoque'

In his *Evolution de la Troisième République*, published in 1921, Charles Seignobos wrote, 'In no other period has French society changed so rapidly as during the last fifty years'. This verdict needs closer examination, but in itself it is not surprising, since Seignobos witnessed such enormous changes that he could hardly have failed to have been amazed by them. Production had made astonishing progress with the stimulus given by science and technology. The use of new sources of power, electricity, oil and gas, led to what has sometimes been called the 'second industrial revolution'. But even more remarkable was the progress made in the realm of communications. Nobody who had seen within a few decades the spread of the bicycle, car, aeroplane, telegraph and telephone could doubt that they were seeing a revolutionary change in the conditions of life.

As Seignobos himself wrote, 'The material life of Frenchmen improved through the vast increase in the amount and variety of goods and services.' The consumption of goods increased significantly. The consumption of wheat only progressed slightly (250 litres per person per year in 1860, 323 in 1885, 325 in 1910) as did the consumption of the potato (133 kilos in 1860, 141 in 1882, 192 in 1910) but this was because Frenchmen were turning towards richer and more varied foods. The amount of meat consumed was only twenty-six kilos per person per year in 1862; it had risen to thirty-three kilos in 1882, thirty-six in 1892 and forty in 1814.

The amount of sugar consumed was 6.5 kilos in the 1860s but this had more than doubled by the 1900s and amounted to fourteen kilos and by 1914 was seventeen kilos. Goods coming from the colonies were also more in favour — the amount of coffee consumed trebled in fifty years, and the amount of cocoa more than trebled. Unfortunately amounts of alcohol consumed also rose. Around 1875 it seems that in terms of pure spirit the average consumption per head was 2.8 litres. This had risen to 3.6 litres in 1880 and reached 4.5 litres in 1890. The standard of clothing also improved. Around 1865 the average amounts used, per head, per year, were 2.6 kilos of wool and 1.9 kilos of cotton. In 1885 these amounts had doubled and by 1914 the averages were 6.6 kilos of wool and 6.7 kilos of cotton.

Fig. IV.1   Savings bank deposits, 1835–1913

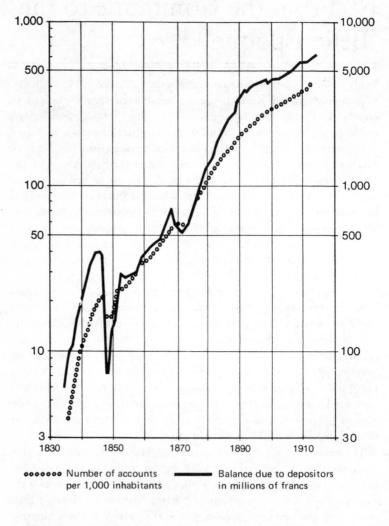

○○○○○○○ Number of accounts   ▬▬▬▬ Balance due to depositors
per 1,000 inhabitants   in millions of francs

The cost of living rose, but people were still able to save. The balance of deposits in the *Caisses d'epargne* (savings banks) stood at around 550 million francs during the early years of the Third Republic. It increased to 2,000 million francs in 1884, 3,000 million francs in 1891 and 6,000 million francs in 1913. These were only the savings of ordinary people. There were also, of course, massive investments elsewhere.

Is Seignobos' statement justified by these statistics? Was French society changing as 'rapidly' as he imagined? A look at neighbouring countries, in spite of the inadequacy of statistical information, raises a few doubts. If one takes a broad look at working populations, by sectors, one finds that the size of the primary sector in France was reduced by 12 per cent between 1876 and 1906, but in Germany it was reduced by 18 per cent, in Switzerland by 27 per cent and in England by 38 per cent. The size of the secondary sector grew by 6 per cent in France, by 8 per cent in Germany and by 9.5 per cent in Switzerland. The tertiary sector increased by 13 per cent in France and 16 per cent in England, but in Germany it increased by 25 per cent and in Switzerland by 28 per cent. Although these figures are not as accurate as one might wish they do help put France's social changes in a comparative European context. But the comparison between the USA and France is more striking. In the USA there were much more profound changes. The primary sector was reduced by 36 points, the secondary sector was increased by 26 points and the tertiary sector was increased by a significant 42 points.

France at the end of the nineteenth century was still largely a nation of peasants. According to the census of 1891 (the last census to give information of exactly this sort) the size of the population living off agriculture (that is to say where the head of the family had an agricultural occupation) had increased to 17.5 millions, which was 46.5 per cent of the total population. Industry occupied 9.5 millions (25 per cent of the population), commerce and transport 5 millions (13.5 per cent of the population), the liberal professions 2.5 millions (6.6 per cent of the population) and those living off investments numbered 2 millions (5.7 per cent of the population). At the end of the nineteenth century agriculture was supporting as many people as all the other activities put together.

To get an exact idea of the evolution of the working population one would need comparable censuses for 1872 and 1911. Unfortunately these censuses were conducted in different ways and are not strictly comparable. As a second-best the censuses of 1866 and 1906 may be used since they were conducted on identical lines. The results of this comparison are to be seen in Table IV 1 below.

It can be seen that the two sectors where there was a decline in numbers were agriculture and domestic service. These two sectors were connected, since sons, and especially daughters, of peasants often became domestic servants. Of the growth sectors, the industrial sector was making the slowest progress whilst the distributive sector (in

Table IV.1 Growth and change of the working population

	1866	1906	Index of growth (100 in 1866)
Agriculture, fisheries, forestry	49.8%	42.7%	86
Industry	29.0%	30.6%	105
Transport and carriage	1.7%	4.3%	253
Trade, banking, service industries	6.4%	9.9%	155
Domestic labour	6.4%	4.6%	72
Professions and public service	6.7%	7.9%	118

commerce and above all transport) attracted more and more workers. But despite the changes which had undoubtedly taken place, one can hardly say that the basic structure of the working population had been transformed during these forty years.

The numbers and relative status of those within the different sectors of the working population had not significantly changed. After 1866 the censuses give information on 'positions with the professions', and a comparison between 1876 and 1911 is thus possible. Numbers in all categories except domestic service increased, indicating a growth in the size of the working population. But within the working population there were proportional changes from category to category and here the most notable feature was the growth in the number of employees, although the disequilibrium between workers and employers as a whole was slowly being reduced.

The social structure of France remained basically stable, for a variety of reasons. There were no longer the great transfers of land which had been characteristic of the revolutionary period and although the peasants were as keen as ever to acquire more land, and if possible to get it at the expense of the nobility and the bourgeoisie this was a slow,

Table IV.2 Working population: status categories

	1876	1911	Index of growth (100 in 1876)
Employers	6 393 000 (40.5%)	8 582 000 (42.2%)	104
Employees	772 000 (5%	1 869 000 (9.3%)	186
Workers	7 653 000 (48%)	8 933 000 (44%)	92
Domestic workers	1 015 000 (6.5%)	929 000 (4.5%)	69

piecemeal process. In addition, after 1873 the remarkable prosperity of the Second Empire gave way to a period of relative economic stagnation which lasted until the last years of the nineteenth century. The fall in prices, of about 40 per cent between 1873 and 1896 discouraged producers. Industrial growth continued, although at a slower rate, but there was a crisis in agriculture due to two main factors. First there was the competition of foreign corn produced cheaply and transported cheaply by a growing merchant navy. Secondly there was the damage to the vines in wine-producing areas, caused by the disease phylloxera from 1876 to 1890. A period of prosperity followed between 1896 and 1914 but the wine-producers were unable to profit from it, and this period of prosperity did not bring as much profit as did the benefits accruing from the Second Empire. It has been calculated that between 1880 and 1914 the profits made by owners or proprietors increased by 13 per cent in agriculture and 57 per cent in industry. But between 1850 and 1880 these profits had multiplied by 2.5 times in agriculture and 4.2 times in industry.

The fluctuations taking place within the economy had a result which was a further reason for the static character of French social structure in this period. Méline and his successors adopted a protectionist economic policy which entrenched a society of small producers and sellers. This in itself reinforced the idea that social harmony had been achieved in France and contributed to a feeling of smugness, making change seem unnecessary and unwelcome.

Another factor in the stability of French society may be found in the attitudes of French entrepreneurs. Up to the time of the first world war they seem to have been very conservative, to have been devoted to the idea of the family firm, and therefore tended to be rather narrow-minded, opposing any outsider. They were reluctant to accept investment from anyone outside the family and even opposed expansion of the firm in case it should grow too large to be controlled by the family or handed down intact. There was therefore little taste for expansion. There were pioneers in new industries who were prepared to take a risk and who had secured real achievements in new sectors − rayon, aluminium, electrical engineering, the car industry and the cinema. But the net results of this do not seem to have been long-lasting. In 1914 the older industries were still dominant − the textile and clothing industries still employed one-third of industrial labour − and the small type of enterprise still predominated. In 1906 half of the total industrial labour force was employed in establishments of from one to five employees. Large-scale establishments with more than one hundred employees accounted for only one-tenth of all workers.

When these factors are taken into account French society at the turn of the century may be seen in rather a different light. The significant features are not the changes of a rather limited character in the distribution of the working population between various economic sectors, but the struggles between social groups in their attempts either to rise to power, or to seize power. In a speech made in Grenoble in 1872 Gambetta announced 'the arrival and presence in politics of a new social stratum . . . ('d'une nouvelle couche sociale') which is by no means inferior to its predecessors'. Here Gambetta had posed the basic problem which was of much greater significance than the character of institutions. It was the question of the replacement of the old ruling classes by the new.

1. The new social strata

When he used the deliberately vague expression 'une nouvelle couche sociale', Gambetta did not have a precise, limited social group in mind. Rather he was thinking of a complex amalgam of old social strata and new ones, created by the economic growth of the period of the Second Empire, the development of new techniques and the quickening division of labour. Their intellectual and material independence were forces enabling them to evade the ascendancy of the *grande bourgeoisie.*

The 'capacités'

At a time when the prestige of science was at its height and when there was a general belief in education as the means by which humanity would progress, it is not surprising to note the increase in status of the educated, of those with professional qualifications. These were the 'able', the *capacités.*

Among the able, the oldest group with a high reputation because of their culture and their independence were the liberal professions. At the head of this group came barristers, who led an active professional life, and were better integrated into urban life than magistrates who tended to come from well-established bourgeois families, and who, because of professional as well as personal taste, tended to live apart, more cut off from the ebb and flow of ordinary life than the barristers. Barristers were professional speech makers and were indispensable in political life. They could run a campaign, chair a political committee or meeting. At times of elections to the assemblies barristers were suitable candidates, and were able to give up their practice if elected and take it up once more if defeated. By introducing universal manhood suffrage the Third Republic opened up a political career, and with it possibilities of social advancement to those possessing the necessary qualifications, of which eloquence was an important one.

Two other professions which had similar positions in society were equally to benefit from the possibilities opened up by the Third Republic. These were the lawyers and the doctors. They often had close links with their clients especially in the countryside and in smaller towns. They were often referred to as the 'family lawyer' or the 'family doctor'. Already during the Second Empire administrative officials had frequently complained in their reports to the central administration of the harmful influence of these 'petty notables' on the electors. They were said to have 'corrupted opinion'. After the fall of the Empire and during the early years of the Republic, lawyers and doctors found their field of action more open because of the removal of a great deal of administrative interference. Their influence was now felt much more widely than before. They were perhaps less well qualified than barristers to be candidates for election as deputies, but they made excellent local councillors, advisers, propagandists, inspirers and guiders of opinion.

The number of lawyers remained fairly static. The number of doctors increased rapidly towards the end of the century. There were now more people to treat. These people had more belief in the efficacy of medicine and they had more means to pay for it. In addition there were more qualified doctors. So much so that the post of officer of health (*officier de santé*) which did not require the holder to have the necessary university training to be a bachelor of medicine was abolished in 1892. In 1876 there were 10,000 doctors; in 1911 there were more than 20,000 and in addition there were 10,000 students registered in the various faculties of medicine.

These were old professional categories. Their basic characteristic was their 'independence' — since those who practised these professions lived off their clients and received fees from them. But by the end of the nineteenth century there were salaried professions which also enjoyed prestige because of the education and ability required to exercise them. Some of these professions were linked with scientific or technical progress: professions such as architects and especially engineers, of whom there were 25,000 by 1914. Other professions were more linked to the diffusion of education. Now that there was a literate public and because the exploitation of advertising was responsible for a reduction in newspaper prices, the press, and particularly the local press, experienced a golden age. After the law of 29 July 1881, which abolished all restrictions on the freedom of the press, the number of publications rose rapidly. The number of provincial daily papers rose from 114 in 1880 to 280 in 1885 and to 302 in 1892. The number of provincial weekly papers rose from 1156 in 1882 to more than 2000 in 1913. There was now a greater need for journalists. Some were impecunious and destined to remain unknown since they were not allowed to sign their articles. But others were powerful and capable of influencing opinion in a particular electoral area, and sometimes in a whole *département*. From 1871 to 1879, years when the future of the republic seemed to be in the balance, there was no republican 'party', but the republic had at its disposal a political press of remarkable efficacy. The spread of republicanism as an ideology was just as much the achievement of these great journalists as of the professional politicians. In small and medium-sized towns the editor of the most widely-read local newspaper was often an important local figure and a force to be reckoned with; a political figure with political power, he also exercised social power since he was able, almost at will, to make and destroy reputations.

The teaching profession benefited greatly from the reforms of Jules Ferry. The number of primary school teachers increased (from 64,000 men and women in 1876—7 to 100,000 in 1892—3 and 125,000 in 1912—13), and so did the numbers of secondary teachers. The improvement in the material conditions of teachers enhanced their social status. Teachers were better paid, were free from the interference of parish priests and mayors (although not from the interference of the prefect). After the law of 1889 they were paid by the state and had received a solid training from the École Normale of their *département*. The teacher was now a person of standing in the place where he taught because he disseminated learning. He was also looked up to because he knew how to deal with officialdom, how to write letters in an acceptable manner, and was a sure guide to the locals in their dealings with a distant, frequently feared central administration. In the countryside he was the equal of the parish priest except in very clerical areas. But he was rarely the equal of the mayor, because his salary was modest and because he was closely dependent on the authorities, since school teachers were not permitted their own trade union. He was a man of standing, but in a limited way. The importance of teachers in grammar schools and secondary schools increased similarly. They were university trained, all were at least graduates, and in the grammar schools most had passed the *agrégation* examination in order to gain a post on the teaching staff of the lycée. They were less closely bound up with local life than primary school teachers and they were usually rather more circumspect. But some played a part in political life. Others were even local political militants, but few became deputies or senators.

Below the teachers in the social hierarchy came civil servants. Having emerged from the masses they helped to swell the ranks of the new social strata. These men were not part of the upper ranks of the civil service, who were still recruited from the *grande bourgeoisie* even after the purges of 16 May 1877, but were minor civil servants. Their number increased, as the concerns of the administration became simultaneously wider and more precise. Estimates of the number of those employed in public and administrative services on the eve of the first world war ranged from 470,000 to 550,000. Their number had probably almost doubled since 1870.

Most came from the lower middle class and many still remained part of that class. Minor civil servants were not well-paid. Sub-clerks in the Ministry of Public Works only received a salary of 800 francs per annum in 1911. Store keepers, earning 1,000 francs, country postmen earning 1,100, customs clerks earning 1,140 francs, all earned less than many workers and substantially less than miners who probably earned 1,500 francs. But there were wide variations in the salaries of civil servants — there were forty grades in 1914. In addition through their work, or the protection they received from higher-placed persons, particularly politicians, the civil servants were able to work their way up the promotion ladder. They also enjoyed the respect of their fellow citizens, although this varied according to their particular branch of the civil service. Those employed in the financial branches, like taxation, or technical (bridges and highways), the Post Office (which together with teaching was the only profession to employ women) and especially those employed in the services of the many prefectures, were held in the greatest esteem. The heads and deputy-heads of the various sections of the prefectures belonged to the group of leading citizens, the notables of small French towns.

A job in the civil service was more or less a guarantee of permanent employment. In the future lay prospects of becoming established civil servants and of a pension. Civil servants were respected and even feared because they represented the state. These civil servants of middle rank were secure. They were almost able to raise themselves to the level of the liberal professions and swelled the ranks of the new *capacités*.

Business concerns

Heads of businesses were obviously not a new group in French society. Yet, as has already been noted, the development of big business and the creation of large business concerns did not have the same degree of 'concentration' as in other countries. The number of small businesses did not decrease, but grew considerably. The census of 1866 revealed there were 1,968,000 one-man businesses. But the census of 1896 recorded 3,436,000 and the census of 1906 3,927,000 although this figure was never reached again. Out of this figure of almost 4 million there were hardly more than a million businessmen employing one or two workers. The rest were men working with their wives (364,000) or working totally alone (2,445,000). On the eve of the first world war, one-man, or family businesses were the rule. They were small-scale from every point of view.

This phenomenon is explained by the growth in consumption and the growing specialization whereby medium and large-scale industrial enterprises become more or less solely concerned with production, leaving marketing to others. Transport and warehousing employed two and a half times as many persons in 1906 as in 1866. There were remarkable developments in trading and above all in the food trade which employed some 600,000 persons. Taxation records indicate that the number of those holding a licence to sell alcohol rose to 482,000 in 1913: one seller for every fifty-three adults.

The building trade was still dominated by small firms. In the *département* of the Isère at the turn of the century there were almost a thousand builders. By far the most numerous category consisted of independent masters working alone, or almost alone. Then came a category employing ten or twenty workers; the largest firms in carpentry, painting, joinery usually employed no more than this; and the same was true of quarrying. There were large-scale businesses in the building trade only in Grenoble where two had more than a hundred employees. It was possible to climb the social ladder by being in the building trade. This was shown by Italian immigrants who rose in prosperity through frantically hard work. They had been setting up in business on their own account since the beginning of the nineteenth century. In 1872 half of the painters in the département had Italian names.

The country craftsman, on the other hand, was in decline. G. Garrier comments:

We find the village craftsman at the height of his fortunes and influence in the middle of the nineteenth century. He held a unique position as the cornerstone of a small closed economy. The opening up of the countryside by road and later by rail dealt him a savage blow. He is no longer the indispensable man, the source of good advice and even the occasional loan. Manufactured goods flow in, better made and cheaper. After their golden age of 1850 and 1860 demand for coopers slackens: 'vin ordinaire' is sold from the vat, the buyer provides the cask and looks after it. The fine wines of the Beaujolais are sold in cask, but the casks get used again and returned empty by rail. The census of 1911 shows a total disappearance of tinmen, coopers, sawyers, tile-makers, shoemakers, carriers, basket makers, rope-makers, well-sinkers; makers of sabots and clogs have become very rare. Skills ancillary to building are only found in market towns, though in 1870 there was a blacksmith, a carpenter, a tiler, a bricklayer, a locksmith in every village and even in every hamlet. In 1906 the village craftsman works alone: he has neither journeyman nor apprentice and it is rare for a grownup son to be working with his father; while forty or fifty years earlier every workshop would have had three or four people working in it. This decline was slow and hardly felt as a crisis. The local craftsman reduced his clientele and his work, gave up his apprentices, lived on his savings and his kitchen garden, discouraged his sons from following him. The exodus of the next generation certainly warranted this decline. (*Les Campagnes de l'ouest, 1800–1870*)

The proliferation of small businesses in cities, particularly in the retail trades, helped wage earners to rise in the social scale. For the ambitious workman a small business was not difficult to achieve. The level of education needed was not particularly high and there was not, as yet, a great deal of competition from the bigger firms. But once this position had been gained there was little question of future economic advancement. As shopkeepers or master craftsmen they rarely saw beyond the village or their own suburb in a town, and as small industrialists rarely looked beyond the *département*.

There was inevitably a lot of competition between these numerous small business men. There were, however, some professional organizations. The first to be founded were in the building trades – in the form of either employers' unions in the different trades, or associations at the level of the *département*. The basic raison d'être was the solid defence of price levels, particularly as far as public works were concerned. Associations of retailers were also formed when the government changed the laws relating to the sale of alcohol, and sometimes there were meetings of federations of retailers, such as the South Eastern

Federation which covered the region around Lyon. By the end of the nineteenth century grocers had formed trade unions in many towns. These professional organizations were involved in a two-sided struggle. They accused the taxation authorities of sacrificing the interest of the small businessmen by over-taxation. They also opposed workers' co-operatives which were accused of deliberately attempting to starve independent businessmen. These two attitudes — regarding the state as an enemy and the workers' co-operatives as an obstacle to the free-play of the economy — were characteristic of small businessmen at this time.

They had therefore something in common but this did not lead them all to adopt the same political views. Some, and particularly those whose finances were rather precarious, were obsessed by fears of social collapse, and dreading any form of disorder that might disrupt their affairs readily joined the ranks of the conservatives. The wealthier and more successful tended to be more open to new ideas. Many of them joined the radicals in a rather unmilitant way. At the beginning of the twentieth century many were attracted to socialism. Some builders even became heads of local branches of the socialist party. Perhaps this was a result of their experience as young workmen. But many found the socialist party too authoritarian. They preferred to vote for 'independent socialists'. In this way they could show their approval of the latest ideas yet not vote for a party which might endanger the status quo.

The peasants

The peasants were slow to change. The change was indeed so slow that many contemporaries failed to notice it. But the countryside changed between 1870 and 1914. The forces of change were not new, but their impact was increasing with the passage of time. One of the most important of these forces was the rural exodus. This was almost a self-generating process. It was easier for the poor of the countryside to move to the towns in search of work if relatives or friends were already there and were able to help them adapt to their new way of life. The fall in the prices of agricultural produce in the third quarter of the nineteenth century added to the economic pressures behind the rural exodus. The introduction of universal military service added a psychological impulse, when the young peasant first came into contact with the young city dweller, and the tinsel pleasures of the garrison town made city life appear so seductive.

Those peasants who stayed on in the towns after their military service were generally the poorest: the sort who up to 1850 had generated a climate of unrest and awkward demands which in periods of economic or political crisis could become dangerous. After their departure peasant society presented a less threatening aspect. 'Emigration has cleansed it, bled off the poorest and the most dangerous blood' — also some of the best blood: for many of the better-off steered their more intelligent offspring, those noted by their teachers for brightness and industry, into urban careers, especially the unpopular but envied civil service.

The rural exodus was part cause and part result of technical progress in the country: result, because labour-saving machinery threw up a surplus of labour for the towns; cause, because eventual scarcity of labour resulted in a rise in wages and forced the farmer to invest in more machinery. Agriculture was steadily becoming more mechanized: improved ploughs, mechanical seed-drills and harvesters were widely used. The use of chemical fertilizers increased sixfold between 1866 and 1913. But technical progress was sporadic; many could not afford it, and it came mainly from the scattered initiatives of enterprising individuals. There was almost no education in agricultural techniques, which might have led to a more general adoption of machinery. The sons of peasants rarely attended institutions of higher education where agriculture was taught. There was one instructor in agriculture in each *département*, but his viewpoint tended to be more that of the administrator than the practical farmer, and agricultural instruction was in general not taken very seriously. Hence technical advance in the countryside was uneven in its results. The Third Republic did little nore than the Second Empire to encourage it, confining its effort to the support of agricultural exhibitions and local shows. Technical progress was an added factor in widening the gap between large and small scale farmers.

The change from a subsistence to a market economy had the same result and exposed the peasant to troublesome fluctuations. He had for long been content to bring his produce to the nearest market to sell direct to the consumer. But at the end of the century things began to change and the consumer tended to go to the specialist shopkeeper. The peasant, especially if he specialized in a few products, found himself up against, not the consumer, but the bulk-buying middleman, much shrewder and more formidable than the consumer. These kinds of marketing enhanced the disparity between the small scale grower who had to make a quick sale and the larger one who had reserves to fall back on.

Uncertainty was now the lot of the peasants. Improved technique had reduced the old uncertainties caused by the weather. But the new uncertainties of the market and competition between peasants needing to sell had replaced the old ones and could be particularly dangerous at times of low prices. Peasant society became diversified, a diversity based on levels of expertise, and the result was an intensification of peasant individualism. Diversity, too, characterized the French countryside. There was economic diversity according to the size and value of holdings. At the top of the peasant hierarchy were the big farmers, large scale agricultural entrepreneurs with capital available, or, more rarely, big proprietors cultivating their own land. The rich agricultural entrepreneur would use the latest machinery and would employ a numerous labour force. In 1906 there were nearly 250 large scale establishments each employing more than fifty wage-earners. These were large-scale farms directly associated with processing plants such as distillers, mills, and beet sugar factories. There were 45,000 holdings employing from six to fifty wage-earners and 1,300,000 employing from one to six wage-earners. At least one-third, and possibly two-fifths of the farmers employed some labour.

It seems surprising that contemporaries attached so little importance and made so little mention of this class of master farmers. They were obsessed by the idea that there was a kind of ideal peasant whose virtues they extolled and who, it was said, would form the basis of an ideal democratic society. This was the peasant proprietor working his holding with his family without employing any 'hirelings'. But often this romanticized peasant proprietor did not exist. Contemporaries rarely mentioned the hard, dirty work undertaken by women who had to run the house, tend the farm animals, and bring up the children who left school and were set to work at the age of thirteen. The agricultural inquiry of 1909 praised family farming and claimed that this way of running a farm obtained the best results and even fared best during periods of crisis.

At the beginning of the twentieth century the majority of farms were run by families. There were probably between 2 and 2.5 million of them. They were sometimes run by the owners, sometimes by tenant farmers or sharecroppers. The material condition of the exploiters varied as widely as that of their lands. Mixed farming partly for subsistence meant that some were not particularly well-off. Specialization paid off in some cases if the land was suitable and economic conditions were favourable. But it is impossible to generalize. Agricultural development reached different levels in different parts of France.

Along with this economic diversity went an increasing degree of geographical diversity. As different parts of the countryside emerged from their isolation and were drawn into the mainstream of commerce, local specializations emphasized the differences between areas that were more richly endowed by nature or better exploited and the less fortunate ones. The lands of the north and the Paris basin producing corn and sugar beet were the most 'advanced'. There was prosperous agriculture on the limey soils of Flanders, Hainaut, the Cambrésis, Picardy, the Vexin, Soissonnais, Valois, Brie and the Beauce. They also benefited from the proximity of the urban centre. These lands were usually being run by large tenant farmers, but sometimes owners farmed them directly. On the eve of the first world war this agricultural area could hold its own with the best lands in England and northern Europe.

The areas of mixed woodland and pasture (the *bocage*) were rather more complex. Their progress had often been retarded because of their isolated character. But prosperity followed the advent of more specialized agriculture. Normandy specialized in dairy farming and supplied the needs of the Paris region for dairy products. Farmers.and landowners grew rich as a result, and tended to become a kind of local bourgeoisie whose wealth also tended to make them conservative politically. But there was a different kind of development in the area around Charentes. Before 1800 the 120,000 hectares of vine land made this area the second most important vine-growing area in France after the Gironde. But most of the vines were destroyed by an epidemic of phylloxera and in 1892 there were only 30,000 hectares under viticulture. The initiative of a peasant from Surgères, who started the first dairy co-operative in 1888, transformed this old vine-growing region into a land of dairy farming. In 1893 the Central Cooperative Association of dairy farming of the Charentes and Poitou regions was founded on the pattern of Swiss co-operatives. As early as 1899 the association had organized a system of refrigerated vans to transport milk to Paris. In 1906 a professional dairy-farming school was established at Surgères which played a part in training future dairy production managers. This co-operative had saved the region and saved the small peasant proprietors.

Agricultural specialization also changed the character of two areas in the south: the Rhône plains and Lower Languedoc. The plains of the Rhône were improved by the drainage of marsh land and the watering of dry land by water from the river Durance, distributed through canals. The cost of this scheme and of the irrigation water meant that the farming had to be profitable. This was possible when rapid means of transport were available. These allowed distant markets to be reached — in Paris and even in Germany, Switzerland, the Low Countries and England. The small proprietors specialized in producing fruit and vegetables. On the eve of the first world war the plains of the Rhône were prosperous. The rural exodus had stopped and there was even some re-population in the area.

In Lower Languedoc phylloxera again led to a change in the economic character of the area. Before 1870 vines had been cultivated on the hills by small proprietors while the lowlands were relatively neglected. But between 1870 and 1880 the vines on the slopes were ruined. The first method used to combat phylloxera was winter flooding, so vines were planted on irrigable ground, i.e. the plains. There the land cost almost nothing; but re-establishing the vineyards needed heavy investment with no return for several years. This favoured vine-growers who were already well-off and rich town-dwellers who employed labourers to do the work with more specialized equipment. The smaller vine-growers who remained on the hills planted at great cost American varieties which were resistant to phylloxera but the yield was not as great as that of the vineyards of the plain. The small vine-growers of the plain and the hills formed co-operative associations to combat the competition of the larger vine-growers. But after 1900 they were hit by over-production and added to this was competition from the development of the vines of Algeria. They formed a defence committee in 1907; there were mass demonstrations which developed into riots in Narbonne and Perpignan and even into a mutiny of soldiers in Béziers. The intervention of the government and a rise in prices after some bad harvests led to a calmer situation in subsequent years.

Specialized agriculture was not adopted everywhere. Some areas resisted it, and there agriculture in the early years of the twentieth century remained substantially as it had always been. This was true of much of Provence, inland Brittany, Champagne and Lorraine; these were still regions of subsistence economy. Even some areas where the soil was rich maintained mixed farming. Here, in areas such as the Limagne or Aquitaine, there was less risk than elsewhere, but by maintaining this kind of agriculture returns did not increase significantly. Again there was not much change in the character of agriculture in mountainous regions.

The political tendencies of the peasants varied as much as their economic condition. Unlike the working classes they provided support for every conceivable political movement. In the first elections under the Third Republic, those of 1876 and 1877, when there was a definite confrontation between right and left, the peasants were divided. Western rural France voted for the right; eastern rural France (from Lorraine to Provence through the Massif Central) for the republicans. In 1914 the right only controlled western inland Brittany, the Basque country, the southern part of the Massif Central, and some Alpine départements, but it had regained Lorraine and Champagne. But other rural areas either remained republican or were gained by the republicans (areas such as the south-west, Languedoc and the Aquitaine basin). But these changes in political behaviour did not coincide with changes in the economy. Modernized regions maintained their traditional political attitudes (Normandy for example, remained conservative, and the plains of the Rhône remained republican) or moved to the left like the Languedoc. But areas of mixed farming varied in their political support, the north-east moved towards the right, the south-west towards the left. Remarkable as it may seem there was never a 'peasant party'. Indeed no party could ever claim to be the mouthpiece of the peasants. The variety of conditions and interests constantly being widened, meant that all political parties had a chance of drawing support from the electors of the changing peasant world.

Variety characterized the peasantry. And even if the richer peasants were tending to live like bourgeois and the poorer peasants remained much as they had been, they were all individualists. All members of the community — peasants, tradesmen, artisans, entrepreneurs and members of the liberal professions — realized that their place in society depended on the efficacy and intensity of their own efforts. They had, in the final analysis, to depend on themselves if they wanted to rise in society. But they already knew that education was necessary if one wished to rise in society, which is why they were so anxious to assure it for their children. Fortunately this coincided with the concerns of the political leaders of the republic, and particularly with those of Jules Ferry and his associates, even if they were more intent on producing good citizens than training people for a profession. The success of Ferry's schemes is largely to be explained by the demand for education, since the machinery of state was insufficient to enforce school attendance even if the law required it.

Primary schools gave children the rudiments of an education which were necessary in order to practise a profession. But once these rudiments had been attained it was possible for the diligent, intelligent child noticed by the schoolmaster to rise to higher things. He could enter the higher elementary school from which many pupils eventually entered the public services. He might even go to the *école normale*, the teachers' training college of the *département* and from there become a teacher. But it was also possible to go to secondary school and from there enter the professional bourgeoisie by exercising a more important profession. Social betterment through education is an original feature of this period: it might be gradual or swift, either stopping at the first generation at the level of petty functionary or teacher, a well respected stage, or leading the more brilliant pupils to university and the higher civil service examinations. The cleverest and most deserving children could win state scholarships. The *boursier*, the clever scholar from the poor family, gaining the highest positions in the state by his talents, stood in France, like the myth of the self-made man in America, as the symbol of a society in which advancement was open to all.

For the individual, rising in society meant a good school record; in the family it involved attention to Malthusian principles. State scholarships were only for a few and were best suited to the children of wage-earners. For the rest the family heritage (trade, business or property) determined social status. If the inheritance was divided the next generation might regress rather than progress. The provisions of the Civil Code regarding inheritance therefore led, indirectly, to family limitation, at least among the property-owning section of society. There was therefore a marked fall in the birth rate, perhaps attributable to the behaviour of the new élites in society.

Another influence making for a decline in the birth rate was the turning away from Christianity which was noted in several regions in France (Aquitaine, Poitou, the Limousin, and the Paris basin apart from Lorraine), and above all in towns both large and small. Some observers held that religious observance had for long become somewhat superficial for a good number of roman catholics. It had become an aspect of social conformity. When the republic began its anti-clerical legislation, which developed into the separation of Church and state, this produced a new kind of social conformity: it was now the done thing to stay away from church. There seems to have been a close link between the decline in clerical recruitment which was particularly marked from 1900 onwards, the anti-clerical measures of the government and the general 'spirit of the country'. The towns had been hostile towards the Church for some time because of the antipathy of the workers and the diminishing number of priests. But there was a growing hostility in the villages too because of the conflicts between priests and teachers who were now free from clerical control and whose teachers' colleges had encouraged anti-clerical tendencies. This 'dechristianization movement' affected men more than women. Women read little, rarely went out, were kept out of controversies and were generally more under the influence of the clergy, and the men seem to have shown little concern over this. André Siegfried remarks, 'Even an anti-clerical Frenchman feels happier about his wife if the curé is keeping an eye on her – especially if she's pretty.'

The lay schools seem to have provided another faith for the irreligious. There was now faith in reason, and in progress, and a belief in the desirability of knowledge. This was an echo of the positivism of Auguste Comte, who, with Taine and Berthelot, were the representatives of a generation which had complete faith in the power and even the beneficence of science. Positivism had gained a hold over the universities, had influenced education and thus reached as far as the primary schools where, if nothing more, it had been reduced to a belief in rationalism and secularism. The new social élites were well served by this confidence in progress, and belief in science as the means to achieve this progress. They were also drawn towards radicalism which, said Léon Bourgeois, 'tended to organize society politically and socially according to the laws of reason'. Gambetta had put his faith in the new élites, the *couches nouvelles* and he was to be proved right since they were firm supporters of radicalism during the Third Republic.

But the character of radicalism changed. Early radicalism, of the days towards the end of the Second Empire, as expressed in the Belleville programme (1869), was little more than a general call for basic liberties and a statement of belief in popular sovereignty. It was a question of founding democracy and the rest would follow in its wake. Gambetta believed that once universal suffrage had really established itself it would get rid of the impediments to the realization of the Belleville programme, and would lead to the achievement of these basic liberties. But at this point radicalism was the same as republicanism and if its programme was realized by Jules Ferry rather than Gambetta, this was because personal rivalry had excluded Gambetta from power. The later radicalism of the 1880s was characterized by its impatience with the compromise attitude of republicans which was preventing the immediate institution of a great republic free of the influence of outmoded social institutions. These radicals were hostile to the Church, and demanded the separation of Church and state. They opposed financial empires and called for nationalization of the railways. They were hostile to the rich and called for a graduated income tax.

Once in power the radicals organized themselves and their programme (the republican-radical and radical-socialist party had been founded in 1901). The radicals' aim was to establish a republic which would be the heir to the traditions of the Revolution. The basic institution of the Republic would be the school, which would spread knowledge. Guarantee of the integrity of private property would guarantee the independence of citizens. Agrarian problems would be solved by protecting small landowners. The workers would be able to throw off their fetters by becoming craftsmen, and unity between citizens (*la solidarité*) would solve social problems. These beliefs inevitably appealed to the new élites because they appealed to their interdependent attitudes, to their desire to secure respect for humanity but also because of their fear of social revolution. It seemed to combine the socialist ideal of state control and the rights of the individual as against those of the community. This put to one side the menace of the class struggle which would have badly hit the new élites.

But radicalism was threatened by the development of two streams of thought within the movement — a jacobin stream and an egalitarian stream. The first had deviated into Boulangism and nationalism; the second insisted on the label 'radical-socialist', rejecting mere reforms. Faced with these threats pre-war radicalism became inward-looking and adopted a radicalism of negation: refusal to change the existing social order: 'The party is firmly attached to the principle of private property which it has no intention of suppressing' (1907 programme); refusal to admit the existence of a social problem: 'The party rejects the idea of initiating class struggles among our citizens'; refusal to assume authority. With the separation of Church and state in 1905 the force of anti-clericalism was more or less spent. French radicalism tended to be traditionalist, self-satisfied, making gestures towards the left but in reality being socially conservative. Reforms were often talked about, but nothing was really done. As André Siegfried remarks, 'It is amazing how comfortably the vanguard of this body reclines on the existing social order. In this democracy which is ideologically so advanced and practically so moderate a political takeover would seem so safe and easy within a social framework that eschews change.' This was, after all, the framework which allowed the new élites to rise.

2. The grande bourgeoisie

By the turn of the century Gambetta's prophecy seemed to have come true. The new social élites had come to power through the radical party which represented their interests. This situation had been developing since 16 May 1877. The *grande bourgeoisie* had attempted to keep power in its own hands but universal suffrage had decided otherwise.

Within two years the republicans had gained control of the Chamber, the Senate and the Presidency of the Republic. This was now a 'republic of republicans'. But would the *grande bourgeoisie* allow itself to be deprived of its supremacy in the state just as fifty years earlier it had deprived the aristocracy of its supremacy? Would it surrender its control of political, economic and social power?

Their loss of political power was much less complete or swift than their own contemporaries realized, for they had no intention of abdicating and fought a strong rearguard action. Their worst setback was over their control of the executive, lost to the republican 'opportunists' and later to the radicals. The latter were openly hostile to them, while the 'opportunists', who had no objections to them as a class, and were more interested in purging the republic of royalist sentiment, tried to win them tactfully over to the support of the régime. Yet ministerial instability often served the interests of the *grande bourgeoisie* in that they occasionally managed to wangle the appointment at the head of a ministry of someone who was not particularly hostile to their interests. This was the case with Charles Dupuy, Jules Méline and, after the period of the radical cabinets, Raymond Poincaré. Maurice Rouvier even defended their interests during his two ministries, the first from May to December 1887, the second from January 1905 to February 1906. He was also Minister of Finance for several years and in the cabinets of Tirard, Freycinet, Loubet and Ribot (February 1889 to December 1892) and again in Combes' cabinet from June 1902 to January 1905. It was largely due to the skill of Rouvier that they escaped the threat of a tax on incomes which would have threatened the privileged position they held through their control of large personal wealth.

Rouvier achieved only the postponement of this measure, which was finally adopted in July 1914. However he had been able to achieve this because he had support in the assemblies. It is generally agreed that the *grande bourgeoisie* lost control of the legislature. Certainly they soon lost strength in the Senate which, under the Third Republic, became the preserve of republicans who had made a specialized profession of politics. This sort of professionalism neither suited the *grande bour-geoisie* nor attracted them, demanding as it did flexibility, patience and powers of persuasion in which they were apt to be lacking. But the Chamber of Deputies was more accessible, and the democratization of this body was much slower, as will appear from Table IV.3.

If there had been real conformity of political views among them the *grande bourgeoisie* could have dominated the Chamber: coalition with

Table IV.3 Social origins of deputies

Election of	1871	1893	1919
Nobility	34%	23%	10%
Upper middle class	36%	32%	30%
Middle class	19%	30%	35%
Lower middle class	8%	10%	15%
Working class	3%	5%	10%
TOTAL	100	100	100

Source: DOGAN, M., *Les Hommes politiques et l'illusion du pouvoir.*

the nobility would have sufficed to block any legislation that endangered their interests. But there was no such conformity; Caillaux, the keenest champion of income tax was himself a member of a *grande bourgeois* family. Even so, their differences were not so numerous as to diminish their influence in the assembly very noticeably.

It was with still greater ease that the *grande bourgeoisie* maintained its hold over the important administrative bodies in the state. This was particularly important during a period of ministerial instability when ministers had barely the time to decide on any large scale plan, let alone put it into effect. Until Jules Ferry came to power in 1880 the administrative personnel was anything but republican. Seignobos commented,

> All the civil servants of the Empire remained in their places apart from a few hundred prefects, subprefects and public prosecutors. These civil servants continued to run the public services, the army, the gendarmerie, the navy, the law offices of the state, taxation direct and indirect, the postal service, bridges and highways and education. They alone knew their way through the arsenal of police and finance regulations which had been accumulated since the Ancien Régime and which could be used by the administration at will against its opponents, and which it might choose to ignore if its friends were involved. They could have subordinates moved or dismissed, promoted or demoted. A secret report from their hands could make or wreck a subordinate's career.

The republicans very quickly tried to purge the service, and administrative despotism was reduced to the extent that politicians now began to stand up for their constituents and managed to gain the ear of ministers. There remained the problem of how to replace the former officials, particularly at the top. The young *grande bourgeois* were in the best position to gain these posts because of their wealth, their intellectual training, and their connections. In short they knew what was what. Many had trained in the *Ecole libre des sciences politiques* which had been created by Emile Boutmy in 1871 and they snapped up most of the diplomatic posts, and, which was especially important for the defence of the interests of their class, many became inspectors of finance. As high-ranking civil servants, leading technicians and ministerial advisers they were to have an important influence on the formulation of French economic policy.

The *grande bourgeoisie* therefore probably maintained a stronger position in the state than has often been claimed. They owed this partly to their own abilities and tenacity but also because of the unconscious help they received from their opponents who never managed, or desired to point to them as an enemy to be removed. Until about 1885 the republicans ran their electoral campaigns on old themes such as those of 1789, calling on the electors to form the Third Estate against the aristocracy and the clergy. These political themes were long outdated, though the 'opportunist' provincial press continued to harp on the 'hateful yoke' thrust on his 'serfs' by the feudal lord, and the tyranny of the 'confessional ticket'. Later, republicans and sometimes radicals too were terrified by the progress made by socialism, and in order to prevent social disruption called on all property-owners to unite. They even called the projected income tax an instrument of the 'fiscal inquisition'.

But the essential foundation of the power of the *grande bourgeoisie*, its economic strength, was never really effectively challenged. 'Their opponents never understood on what ground the fight should be carried on. They thought a political victory was enough . . . but if this dominance is to be broken its economic basis has got to be attacked' (Lhomme). For a long time the radical party had called for the abolition of monopolies but it never did anything about it. There was, admittedly, the unfortunate nationalization of the Western Railway in 1908. This might have worried the *grande bourgeoisie* but for the fact that the company was in serious financial difficulties. The taxpayer now had to support them. Such was the only kind of state intervention in the economy the middle class could allow.

Private free enterprise was left relatively untouched, but the economic power of the *grande bourgeoisie* could be threatened by changes in the character of capitalism and by general movements of the economy. French capitalism followed the general patterns of change of world capitalism, but much more slowly. 'Concentration' only developed in certain sectors — in the iron and steel industry, in the chemical industries and in banking where the big Parisian deposit banks took over provincial banks. The tendency of big businessmen was less towards 'concentration' than industrial agreements (*cartellisation*) in order to maintain profits by dictating prices. This was done by fixing production levels and dividing markets.

In common with most other countries there was a 'depersonalization' of ownership. Joint stock companies with anonymous managerial boards, were replacing singlehanded entrepreneurs. Some of the old businesses remained family concerns (the Wendels and Schneiders in metallurgy, the Darblays in the food industry) and there were pioneers such as Louis Renault and Marius Berliet in new industries. Business was favoured by the formation of a nationwide system of credit which replaced the previously regional character of credit. This provided heads of business with cheap money. As banks developed the practice of short-term loans and increased their funds by freeing capital tied up in industry, they gained the confidence of depositors who, by investing their savings in the banks, put them at the service of business entrepreneurs.

Again the movement of the French economy followed general world wide patterns. There was a period of stagnation and a fall in the profits of all sectors from 1873 until the late 1890s. This caused difficulties throughout the economy. But from 1896 until 1914 there was a period of economic expansion. The iron and steel industries made the highest profits of their history during this period: some made profits of over 100 per cent. Banking flourished too. Turnover and profits of banks and iron and steel industries were at their highest in the immediate pre-war years.

This mood of buoyant optimism in business, helped on by a policy of rearmament, was the background of the *Belle Epoque*, — a *belle époque* indeed for those who wielded economic power.

But the *grande bourgeoisie* did not have the same degree of control over society as it had over the economy. It still had some social power, and this was favoured by the press which played a part in moulding public opinion. The end of the nineteenth century saw the triumph of the big newspapers modelled on the English and American press, with their huge printing numbers, their wide scope and coverage of a host of subjects, their publicity and their alleged political impartiality. The five big Parisian newspapers, *Le Petit Journal*, *Le Petit Parisien*, *Le Matin*, *Le Journal*, and *L'Echo de Paris* — whose political bias was more marked – had a circulation of five million, and thus managed to smother the left-wing press. They supported the *status quo* and with it the interests of those who financed them, the *grande bourgeoisie*.

The *grande bourgeoisie* lost control of education, particularly state education. The universities in particular were the institutions whose spirit was most hostile to their interests. Their recruitment processes were democratic. They took an independent stand towards the Church. They attached great importance to rationalism, free investigation and free inquiry. And the *grande bourgeoisie* regarded the publicly-educated young with fear. This fear of the educated explains a change in the intellectual behaviour of the *grande bourgeoisie*. They welcomed the anti-positivist, and even anti-scientific reaction of the early years of the twentieth century. Doubtless the society women who flocked to Bergson's lectures at the *Collège de France* lacked the philosophical background to understand the master's teaching; but their mere presence, their intellectual snobbishness, bore witness to the importance of the new mental climate, as did on a lower level the success of a novelist like Paul Bourget. They were prepared to turn their backs on their former espousal of 'reason' and 'progress' because these might serve the interests of other social classes whose rise they feared.

3. The working-class movement

The proletariat had suffered from the industrial revolution. Those who profited from it considered that their growing class consciousness posed a threat to the established order. The failure of the Commune and the repression which followed it had damped down the danger for a few years. But the danger was still there. There was a worker problem on three levels: their material condition, their ideology and their action. The considerable rise in wages noted under the Second Empire resulted from widespread prosperity, and the workers had gained their share of this. But what became of them with the economic setback of 1873 and the twenty-three years of depression that followed?

It is possible to follow movements with reasonable precision because the available statistics are reliable. Surprisingly, perhaps, nominal wages continued to rise, although at a lower rate than before. Between 1873 and 1900 the average wages of a miner rose 30 per cent, of a Parisian building worker 34 per cent, of an unskilled labourer 40 per cent. The rise tended to be lower in the traditionally better paid professions, since margins tended to be reduced. On the whole the average all round increase was probably about a third. With the return of prosperity in 1900 wages increased again – about 10–20 per cent in ten years. The wages of Frenchmen, however were lower than those in England and much less than in the USA. For instance a London bricklayer earned 28 per cent more than a Parisian one, and a New York one three times as much.

But in order to discover the movement of real wages it is also necessary to bear in mind movements in the cost of living. The cost of living fell by about 10 per cent between 1873 and 1896, largely because food prices fell and rents remained fairly static. Purchasing power had therefore risen by between 40 and 45 per cent. After 1900 the cost of living rose at almost the same rate as nominal salaries. As a whole it seems that the workers were rather better off on the eve of the first world war than on the eve of the Franco-Prussian War of 1870. But had the worker paid for this improvement by having to take on more work or by a lengthening of the working day? We know nothing about conditions in small workshops and businesses. Were bosses more demanding, or workers slacker? In large firms the introduction of more sophisticated machinery meant stricter coordination of effort, more pressure on workers for more concentrated work periods. The evidence from militants leaves no doubt of the workers' sense of oppression. Factory work was labelled 'prison labour'.

The length of the working day did not increase. For some it shortened. The law of 19 May 1874 forbade the employment of children of less than thirteen in industrial work; upwards of thirteen they were not to work more than twelve hours per day. The twelve hour working day seems to have been the norm. The law of 2 November 1892 changed the provisions of the law of 1874. Children between thirteen and sixteen were not allowed to work more than ten hours per day; young persons between sixteen and eighteen were limited to eleven hours per day and not more than sixty hours per six-day week; girls over eighteen and women were limited to eleven hours per day. The law of 30 March 1900 stipulated that young persons and women should not work more than ten and a half hours per day from 1902, ten hours from 1904 and for the first time the hours of men were reduced to the same level if they worked in the same place as women and young persons. The law of 29 June 1905 reduced the length of the miners' working day to eight hours. On the eve of World War I there seems to have been an average working day of ten hours. This was certainily the case in three-quarters of industrial establishments. Workers' organizations demanded an eight hour day on the basis of eight hours work, eight hours rest and eight hours leisure.

By the law of 9 April 1898 the government also laid down that social insurance against accidents at work should be the responsibility of the employer. The employer had to make a payment to workers prevented from returning to work through such an accident. Employers had also to pay for doctors and drugs, and in the case of death had to provide a pension for widows and children. The principle of old age pensions was set out in the draft of 1906 and the scales laid down in the law of 1910 which established old age pensions: wage earners who had earned less than 3,000 francs per year received a life annuity of sixty francs per year after sixty-five provided they had deposited at least thirty annual sums of nine francs for men and six for women. The employer had to match this sum for each employee and the state would make up the rest. This law was badly received by all, and especially by the workers' unions who resented the idea that they should contribute anything. They considered it to be a swindle and three-quarters of the wage-earners refused to join.

Despite this social legislation, which was not as advanced as in some other countries such as Germany, and despite the undoubted rise in the standard of living, the condition of the workers remained precarious. Work exhausted them and reduced their resistance to illness and infection. Unemployment was always threatening. Their situation under the law was weak: individual contracts with their employers were the general rule. There were no collective contracts except, after 1891, in the coal-mining areas of the north. There could be no argument about the terms of a contract; the rules of the firm were made by the employer. Relations between employers and workers, in spite of a law of 1892 instituting a purely optional arbitration, were simply those of opposing forces.

The collective organization of their interests was therefore vital to the workers. It developed in two spheres — the trade-union sphere and the political sphere. Not all workers' organizations were crushed with the Commune, despite legislation outlawing them. There were *chambres syndicales*, workers' trade-union chambers, throughout France. After 1876 the government gave them more favourable treatment. The republicans had gained a majority in that year and, again in 1876, there was the first National Workers' Congress in Paris with representatives from trade-union chambers, and also co-operatives which had been influenced by the ideas of Proudhon. This Congress demanded the end of legislation against workers' movements and the formation of new co-operatives. Jules Guesde, the head of the French workers' party, regarded this Congress as a great political event. For the first time, he said, the workers had met as a national group.

The second Congress met in Lyon in January 1878 and called for a federation of trade unions. But there were divisions between moderates (Proudhon co-operatives) and extremists (militant collectivists) and although the moderates were successful in having this resolution passed in Lyon the extremists had their way in 1879 at the Marseille Congress where the principle of a 'federation of the socialist workers of France' was accepted, and this was to be nothing less than a political party. This triumph of the collectivists committed the movement to political action. But at the fourth Congress in 1880 there was a split between the moderates (syndicalists) and the extremists (collectivists). After this the two groups held separate congresses and this weakened the working-class movement.

The law of 1884 gave legal recognition to professional trade unions, provided a copy of their rules was deposited together with the names of those who ran them. But the unions had not waited for state authorization, which merely legitimized a fait accompli, and they refused to comply with what they judged to be a sort of police inquisition. So they continued, as before, to exist on the margins of legality. The next step in their laborious progress was against the employers, a tougher obstacle than the state. These refused to recognize their existence or to negotiate with workers' organizations especially at a time when economic difficulties were leading them to attempt to lower wages. There was an increase in strike action, accompanied occasionally by bloodshed. This was so effective that action to lower wages was inhibited, and there was even a steady increase.

There was also the question of organizational form. There were two sorts of organizations developing: trade federations (*fédérations de métier*) and labour exchanges (*Bourses du travail*). The first national trade-union federation was founded in 1879 by the hat-makers; workers in the book trade founded one in 1881, miners in 1883, railway employees in 1890. The first *bourse du travail* was founded in Paris in 1887. Others followed in Nîmes, Marseille and Saint-Etienne. By 1892 there were fourteen and the Congress of Saint-Etienne founded the Federation of *Bourses du Travail*. Fernand Pelloutier became its general secretary in 1895. But these two organizations drew closer together. In 1895 the Federation of *Bourses du Travail* and the Federation of Trade Unions held a joint congress at Limoges which led to the foundation of the General Working Confederation (*Confederation Générale du Travail*, the CGT). This union remained rather shaky with those who favoured a vertical organization in federations opposing those who wanted a horizontal structure of *bourses du travail*. After Pelloutier's death real unity was achieved in 1902, the *bourses du travail* losing their autonomy, and the CGT ruled the dual body, vertical (the federations functioning through industries and not crafts) and horizontal (but with departmental unions instead of *bourses du travail*). This marked the triumph of revolutionary syndicalism, whose aim was to make trade unions not just an institution for the defence of workers' interests but the basis of a new kind of state. They favoured direct action by the workers to gain their ends, with the use of violence if necessary. The final means of workers' action would be a general strike which would be 'social revolution'. This would be an action independent of political parties for the revolutionary syndicalists shared Proudhon's abhorrence of parliament. The Charter of Amiens (1906) affirmed the complete independence of syndicalism from political parties.

The syndicalists' distrust of politics was partly to be attributed to the disappointing performance of the socialist movement which for a quarter of a century (1879–1905) had been torn apart by controversy, bitter personal and doctrinal differences. Only in 1901 did the five socialist groups merge into two, the *Parti Socialiste Francais* of Jean Jaurès and Jules Guesde's *Parti Socialiste de France*, and only in 1905 did they finally unite as the *Parti Socialiste Unifié* (SFIO), the French section of the Workers' International. From then onwards socialism gained supporters: 35,000 members, 830,000 votes and fifty-one deputies in 1906 and 90,000 members, 1,400,000 votes and 103 deputies in 1914. But this success did not draw the syndicalist movement into the socialist movement, as Jaurès had hoped. In February 1912 the general secretaries of the CGT, Griffuelhes and Jouhaux, drew up a new, solemn declaration of 'total independence from parties and groups' in a document called the 'Encyclical' by the syndicalists.

This specifically French phenomenon of schism between syndicalism and socialism had dangerous results for the workers' movement. The syndicalists allowed themselves to be frozen into abstract attitudes of working-class sectarianism which isolated them in a sort of intellectual ghetto. The socialist party, on the other hand, could not count on solid support backed by subscriptions from the syndicalists and were forced to look for members, and above all electoral supporters, in other classes, especially the petty bourgeoisie. The electoral map of 1914 shows that the socialist party drew support from traditional left-wing voters, who probably regarded the socialist party as less the party of the workers than a kind of adventurous continuation of the radical party. The lack of vitality of the socialist party had its origin in the obstinate

Fig. IV.2   Elections of 26 April 1914: the extreme left

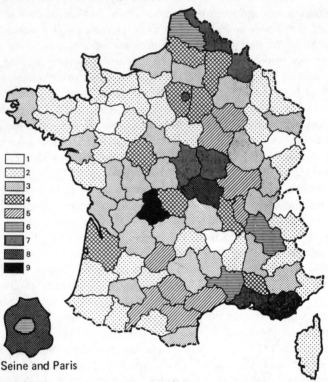

Seine and Paris

The extreme left comprised the *Parti Socialiste Unifié* and the *Parti Ouvrier*.

1. None
2. Less than 5% of electoral vote
3. 5–10% of electoral vote
4. 10–15% of electoral vote
5. 15–20% of electoral vote

6. 20–25% of electoral vote
7. 25–30% of electoral vote
8. 30–35% of electoral vote
9. .35–40% of electoral vote

Source: Fr. Goguel, *Géographie des élections françaises de 1870 à 1951* (A. Colin).

isolation of the syndicalist movement. And this prophylactic isolation did not, as expected, render the syndicalists any less liable to divisions and dissensions since the split in the socialist party in 1920 was almost immediately followed by a split in the syndicalist movement.

The explanation of the intransigence of the syndicalists, of their refusal to co-operate, lay in the origins of the workers' movement. This had, at first been led by educated workers who dreamed less of improving the material conditions of their fellows than of creating a new, better world where the proletariat would not exist and where man would not be exploited by man. Their ideas were global rather than local.

Another reason was that the workers' movement did not embrace all the workers. There were a few hundred thousand trade unionists for several million workers. This was a peculiarly French situation. In 1911 there were 700,000 members of the CGT: seven for every 100 workers. In England there were 4 million – twenty-five trade unionists for every 100 workers. In Germany there were 4.5 million – twenty-eight trade unionists for every 100 workers. Even Italy, despite its economic backwardness, had a higher proportion – 11 per cent of wage-earners. Like all minority movements French syndicalism veered towards extremism.

Finally there was the attitude of the employers. Their absolute, obstinate refusal to recognize the existence of trade unions, their use of brutal and hypocritical methods to destroy workers' organizations were largely responsible for the hardening of syndicalist opinion and for the spirit of desperation with which the workers' class struggle was invested.

4. Conclusion

During the immediate pre-war years the social climate deteriorated seriously. The big strikes of miners in 1906, post-workers in 1909 and railway employees in 1910 were severely repressed by Clemenceau and Briand but paralysed the economy for a time. Syndicalism even infiltrated the civil service despite government warnings of the incompatibility of syndicalism and service to the state. There were some syndicalists who espoused pacifism and anti-militarism, and the CGT Congress of 1913 advocated refusal to serve in the army in case of war. The foundations of society seemed to have been shaken during these years which, for the bourgeoisie were years of fear.

Nevertheless, after the catastrophe of World War I, this same period became known as *La Belle epoque*. What features retained in the collective memory of the French could justify such a title? There was of course the glittering life of Paris, attracting kings, grand dukes, the idle rich, and haunting the dreams of provincials. The surface shimmer of a society of snobs, stars, men of the world, prostitutes, a society whose standards were set by wealthy aristocrats brought up in hereditary idleness. The 'city of light', setting its imprint on fashion, literature, art, the theatre, a make of car, a new health fad. The triumph assured for some second-rate plays or some ludicrous fashions may give rise to doubts about its taste; but the glamour remained.

But the real justification for the term *La belle époque* lies in the realm of economic prosperity. All sections of society benefited, although unevenly, and abject poverty became the exception rather than the rule. There developed a certain style of life, a taste for careful work, for long conversations and for intellectual intercourse. Frenchmen felt they lived in a privileged country, in a country whose civilization was the subject of universal envy. And this kind of feeling bred a profound patriotism due to be revealed during the war. There was a great nostalgia for *La Belle époque* after the cruel upheavals of the war. It was regret at the passing of a certain stability (especially monetary stability), a cult of the golden mean which, amid the tribulations of a later, more difficult period, appeared to have been a time when life was simple but yet happy.

documentation

Social class and politics

In the nineteenth century the various social classes were, politically, sharply divided into two groups — for and against the spirit of 1789. Provided they were not affected by the powerful political influence of the Church, peasants and village craftsmen were devoted to this spirit. Even today the psychology of the peasant continues to reflect a fear of the Ancien Régime, now utterly chimerical. This results in an instinctive resistance to the influence of presbytery and château. Today noble and priest are at loggerheads, but in most *communes* there remains a permanent feud between people and authorities.

The industrial worker began by sharing the same attitudes, by espousing the spirit of the Revolution, with an even stronger ideological attachment. Apart from the idea of the class struggle, an idea of foreign origin which developed rather later, there was an independent French workers' movement whose ideals still exist today. I can remember a time not so distant when workers were simply 'republicans'.

These were basic elements of the left. To them may be added the minor civil servant who originated from the popular classes, and still shared their attitudes and manners. He felt looked down upon as a newcomer to the administration, whose upper ranks seemed to be dominated by the haughty upper classes. He felt that the Republic was his republic and would release him from this. During the early years of the Republic, when the régime was still establishing itself, the schoolteacher and the postman were unrivalled republican militants in the villages. In addition the Republic was supported by the middling and lower bourgeois some of whom were, admittedly,. rising but many of whom were jealous of the snobbery of the rich and thus favoured an egalitarian society. These groups gave the young Republic a spontaneous, but solid support.

But there were groups whose aims clashed with the spirit of 1789. There was the Church.[1] The Church would not support the complete independence of political society in the state. It was prepared to support almost any political authority but it must have divine approval for it to be legitimate. Inevitably it was opposed to popular sovereignty and the secularization of the state. From the point of view of doctrine

[1] This section on the Church is taken from an earlier part of the work by Siegfried.

there seemed no possible way of reconciling the Church's viewpoint with that of revolutionary secularism. Then there was the nobility which inevitably favoured a hierarchical society such as still existed in some areas. The bourgeoisie, and especially the *grande bourgeoisie*, tended to have become in its turn a bastion of the status quo. These three groups had their supporters even if unwilling ones. There were the catholics devoted to their priest; the poor aided by the Church and the rich; tenant farmers afraid of their landlords; village tradesmen afraid of losing custom, even workers feeling dependent on the good will of their employers. Where the character of society was still hierarchical the spirit of 1789 lost its force and other principles determined political attitudes. The influence of a hierarchical society still existed. Many of the popular classes always hoped for the coming of an egalitarian society, but the more educated knew this was a utopian ideal and, since life had to continue, recognized that discipline was still important.

People inevitably ranged themselves on both sides. The smaller fry hung together, as did the rich and powerful. A spontaneous division sprang up in every *commune* between the 'party' of the schoolteacher who wished to 'liberate' the people and the 'party' of the priest, the noble, or the rich bourgeois, the 'hierarchical' party wishing to keep the people in subjection believing them incapable of managing themselves, let alone of governing the country.

There were thus two outlooks which are difficult for Frenchmen to judge objectively . . .

ANDRÉ SIEGFRIED, *Tableau des Partis en France* (Paris, Grasset, 1930) pp. 66—70.

Bursary holders ('boursiers')

Every social class is represented among the young provincials who roam the purlieus of the Quartier Latin, but law and medicine are closed to all but those with private means. The same is almost true for would-be engineers or higher civil servants. Those entering the army are trained elsewhere, but the traditional core of the army is still to be found among some 20,000 noble and bourgeois families.

Teaching is the one career recruited almost exclusively from the portionless *boursier*. Eight or nine out of ten students at the *Ecole Normale Supérieure* are supported by state bursaries won against strong competition. Those who did not pass in are assisted in degree courses, higher degrees, travel, further education. Training colleges for primary teachers are more democratic institutions. Members of rich or even well-to-do families are rare in any of the three branches of the teaching profession. Of all the liberal professions that of teaching alone is almost exclusively manned by the 'new educated'.

The new men remained unassuming until the end of the nineteenth century, and so, intrinsically, they still are; but three events with which they had no direct concern have given them a new and important social status. These are the Dreyfus affair, the political defeat of the Church and the coming of the radical republic. The Dreyfus case was basically a struggle between the intellectuals and the military; the defeat of the Church enhanced the standing of the lay administrator; the 'radical republic', born in 1898, inevitably drew its strength from these new men.

This was not a political movement of Parisian origin, but emerged from the provinces, where revolutions start today. In Paris the strongholds of the intelligentsia are the *Académie française*, the *Institut*, literature, journalism, the Bar. The universities come a bad second, and the teacher counts for nothing. But in the provinces teachers are the intellectual élite and in the villages, with the curé out of the way, there is only the village schoolteacher left.

ALBERT THIBAUDET, *La république des professeurs* (Paris, Grasset, 1927) pp. 120–23.

Lay school-mistresses in a rural environment

'I began my school teaching in a *commune* in the Médoc some ten years ago. My head-teacher and I had a lot to put up with from religious fanaticism and from a municipal council of clerical sympathies totally hostile to us. When we complained about our accommodation which was like a shanty open to all the elements we were told that "a cowshed would be good enough for these hussies".'

'In the church we had to sit right at the back in a dark corner against the wall. They would have put us outside if they could. But when, finally, the church and local administrative authorities in their wisdom said we were respectable, everyone else agreed. We certainly had to pay much more for our food than anyone else, although we were never actually refused it.'

'But in the north of France poor school-mistresses who through no choice of their own had to replace the nuns whose school had been secularized, were refused necessary food stuffs by the locals: bread, milk, butter, vegetables. Nobody would sell them anything and they were obliged to buy elsewhere.'

'Abuse of all kinds is thrown at us: blasphemous education, atheistic education, Godless schools . . . and others. All these things are forever being hurled in the faces of teachers, especially women teachers, and if I repeated every word of abuse you would be astonished. We are accused of being part of a "government of freemasons, of Jews, of thieves" as if we ourselves and not universal suffrage had formed the government. The schoolmaster can say that we have the government we chose, but the schoolmistress can say nothing. She must lower her eyes, blush and remain silent. If she said that she had no right to abuse those who paid her, she would be accused of meddling in politics and even of being a second Louise Michel.'

Lettres d'institutrices rurales d'autrefois, rédigées a la suite de l'enquête
   de Francisque Sorcey en 1897.
   Introduites et commentées par Ida Berger.
   Association des amis du Musée pédagogique, Imp. Nat., s.d.
   pp. 44—45.

Religious practice in the département of the Nièvre at the beginning of the twentieth century

What kinds of religious behaviour are there in the *département*? What are their characteristics? And which strata in society practise them? It is possible to distinguish various attitudes: the attitude of the declared atheist or man practising another religion — men outside the Church; the attitude of the indifferent conformist; and finally the attitude of the regular church-goer who may even be devout.

The number of those outside the Church, of those refusing the aid of the Church even to be buried, have always been in a minority in the Nièvre. They were of course notable in the public eye, but not particularly notable in themselves. But this attitude often ran counter to their family history and their education, and rarely persisted until death. They even took a certain pride in the fact that their wives practised religion and that their children took their first communion and they almost always insisted that their children were baptised. They were not therefore independent of the Church even if they were not themselves practising christians. And the Church had no competition for the care of souls . . . Whatever may have been the strength of anticlericalism in the Nièvre, no 'missions' were sent there. The real weakness of the Church was elsewhere.

But the christian population of the Nièvre lived at a distance from the Church, far removed from its influence and its rules. Its religious conformity was seasonal. Religious practice was no more than attachment to a tradition. The inner significance of religion had disappeared. Faith was often lacking and religious rites were more a superstition than a sign of a religious frame of mind. They were part of respect for the demands of society, part of human respect which was so much part of the temperament of those who lived in the Nivernais. The conformity was seasonal, in that attendance at church had fallen off and for many was limited to four occasions – baptism, first communion, marriage and burial.

Religion was respected, but it was hardly part of daily life. Daily life was more dominated by scepticism, propped up by materialism and indifference – the product of a fruitful land. The clergy were reduced to performing rites only they could perform and had lost their sense of mission. The Church had ceased to be a spiritual guide and mentor.

In 1886 96,200, 35 per cent of the population, took communion on Easter Day. In 1909 the number of those taking Easter communion was only 58,000 and only about 41,200 regularly attended church. These two figures give some idea of the number of the practising christians of the *département*, of those who had remained attached to the Church for reasons other than mere conformity.

The Church could have political influence over these people alone. Those taking Easter communion only amounted to 19 per cent of the total population. Since children under seven and even eleven did not take communion, about 20 to 25 per cent of the population over this age took Easter communion in 1909. These might be influential in lay matters especially if many were men. Ecclesiastical statistics do not provide the necessary figures for attendance at communion, but they do give figures for attendance at mass. There were fewer attenders at mass, probably 13.5 per cent of the total population, and of these there were not many men: possibly 2.5 per cent of the total population. Roman catholicism was almost becoming a religion for women. Only one man in thirteen attended mass.

There were few religious extremes in the Nièvre, as far as atheism on the one hand and devotion on the other were concerned. Religious behaviour was moderate. The majority were only 'seasonal' church attenders but there was a minority, largely of women, who were regular attenders. The Church was everywhere, but its influence was slight.

This was the general picture; but in some areas, and in some sectors of society the Church's influence varied. This was partly because of different approaches by the Church to the decline in religion at the end of the nineteenth century. The Church retained the fidelity of certain areas, and certain sectors of society. These seem to have been the 'privileged' in both town and countryside.

In the countryside the more prosperous landowners were often united with the Church and thus were regular churchgoers. So were those dependent on them. It seems that landlords were still able to influence their tenant-farmers and farm-workers, particularly if the landlord was a noble. And there was a considerable amount of land owned by the nobles in the Nièvre. In the towns the regular attenders tended to be from the middling and lower bourgeoisie. They were well-off financially and drew large rents from the surrounding region. They tended to be linked with the men of law and sometimes even with the nobility. But the commercial bourgeoisie was not conservative, unless individuals had marriage links with the more conservative forces of the bourgeoisie and nobility. The commercial bourgeoisie were often radicals, more influenced by new ideas and much less attached to the Church than others. But in the towns and in the countryside family and local traditions were still very important dererminants, especially among the lower classes who seemed to have been largely seasonal attenders.

Those who did not attend church at all were in a minority. In town and country they tended to be chemists, insurance agents, teachers, doctors and sometimes veterinary surgeons. They were drawn from the liberal professions, the commercial world, the civil service and sometimes from landlords with an anti-clerical background. They were rarely drawn from the upper classes.

J. PATAUT, *Sociologie Electorale de la Nièvre au XX$_e$ siècle, 1902—1951* (Editions Cujas) pp. 63—8.

Taxation law of 15 July 1914.
(Articles 5—17 establish a general tax on incomes).

Article 5 — A general tax is imposed on income.

Article 6 — This tax is due on 1 January each year and is to be paid by all those whose usual place of residence is in France.

Article 7 — If the taxpayer has one place of residence only the tax is payable at that place.

— If he has several places of residence, the tax will be payable at the place where his main premises are to be found.

Article 8 — Each head of family is liable for taxation on his personal income and on those of his wife and children living with him.

— Nevertheless tax payers may ask for separate assessments, 1) if the wife and her property are separate from the husband, 2) if the children or other members of the family, except the wife, have an income from their own work or if they have an accumulation of wealth separate from that of the head of the family.

Article 9 — The following are exempt from this tax:

(i) — Those whose taxable income does not exceed the sum of 5,000 francs plus the allowance stated in Article 12 below.

(ii) — Ambassadors and other foreign diplomatic representatives, consuls, and consular agents of foreign nationality, but only insofar as these financial advantages are permitted for French diplomatic agents and consuls.

Article 10— The tax is calculated on the total net income of each taxpayer. The net income is determined according to the amount of property and capital owned by the taxpayer, the post or profession he holds, the salaries, wages, pensions and annuities he receives and financial benefit he may derive from any profitable task he may undertake. The following may be deducted from the revenue:

(i) — Interests on debts and loans.

(ii) — Arrears due on fixed annuities paid by the taxpayer.

(iii) — Other direct taxes paid by the taxpayer.

(iv) — Losses incurred by an agricultural or industrial concern. The amount of income from diverse sources for the year is calculated according to the total of the incomes for the previous year.

Article 11 — For those who do not live in France, but who have several properties in France, the taxable sum is fixed at a sum equal to seven times the rented value of this/these residence(s), unless the revenue(s) gained by the taxpayer from property, developments, or professions in France is higher than the said sum in which case the latter figure will form the basis of the sum of taxation due.

Article 12 — Married taxpayers may deduct 2,000 francs from their incomes as an allowance for taxation purposes.

In addition the sum of 1,000 francs may be deducted for each of the taxpayers dependents, up to five dependents.

Article 14 — Each taxpayer only pays tax on that portion of his revenue (after application of Article 12) which exceeds the sum of 5,000 francs.

Article 15 — The tax due will be one-fifth of the revenue between 5,000 and 10,000 francs; two-fifths between 10,000 and 15,000 francs; three-fifths between 15,000 and 20,000 francs; four-fifths between 20,000 and 25,000 francs. The taxable total will be the surplus revenue thus calculated plus 2 per cent.

Article 16 — Those liable to pay this tax will make a declaration of their total revenue with the option of making a detailed declaration of the composite elements of the revenue.

Article 17 — The inspector will verify the declarations on the basis of those figures he already has in his possession or may be communicated to him, such as the tax statistics for direct taxation and other incorporated taxes, and the statistics gathered by other public authorities. The inspector has no right to demand any title or deed, book or any document. The inspector may adjust the declaration but in this case he must indicate to the taxpayer the constituent elements of the basis on which he is taxed. This must not be done before the tax register is compiled.

On the importance of keeping accurate accounts
12 December 1886

My dear Julie,

You will shortly receive some account books that I am giving you as a wedding present.

The bigger of the two is for keeping a monthly account of expenses arranged under different headings. On the left hand side of the page there is a column for receipts and one for money laid out. You will therefore be able to keep a record of each and every receipt and expenditure and to add them up each month.

The smaller of the two books is divided into two parts. The first is for recording receipts and expenditure over a whole year. It is, I might add, more useful to make your financial year run from a point within the year, for example from 30 September, than from the end of the year, because there are always bills straddling the year's end and the new year. Assuming you use this date, you will keep the first two pages blank and then fill them with your expenditure for 1886—7 and then, starting at 10 October 1887, at the end of each month, you will transcribe the monthly totals on each line. When the totals for the twelve months from 1 October 1887 to 30 September 1888 are entered you will add up all the columns at the bottom of the page and you will have the total receipts for the year and the total expenditure as well as the separated expenditures. As a check the sum of the receipts plus cash in hand at the beginning of the year ought to equal the total of investments, plus cash in hand less expenditure at the end.

The second part of this book contains only blank paper. It is for recording at the year's end a detailed inventory of your assets. On the first page you should begin by writing down what you have when setting up house. I suggest that you then put underneath this your initial expenses: cost of marriage settlement, trousseau, honeymoon, furniture, etc. This will amount to a lot, however economical you may be. If all these expenses are deducted from your total fortune you will have the capital remaining to you when you arrive in Tunis, and which you will be able to add to, year by year, in order to provide your daughters with dowries.

But your fortune will vary not only with the level of your expenditure and receipts, but also with the rise and fall in the value of your investments. In order that you may know your real financial position you must note in this second part of the book each of your investments and its actual value at the time, according to its quoted price on the stock exchange. Investments can always go down in value. You have seen this happen with some of mine. We delude ourselves if we think we shall always be equally well off because we have held on to all our shares.

I think it is important to keep proper accounts. If you do it carefully and try to find out the causes of variations over the years you will find it a far from tedious task but actually a very fascinating one from which you will learn a lot.

I am not overestimating the value of my gift. It will not hold pride of place among those you will receive. But one mustn't always go by appearances. It will be a serviceable daily help and if you interpret it properly it will give you good advice.

Your affectionate uncle

Copy of a letter dated 12 December 1886
M. PERROT, *Le mode de vie des familles bourgeoises* (Colin, Paris)
pp. 264–5

Law of 21 March 1884 relating to the formation of trade unions

Article 1 — The law of 14–17 June 1791 and article 416 of the Penal Code are repealed.

Articles 291, 292, 293, 294 of the Penal Code are no longer applicable to trade unions.

Article 2 — Trade unions or professional associations (of even more than twenty persons exercising the same profession, similar trades or related trades leading to the production of specific products) may be freely founded without governmental authorization.

Article 3 — The trade unions will concern themselves exclusively with their economic, industrial or agricultural interests.

Article 4 — The names of those running the association, in addition to a copy of the statutes of the association, must be deposited with the administration.

Article 5 — The trade unions who have followed the above regulation may work together in defence of their economic, industrial, commercial and agricultural interests.

Combinations of unions taking advantage of this provision must jointly deposit their names with the administration. They may not own property nor may they initiate judicial proceedings.

Article 6 — Individual trade unions of employers or workers may initiate judicial proceedings.

They may use money coming from subscriptions.

They may only own sufficient property for their meetings, libraries or courses of professional instruction.

No authorization is required for them to set up mutual aid and retirement funds between members provided other provisions in the law are observed.

They may set up, and administer, information boards for those seeking to employ and those seeking employment. They may be consulted on all disputes and other matters relating to their trade.

In disputed matters the opinion of the trade unions may be placed at the disposition of the disputers who may have a transcript of the said opinion.

Article 7 — Any member of a trade union may withdraw at any time despite any trade-union regulation to the contrary. He is, however, liable to pay the subscription for the current year.

Any person who withdraws is still eligible to benefit from any mutual aid or retirement fund to which he has contributed.

Article 10 — The present law is applicable to Algeria.

It is equally applicable in the colonies of the Martinique, Guadeloupe and of the island of Réunion.

The Amiens charter

Agenda adopted at the fifteenth National Congress of the CGT held in Amiens 8—16 October 1906.

The congress confirms article 2 of the statutes of the CGT which states that: 'The CGT unites all workers, regardless of political belief, who are aware of the struggle to be fought in order to abolish the categories of wage-earners and employers . . .'

The congress believes that this declaration recognizes the class struggle in the economic sphere which groups workers together against any form of exploitation or oppression — either physical or mental — which may be employed by the capitalists against the working class.

The congress specifies this theoretical declaration by the following details:

In its day-to -day demands the union movement seeks to achieve the coordination of the efforts of the workers in order to increase their wellbeing through achieving immediate improved conditions such as shortening of the working day, increases in wages etc. . . .; but this is only one aspect of the work of the union movement. It seeks to achieve complete emancipation of the workers and this can only be realized by dispossessing the capitalist classes. It advocates the general strike as one way of achieving this and envisages that the unions, which today are units of resistance, will in the future become units of production and distribution and they will form the basis of social reorganization.

The congress declares that its immediate and future tasks spring from the fact that the working population is wage-earning and this factor means that all workers whatever their political beliefs must belong to the trade unions which are fundamental institutions for them.

As a result the congress asserts that the individual union member has the right to pursue his independent political beliefs outside of the union, provided he does not introduce them into it.

Independent groups or parties may strive for social change in their own right but they are separate from the union movement whose avowed single purpose is to act directly against the employers, for only in this way can the union movement reach its fullest potential.

Chronology of the workers' movement, 1870—1914[1]

1870   July: Franco-Prussian war.

   23 July: First manifesto drawn up by Karl Marx in the name of the General Council of the International.

   4 September: the Republic.

   9 September: Second manifesto on the war drawn up by Karl Marx in the name of the General Council.

1871   18 March: Thiers orders the regular army to recapture the field guns removed by the National Guard. The crowd resists. Thiers orders the evacuation of Paris.

   23 March: The Federal Council of the Paris International publishes a manifesto calling on all workers to support the Central Committee of the Commune and outlines a plan of reforms.

   26 March: Elections: out of eighty elected, twenty-five are workers and among these were leaders of the International — Varlin, Camelinat, Benoît Malon, Leo Frankel.

   March—May: The Central Committee governs Paris. Leo Frankel, member of the Commission of Work and Exchange, tries to introduce socialist measures. He favours workers' co-operatives and organizes *bourses du travail.*

   22—8 May: The troops from Versailles re-take Paris. There are 107,000 victims, mostly from the working class.

   30 May: Marx drafts *The Civil War in France* as an official document of the International.

1872   14 March: Thiers secures the passing of the repressive Dufaure law on the International.

   3 May: Commission of inquiry on working conditions in France.

   28 August: Foundation of the moderate Workers Union Circle controlled by Barberet. Vaillant replies to him from Belgium in the name of the *Communeux.*

1873   Workers' delegation at the Universal Exhibition in Vienna; fall of Thiers; monarchists gain power.

1874   Law on the hours of work of women and children and setting up of the Inspectorate of Work (*Inspection du Travail*).

[1] DOLLEANS (E.), CROZIER (M.), *Mouvements ouvriers et socialistes Chronologie et bibliographe*, Les Editions Ouvriers, pp. 85—86, 159—162, 223—228.

1875   Wallon's amendment recognizes the existence of the Republic.
1876   Workers' delegation to the Universal Exhibition in Phila-
        delphia.
        National Workers' Congress in Paris.
1877   Crisis of 16 May. Ministry of Moral Order.
        Republican elections.
        18 November: Jules Guesde founds the first socialist news-
        paper, *L'Egalité*.
1878   First workers' candidates for municipal elections in Paris.
        'Moderate' Workers' Congress in Lyon.
        15 September: Guesde, Fournière, Labousquière are among
        thirty-five other organizers of the forbidden inter-
        national congress who are arrested. They bring out
        the manifesto: Address and programme of French
        revolutionary socialists (*Programme et a dresse des
        socialistes révolutionnaires francais*).
1879   20 April: Blanqui elected deputy in Bordeaux.
        Amnesty is voted.
        Foundation of the first national trade union by the hatters.
        National Congress in Marseille consisting of delegates from
        professional associations, Socialist study societies
        and anarchist groups. The collectivists are
        triumphant. Foundation of the POF, *Parti Ouvrier de
        France* (French workers' party).
1880   Guesde visits Karl Marx.
        Congress in Le Havre. Mutualists withdraw but do not succeed
        in holding their organization together.
        21 November: Jules Ferry tables a bill on trade unions.
1881   15 March: Allain Targe's report on the Trade Union Bill.
        Blanquist *Comité revolutionnaire central* is founded.
        Foundation of the National Federation of Bookworkers.
1882   At the POF congress in Saint-Etienne moderates (*les possi-
        bilistes*) withdraw under the leadership of Paul
        Brousse and found the *Fédération des travailleurs
        socialistes de France.*
1883   Foundation of National Federation of Miners and a Federa-
        tion of Casters.
1884   The law on trade unions which, at last, gives them legal
        recognition.
        Eighteen workers elected to the chamber. Strike at
        Decazeville.
1886   First national trade union congress at Lyon, where it is

decided to create the National Federation of Trade Unions. Discussions took place on the law of 1884.

1886—9   Crisis of 'Boulangism'. *Fédération nationale des syndicats* meets at Montluçon.

1888   Formation of the national federation of underground workers. First electoral successes for the socialists. Winning of mayorships of Saint-Etienne, Commentry, Narbonne and Saint-Ouen.

28 November: Third *Fédération nationale des syndicats* congress at Le Bouscat. Resolution on the general strike is voted.

1889   January: Electoral success of General Boulanger in Paris.

1 April: The General flees to Brussels.

Universal Exhibition. Celebration of the hundredth anniversary of the Revolution of 1789.

Two international workers' congresses held in Paris. Foundation of the Second International. Foundation of association of printers from different countries.

1890   Piou and de Mun lead the *'ralliement'* of Catholics to the republican régime.

First French celebration of May Day; several strikes and other incidents.

Foundation of the federation of railway employees.

1890   Extremists break away from the Federation of French Socialist Workers at its Congress in Chatellrault and form the Revolutionary Socialist Workers' Party (*Parti socialiste ouvrier revolutionnaire*: PSOR)

1891   First collective bargaining agreement in the coalmines of northern France (the Arras agreement).

Bloodshed in Fourmies on May Day.

Foundation of the national federation of textile trade unions and federation of maritime workers' trade unions.

Second international socialist workers' congress in Brussels.

1892   Founding of the National Federation of *Bourses du Travail* which holds its first congress in Saint-Etienne.

Socialists are elected as mayors in: Marseille, Toulon, La Ciotat, Narbonne, Montlucon, Commentry, Saint-Ouen, Carmaux, Caudry.

Panama scandal.

Strike at Carmaux. The company and the government have to give way. The deputy from Carmaux resigns.

1893 21 January: Jean Jaurès is elected deputy for Carmaux.

   First socialist daily newspaper, *La Petite République.*

   August elections: fifty socialists are elected including Millerand, Viviani, Jaurès, Jules Guesde and Edouard Vaillant.

   September: Congress of Federation of trade unions. Aristide Briand makes his reports on the question of a General Strike.

1892–4 Anarchist outrages.

1894 8 February: Jules Guesde's proposal on the organization of the right to strike.

1894 Press laws of December 1893 and July 1894, sometimes called the 'wicked laws' (*lois scelerates*).

   At Nantes Fernand Pelloutier becomes secretary of the National Federation of *Bourses du Travail* and of the Federation of Trade Unions.

   Voting in principle of the general strike and of the breach with the political parties.

   24 June: Sadi Carnot is assassinated.

   Trial of the thirty: but they are acquitted.

1895 Joint congress of the *bourses du travail* and the trade unions in Limoges when the CGT is founded.

1898 1 October: General strike of railway employees which fails.

   Builders strike in Paris.

1900 Several strikes – bloodshed at some.

   Law of the ten-hour day is voted.

1901 13 March: death of Fernand Pelloutier.

   Law of 1 July on trade unions.

1902 September: last congress of the *bourses du travail* in Algiers.

   At the seventh CGT congress in Montpellier there is agreement and the *bourses* lose their autonomy. Victor Griffuelhes becomes secretary.

1904 Founding of *L'Humanité*, a daily newspaper whose chief editor is Jaurès.

   First congress of Christian trade unions.

1906 April: Courrières catastrophe. Strike in the mines of the Pas-de-Calais. Clemenceau mobilizes 20,000 troops. Further strikes by twenty workers' co-operatives.

   1 May: General strike for an eight-hour day. Troops are mobilized. Violent demonstrations.

Fig. IV.3　Traditional right-wing support

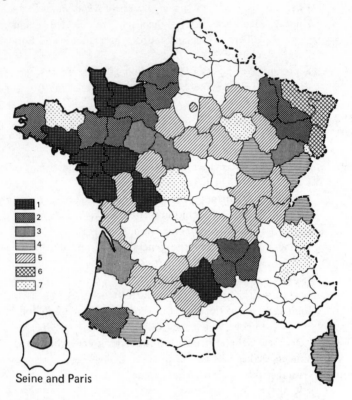

Seine and Paris

Habitual support for right wing since dates given

1. 1871—81.
2. 1885—98.
3. 1902—14.
4. 1919—36.
5. 1946
6. 1919, departments recovered in 1918
7. Uncertain

Source: F. Goguel, *Géographie des élections françaises sous la IIIe et la IVe République* (Paris, Colin, 1970).

Fig. IV.4 Traditional left-wing support

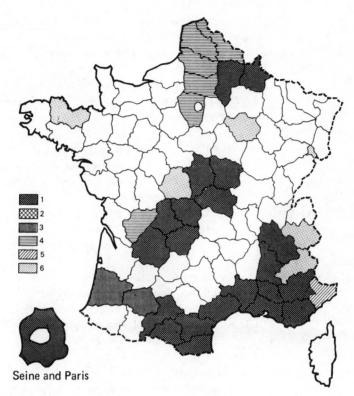

Seine and Paris

Habitual support for left wing since dates given

1. 1871–81
2. 1885–98
3. 1902–14
4. 1919–36
5. Since 1946
6. Uncertain

Source: F. Goguel, *Géographie des élections françaises sous la IIIe et la IVe République* (Paris, Colin, 1970).

October: Clemenceau's ministry: Viviani is made the first Minister of Labour.

October: CGT hold a congress at Amiens. The Amiens Charter is approved by 830 votes to nine.

1907   Paper workers strike at Essonnes. Troops are called in.

Riots in the southern vineyards — Troops mutiny.

1908   Deaths in strikes at Draveil and Villeneuve-St. Georges.

October: CGT hold a congress in Marseille. Idea of general strike again accepted.

1909   March: first postal strike.

May: second postal strike. The new secretary of the CGT, Niel, calls on all workers to back the post-workers, but this is ignored. The strike fails and Clemenceau announces 541 dismissals.

1910   October: General strike of railway employees. Strikers' committee is arrested through orders of Briand and he has 15,000 of the strikers called up into the army.

1911   Building strike.

1912   September: CGT congress at Le Havre. Various trade federations join forces. Syndicalists are successful.

1913   Extraordinary CGT congress which anticipates refusal of military service in case of war.

Metal workers of Seine area and miners of Pas-de-Calais go on strike.

1914   27 July: Workers demonstrate against the war, following the appeal of the Seine Association of Trade Unions (*Union des Syndicats de la Seine*).

31 July: Jaurès is assassinated.

26 August: Guesde and Sembat join the ministry.

V French Society in the twentieth century (1914-1970)

Understandably, nobody realized at the time that 2 August 1914 marked not only the beginning of the war, but also the end of a social and economic order. There had already been considerable changes: gone were the gold franc, the sleepy little towns, leisurely craftsmanship, general economic feather-bedding. Total war, involving a whole industrial economy, paid for by credit and human sacrifice, raised difficult problems that were not solved by the return of an all too brief prosperity. During the 1930s France felt the effects of the worldwide economic crisis which she had managed to escape for a few years. These were slow in manifesting themselves, but discontents were stoked up and led to a near-revolutionary situation in 1936. World War II broke out in an atmosphere of rancour and disillusion. The defeat of 1940 led to the dark years of the Occupation. The hope that one day a fairer social order would exist in France was kept alive by the resistance movement. This was not completely realized at the Liberation, but nevertheless the reforms of 1945 brought some relief and security to the poorest sections in society. The economy gradually picked up once more and, in time, reached a rate of growth that had never been achieved before. With increased automation and the use of nuclear power the character of the new 'society of plenty' will change greatly from what it is now, although the broad outlines are, in some ways, becoming apparent.

1. The upheavals of world war I

The wars of the nineteenth century had a negligible influence on the evolution of French society. World War I, like the Revolutionary and Napoleonic wars, brought about lasting changes.

It soon became obvious that the war would last longer than the anticipated few weeks, and the government realized that for the long haul ahead the liberal economy had to give way to an authoritarian control of production, currency and the division of goods. To ensure victory there had to be state intervention not only in the management of the railways, shipping, raw materials, the allocation of labour, the control of armaments manufacture, but even in finance and housing. This great experiment in controlling the economy had a disparaging effect, in the mind of the public, on the whole dogma of free enterprise.

The state seems to have been too long in acting, and when it acted it often did so badly. There was an enormous wastage of food, clothing, livestock and war equipment by the army authorities. The government was unable to check speculation and profiteering. It only imposed price controls in 1916, having been reluctant to do this previously. The requisitioning of grain was only introduced in 1917, bread-rationing cards in January 1918 and other food-rationing cards in April 1918. This annoyed or exasperated both sellers and buyers. The authority of the state was probably damaged by its conduct during the period. Once the intoxication of victory had worn off, many Frenchmen began to question the ability of a capitalist state to manage the economy.

The demographic consequences of the war were immediately apparent. The population had been appallingly hit. At the time of the armistice France had mobilized 8 million men — 20.5 per cent of the population (to Britain's 12.5 per cent and America's 3.7 per cent). She had lost 1,400,000; a further 3 million had been wounded, and of these 750,000 were total invalids. For every ten men between 20 and 45 years old in 1914, two had been killed, one was dependent on what the state could provide, three were inactive for varying lengths of time. The nation thus depended on the efforts of the four others. But this toll of the war affected the demographic vitality of France. The rate of births inevitably decreased, and although there was a vigorous increase in births after 1918, it by no means made up the gap. The French population had been profoundly affected by the war, both physically and morally.

Another aspect of war was the burden of work undertaken by women. In the countryside the departure of able-bodied men at the very moment of the 1914 harvest mobilized an absolute army of substitute manpower — women, children, the aged. All through the war the fatigue and worry of carrying on farming the land fell upon peasant women. In the towns the effects were dual: essential industries had to be moved from the threatened areas of the north, the east and Paris, or entirely recreated, into the more sheltered areas of the centre and south; and female labour had to be massively recruited — wives of mobilized workers, daughters of artisans and tradesmen. The feminine virtues of carefulness, efficiency and conscientiousness were also deployed in the management of industrial and commercial firms.

The pay-off for the hard work imposed on the female population was, first, and especially for working-class women, the attainment of a standard of living unknown before the war, the assumption of new responsibilities and personal freedom, freedom from outmoded conventions in towns and a new position in the peasant family — irreversible changes of social status.

The material losses were less heavy, although still significant. The currency had been affected. Monetary stability had characterized the pre-war years. The gold standard functioned normally; money in circulation depended merely on the balance of payments and internal trading and was not affected by government finance. After the war the situation changed. By suspending the gold convertibility of the franc the way was left open for large scale borrowing from the Banque de France and hence an inflationary increase in note circulation. These methods were frequently resorted to. From 1914 to 1919 a huge increase in public expenditure up to 210,000 million francs had to be faced. Taxes only brought in 35,000 million, because governments with typical conservatism and lack of responsibility had shied away from asking tax-payers to make the huge sacrifices the occasion demanded. Instead they had recourse to loans, largely from the Banque de France. The result was that the number of bank notes in circulation increased from 6,000 million francs in 1913 to 38,000 million francs in 1920. Inflation had replaced stability and inevitably prices rose and the situation was worsened by shortage of goods and services. Assuming a wholesale price-index at 100 in July 1914, by April 1920 it had risen to 600.

Expenditure abroad also increased. Imports rose between 1914 and 1919. By the end of 1919 they had reached a figure of 117,000 million francs, but exports only amounted to 34,000 million. To fill the gap, loans had to be negotiated with wealthy allies; foreign securities had to be sold by individuals, and the state gave them French securities in exchange, or else compensated them with cash payments. The value of Russian and Turkish state loans were reduced to almost nothing because of the collapse of these powers.

The financing of the war and the inflation which stemmed from it had a profound effect on the level of financial wealth. It has been estimated that the level of financial wealth before 1914 stood at 113,000 million gold francs, but in 1924 it was only 60—70,000 million paper francs — about 15—18,000 million gold francs. Inflation had impoverished those depending on fixed incomes. These had probably been devalued by some 85 per cent. In addition, prices had risen considerably.

A new kind of financial wealth had also come into existence because of the issue of government stock in return for loans. The total value of stocks in 1924 has been estimated at 360,000 million francs (paper

Fig. V.1   Growth of money stock, 1870–1958 (*in thousand millions of francs*)

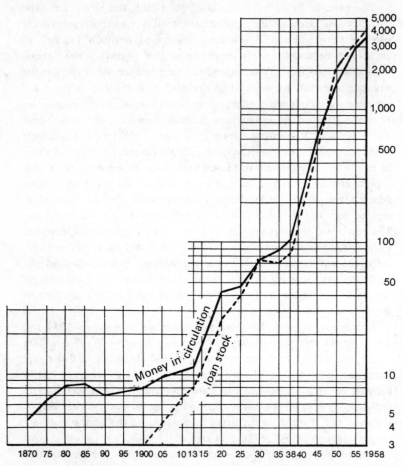

Source: *L'Univers économique et social*, vol. IX of *L'Encyclopédie française*.

currency), equivalent to between 72,000 and 90,000 million gold francs. More than half consisted of government stock, or of stock guaranteed by the state, two-fifths consisted of other French stock and rather more than one-tenth of foreign stock. The percentage of government stocks had risen by 100 per cent since before the war. However, the percentage of other French stock had fallen by 34 per cent and that of foreign stocks by 72 per cent. Financial wealth was therefore dependent above all on public finances rather than being drawn from national or foreign production. This is an indication of the impoverishment of France following the war.

But contemporaries realized that some social groups had profited from the war – the middlemen, producers, merchants and peasants. Food prices continued to rise, above all that of meat. This was particularly annoying to town dwellers. Contemporaries noted that by the end of the war the peasants had improved their standard of living. They ate more meat and drank more wine and more coffee, having accustomed themselves to these habits in the army. They also spent more. Careful observers may even have noticed that many peasants had paid off their mortgages, and that many farmers were buying up land that had formerly belonged to bourgeois. Many townsmen believed that the peasants had become the 'new rich' of the early twentieth century.

The sources do not permit the historian to be precise. Local monographs need to be written before the idea of growing peasant wealth, during and after the war, can be accepted. Certainly the ready market for their products, the steady rise in prices and the shortage of consumption durables allowed them to accumulate wealth – at least in terms of paper currency. But they needed these savings to replace old machinery and equipment, to fertilize soils exhausted because of the lack, during the war, of chemical fertilizers. These were expensive items. But the ability to repay debts was not peculiar to the peasants. They shared the advantage of all borrowers in repaying with paper debts contracted in gold. Although the buying up of land during the war had partly satisfied the desires of the French peasants, it had also absorbed much of their capital and meant that technical developments in the countryside were slowed down. It has been estimated that before the war one agricultural worker fed 4.2 persons. Between 1935 and 1939 he fed 5.1. This was a slow rate of development when compared with America, where the number had increased from 10.2 to 14.8. This low level of technical development was a feature of French agriculture both before and after the war. It seems probable that for the peasantry the most important change was not in their material condition but in their outlook. In 1914 most peasants accepted their condition of life, despite the progress of socialist ideas in some rural areas. But by 1920 they were discontented. They felt the nation owed them a debt which should be repaid, in some way or other, in return for the number that had lost their lives in the defence of the country.

But the results of the war were much more marked in the industrial sector of the economy. Industry had had to meet not only ordinary civilian demands, but also the enormous demands of the armed forces for war material — arms, uniforms and provisions. Mass production was required from industry and the war was to show how ill-prepared it was to meet the demand. The result was a mixture of disorder and improvization, of waste and the wasting of public money on unsuitable goods provided by unscrupulous suppliers. Under such strains many weaknesses of various industries were revealed in an exaggerated, but valuable way.

The rate of production increased. This was partly due to technical progress, itself the product of research, and partly to the greater co-operation between science and industry — the sort of co-operation which was already well-developed in Germany. There was standardization in manufacturing techniques because of the demands of the armaments ministry in conjunction with France's allies. And there was a more economic use of coal and electricity as sources of energy. The use of water-power for generating electricity was increased by 250 per cent. Because labour in factories tended to be in the hands of largely untrained women, this led to various improvements in machinery and sometimes the invention of new machinery. Machine-tools were more widely used. Automation was even introduced into the checking of goods being manufactured.

Industry undoubtedly developed through the impulse of war. This development, as well as the conditions and circumstances under which it developed, led to changes among the employers as well as the workers. After the war the employers appeared to have gained vigour, to be more specialized and to be better organized. Many had gained decisively from the huge orders they had obtained from the government, which had changed them from small to big industrialists. Citroen supplied shells; Loucheur supplied poison gas; Boussac invented cloth for use in aircraft manufacture. Many others became rich very quickly. Some Frenchmen were scandalized by this and labelled the suppliers 'war profiteers'. But it is impossible to measure the profits of war precisely. Some idea may be gained by examining the tax record for assessment for surplus profits tax between 1 August 1914 and 30 June 1919, which reached 17,500 million francs. There were undoubtedly frauds and concealments, making the size of war profits somewhat larger.

There had been more concentration and merging of firms. The following table gives some evidence of this.

The number of small firms decreased, and there was an increase in the medium-sized, large and very large ones. The percentage of

Table V.1 Number and size of firms

Employing	1906	1921	Index of growth (1906 = 100)
1–5	2 132 800	2 064 100	96
6–50	141 100	158 500	112
51–100	5 600	8 200	146
101–500	4 400	6 200	141
501–1 000	428	552	129
1 001–2 000	152	226	148
2 001–5 000	59	88	149
Over 5 000	17	35	205
TOTAL	2 284 556	2 237 901	98

production from these big establishments is an important point on which information is scanty; but, to give one example, immediately after the war 56 per cent of all automobiles were produced by the three big firms.

There is more than one way of amalgamating firms, and it is almost impossible to collect evidence about financial amalgamations organized by investment companies or finance houses that control and direct policy in groups of companies by placing their nominees on boards of directors. For such secret amalgamations there are no statistics and no means of finding any; but the process was well advanced by the end of the war. Instead of thousands of competing firms there grew up networks of firms that were independent only in name. The biggest, most powerful groups were in the newest industrial sectors – the chemical and electrical industries. This was partly because of financial difficulties in the post-war period which hit the smaller companies and made much easier their absorption by the larger, stronger companies.

The efforts of the government to impose a controlled war economy had caused the heads of industries to get themselves better organized. The government had pressurized them into forming groups so as to avoid separate discussions between the directors of national services and individual manufacturers. The latter quickly realized the desirability of forming 'consortiums' so as to get priority treatment over labour and materials. At the end of the war Clémentel, the minister of trade, put forward a plan for a general organization of heads of industry, in which all industries would be comprised in twenty-one groups, and the representatives of these industries should form a kind of general staff directly responsible to the ministry of commerce.

The business world rejected this move. It disliked the idea of state control and administrative interference. But in 1919 they formed their own organization, the *Confédération générale de la production francaise*. This followed some of the government's suggestions, but was strictly independent of the government. There were to be twenty-one groups, formed according to trades. The confederation had a general secretary and various committees which were to coordinate the various activities of the different federations. It proved to be a pressure group, influencing the administration, playing some part in the drawing up of financial, fiscal and monetary policies, by making various approaches to different bodies, submitting memoranda and reports. Its role in the sphere of labour disputes is more difficult to estimate, although its attitudes were clearly revealed when the Matignon agreement was signed in 1936.

But apart from this national confederation, there were still other groups of employers. The *Comité des Forges* had 200 members who, between them, represented capital worth 1,000 million francs, and who defended the powerful interests of the heavy engineering industries. The *Union des intérêts économiques* was founded in 1910 'to defend the general interests of trade and industry in their economic and social aspects' and had distinguished itself on the eve of World War I by carrying on a violent campaign against the imposition of a general tax on incomes. Later it involved itself more directly in politics, and in 1919 prepared the electoral programme of the *Bloc National* party of conservatives, moderates and some radicals which won the 1919 election. The Chamber of Deputies of 1919 was much more sensitive to the interests of employers than the Chamber of 1914.

The position of the workers had greatly changed as a result of the war. Work was much more mechanized than in the past, because of mass production, especially of war materials, and because more unskilled women were employed than before. These workers involved in mass production were called OS after the war, meaning specialized workers (*ouvriers spécialisés*). This category increased greatly in the post-war years, and skilled workers almost disappeared from mass production factories. Other industrial workers did unspecialized tasks such as cleaning equipment or helping in its upkeep. The old structure of work had thus disappeared. Workers now concentrated on one task. Groups of workers no longer had collective responsibility for the execution of a particular task. The idea of progress within this group from an apprentice to a fully qualified worker also tended to disappear.

The inter-war period saw a vast development of the mass production system of small endlessly repetitive work, with its exhausting, dehumanizing effect, turning workers into automata, 'arms without brains'. Security of employment was also affected, for a worker without qualification is an easily replaceable unit. Big firms had less and less need for a stable work force; this labour market was such that in a few days it was possible to hire any number of people to perform single, simple operations. In a recession there would be massive layoffs, with massive re-employment in times of boom. All this conduced to the demoralization of the unskilled workers. The character of their work was demoralizing too. The older type of worker had felt he was making something of value, and if he felt exploited it was in his character as a producer of wealth. Mass production deprived the worker of this distinction, leaving him only with the grievance of under-payment. This is reflected in a linguistic change, where 'workers' and 'producers' are all reduced to 'proletariat', with all its implications of poverty. But although the creation of these piece-workers was largely due to the impact of war, some of the older skilled workers still existed, even in the few very big factories.

The workers' movement remained dominated by the same militant professional workers as before. With victory in 1918 the deep division in the GCT between peace and war supporters was healed. The GCT felt that the working classes should be rewarded for the part they had played in national defence; that peace should lead to the coming of an economic democracy. A national committee of the CGT drew up a list of minimum demands of 15 December 1918, which included recognition of the rights of unions, collective workers' contracts, the eight-hour day, extension of social insurance and nationalization of enterprises. The government only agreed to the eight-hour day, which was incorporated in the law of 23 April 1919. This was to apply in all commercial and industrial establishments without reductions in salary. Agricultural and domiciliary work were excluded.

But although this represented a gain for the workers, the urgent problem of wages remained. Nominal wages had been lowered at the beginning of the war and had only increased again in 1916 and 1917. But this rise did not keep pace with the rise in the cost of living, and by 1918 real wages were between 15 and 20 per cent lower than the 1914 level. This led to a reaction which took the form of revived militant trade unionism; the number of union members increased considerably. Government statistics give a figure of 1,580,000 members, but the figures provided by the CGT show a figure of 2,400,000. The Catholic unions amalgamated and formed the French Confederation of Christian Workers (*Confédération française des Travailleurs Chrétiens*), which had 100,000 members by 1920. The employers were now better organized but were facing a powerful trade-union movement. The *ouvriers spécialisés* were becoming increasingly important and were prepared to resort to violence in order to achieve their aims. A wave of strikes broke out in 1919 and reached its high point in 1920. The strikes began with a strike of railway employees, but the CGT rapidly tried to widen the movement into a general strike and soon miners, sailors, dockers, metal workers, building workers, transport workers, furniture workers and gas workers were on strike. But there was no general strike. And this failure led to a feeling of disillusionment among those who had newly joined the movement in the hope of a quick gain, but who were incapable of prolonged effort. The number of trade-union members fell from 2,000,000 to some 600,000.

This decline in trade unionism was quickened by the schism of 21 September 1921. At the Congress of Tours in December 1920 there had been a split when three-quarters of the members of the socialist party, greatly influenced by the Bolshevik revolution of 1917, and disappointed by their electoral setback in November 1919, turned towards the Third International and formed the SFIC (*Section Française de L'Internationale Communiste*) — the French communist party. Again, as before 1905, the French socialist movement was divided, but this time the trade unions were affected because the Third International demanded that its members infiltrate and take over the direction of the trade unions. The leaders of the CGT sensing the danger, threatened to expel unruly members. But the members of the SFIC replied by founding a new confederation — the CGTU (*Confédération Générale du Travail Unitaire*), which soon belonged to the communist Trade Union International of Moscow. Trade unionism in France became a divided force. The two confederations spent as much time opposing each other as opposing the employers. By 1922 the CGT could only count 400,000 members, although this number did increase subsequently. But the CGTU was even divided within itself and its numbers continued to decline.

Disillusion over trade unionism and the aftermath of the schism threw the workers on the defensive. But the improvement in the economic situation lasting till 1930 enabled employers to increase wages and resulted for the time being in a general easing of social discord.

2.The growth of social discord 1930—45

Most Frenchmen in the immediate post-war period looked forward to a time when their immediate difficulties would be overcome and when the *belle époque* would return. Rapid and on the whole well-managed reconstruction and vigorous prosperity common to most industrial nations seemed to indicate that the good old days were extremely near, though as early as 1926 monetary difficulties made the future appear uncertain. Yet when the world economic crisis broke out in 1929 France managed to escape and even attracted investments because of adverse conditions elsewhere.

But the escape was soon seen to be a temporary one. The first indications that the crisis was affecting France appeared in 1930 when the indices of economic activity began to fall. But the effects of the crisis were not deeply felt until 1932. By then production had fallen by 27 per cent and unemployment had reached a significant level, and 260,000 were receiving aid. France was hit by this crisis later than most countries, but was hit just as badly and indeed sank into a kind of permanent economic crisis which lasted until the eve of World War II. Even in 1938 industrial production was some 15—17 per cent lower than in 1928. Between 1935 and 1939 the number of unemployed receiving state aid never fell below 350,000.

This was a long-lasting crisis and during it nearly all social categories experienced a fall in their incomes, although some were hit more than others. Between 1929 and 1935 total incomes fell by 30 per cent. The smaller enterprises were especially vulnerable because of the competition of their larger rivals, who were better able to withstand the crisis and maintained their previous level of activity. Those employed in the private sector managed to protect their nominal wages. But some were only employed part-time and many, indeed, were unemployed, and these categories undoubtedly suffered a loss in financial terms. Wage-earners in the public sector were hit, not so much by the crisis itself, as by the policy of deflation followed by the government up till 1935. Agricultural earnings fell by 40 per cent between 1929 and 1932, then suffered a worse setback in 1934 and 1935 with a reduction of 60 per cent.

The crisis was political as well as economic. The inability of governments of any colour to plan and carry out a coherent economic policy caused perplexity and discontent, together with an aversion for parliamentary institutions. Fascist tendencies appeared in some rural areas; some of the middle classes were attracted by the 'Leagues'; the formation of the leftist Popular Front attracted the proletariat, many peasants, and others of the middle classes. The years 1934—6 saw an intensification of political embitterment. Riots and strikes in 1934; the Popular Front; the confrontation at the elections of 1936 of two rival 'blocs' of left and right; the victory of the left and the exasperation of the right all heightened the atmosphere of social antagonism.

The explosion came with the strikes of June 1936, a vast spontaneous outbreak of the working classes exhilarated by the electoral victory of the Popular Front. The declared aim of the strikes and the factory sit-ins was to extract more wages from employers, but more fundamentally to gain genuine recognition for trade unions, for worker representation in the entrepreneurial set up, a radical change in the relationship between employers and workers. Actual wage claims were less significant than the desire to put an end to the state of social inferiority to which the working classes confusedly felt they had for so long been subjected. Their victory was sealed by the Matignon agreements of 7 June 1936. These were quickly followed by a series of laws benefiting the workers.

The law of 20 June 1936 introduced an annual paid holiday of fifteen days; the law of 21 June introduced the forty-hour week; and a law of 24 June introduced better procedure for collective bargaining. The trade-union movement gained an unheard-of impetus. The CFTC, which had previously drawn most of its support from office-workers and women, now had more members from the working classes. The CGT increased its membership from less than a million before the strikes to 4 million in 1937. For the first time 50 per cent of wage-earners belonged to the trade-union movement.

The Matignon Agreements were a significant victory for the workers. The employers were humiliated and discouraged, for public opinion seemed to support the workers and to hold the selfish short-sightedness of the employers responsible for the social crisis of June. But the employers quickly turned on their own delegates to the CGPF (*Confédération Générale de la Production Française*). Many failed to realize that membership of the CGPF bound them to the Matignon Agreements. In August 1936 at a general meeting of the CGPF they revised their rules, changed their name to the *Confédération Génerale du Patronat Français* and elected a new council, whose express purpose was to limit the extent of the workers' victory of June.

This new body refused to negotiate with the CGT and claimed that the CGT did not represent the workers of France. They refused to sign any collective agreements on a national scale. Militant trade unionists were sacked from factories. In order to break this employers'

Fig. V.2 Strikers: 1900–1938

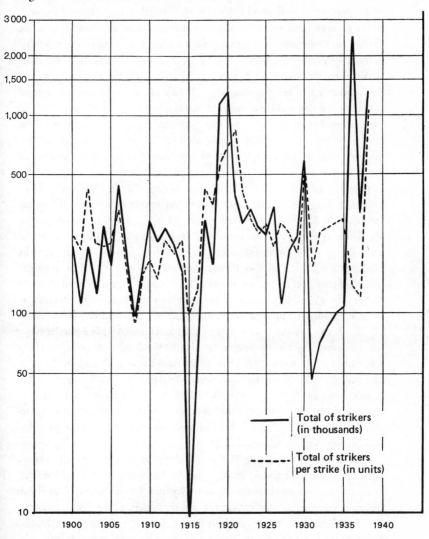

counter-revolution the CGT demanded a law placing the power of hiring and firing labour under the control of the national employment services. The CGPF mounted a violent campaign recruiting practically the whole of its membership in defence of the employer's right to choose his own labour, and succeeded in getting the bill thrown out by the Senate. But the employers were not wholly united. The big employers' fears were soon calmed with the fall of Léon Blum's Popular Front Government in 1937. But this did not calm the anxieties of the smaller and medium-sized employers, on whom the cost of the workers' success weighed more heavily. Many were unable to bear the extra costs involved by the Matignon Agreements, particularly the rise in wages and the shortening of the working day. These employers developed a hatred not only for the workers, but also for the big firms, the 'trusts', whom they suspected of profiting by the occasion to squeeze them out. This may have led some to support the idea of a more authoritarian régime, such as was to be found in some neighbouring European countries. Some may even have developed fascist tendencies.

On the eve of World War II and during the death throes of the Popular Front, the counter-offensive of the employers was in full swing. Inflation had already removed many of the benefits gained by the Matignon agreements. This continual decline in purchasing power led to a feeling of disillusionment among the workers, many of whom left the CGT. When the Daladier-Reynaud government began to consider repealing the forty-hour week, the CGT called a general strike for 30 November 1938. It was badly planned and dubious in motivation – since it seemed to be almost as much against the Munich accord as the repeal of the labour laws – and it failed. This was called the 'revenge for Matignon' by the employers. It also marked the near collapse of the trade-union movement. In early 1939 membership had again fallen to one million. The Russo-German agreement and the war brought further blows. On 14 January 1940 the CGT leaders decided officially to exclude from membership those who continued to support the Soviet Union. This brought a new division into the movement, and resulted in its complete emasculation.

The Vichy episode set the seal on the victory of the employers, although not because Pétain was by inclination or self-interest sympathetic to capitalism. André Siegfried has described his basic political concept as the 'elemental conservatism of a pillar of society'. To establish what he believed to be a balanced order he abolished all trade unions, working-class organizations, and employers' federations, together with strikes and lock-outs. This attempt to endow the country with corporative institutions by means of his Labour Charter (October 1941) had no practical results. But some of his top civil servants, sick of parliamentary impotence under the Third Republic, together with some heads of industry, dreamed up a sort of state *dirigisme*, the principal organs of which were to be the *Comités d'organisation* created by the law of 16 June 1940. These committees were charged with provisionally organizing production in all its aspects — purchase and allocation of primary materials, establishing codes of competition, fixing prices. Production was to be better organized and 'in the interests of enterprises and workers'. But the government nominated the members of committees, and these turned out to be important employers, many of whom had been at the head of their own professional bodies. Although the CGPF had been dissolved, the employers were supreme in the economy.

They shared their supremacy with the régime and shared the opprobrium of the régime. The workers were forced into implacable opposition. As Marshal Pétain's popularity declined, public opinion held that the employers had been the least patriotic of any social group, and were regarded as 'collaborators'. The Resistance prepared sanctions. The *Conseil National de la Résistance* said that after the liberation there would be a 'real economic democracy' in France, and all sources of national wealth, including mines, insurance and banks, would be nationalized. Workers would participate in the running of enterprises. On 14 July 1943 General de Gaulle said, 'The nation will be determined that natural wealth, labour, and technology contribute to the prosperity of all and should not be exploited for the benefit of a few.' The big employers were accomplices of the Vichy régime and were to be the victims of the Liberation.

However, the structural reforms undertaken by the Provisional Government and then the first Constituent Assembly of the Fourth Republic were not solely inspired by a desire for political reprisals. They were the result of considerable thought on social problems and aimed at a better standard of living, greater security and wider opportunities.

Those firms accused of collaborating with the enemy were nationalized, including Berliet (which was later handed back to its owners), Renault and Gnôme et Rhône. The power industries — gas, electricity and coal — were nationalized, as were the big banks — the Banque de France, whose nationalization had already been started in 1936, and the four big deposit banks (*Crédit Lyonnais, Société Générale, Comptoir National d'Escompte*, and the *Banque Nationale pour le Commerce et l'Industrie*); and the thirty-four principal insurance companies. Most of the shareholders were compensated with redeemable stocks. Economists hold that the economic effects of these nationalizations were beneficial. The social effects are rather hard to measure. One important way of analysing the social effects is to examine the management personnel of these new ventures. How different was it from the personnel of pre-nationalization days? At first many new men gained the key posts, men whose political views tended to be in opposition to the interests of the big industrial employers. Subsequently many people who had worked in private enterprises, including top directors, came to play an increasingly important role in the administration of the nationalized industries, and above all, in banking. In addition, the employers gradually recognized that the nationalization was permanent, and reconciled themselves to this.

An order of 22 February 1945 made compulsory the setting up of a *Comité d'entreprise* (a joint committee) in all firms with a hundred or more employees (reduced to fifty in 1946). This represented the fruition of one of the cherished ideas of the Resistance. This was regarded as a step towards what was stated in the preamble of the orders of February 1945 to be 'the association of wage-earners in the running of the economy and in the management of industry.' These committees were to be set up by representatives of the staff and had to work in conjunction with the management in order to improve working conditions, to run the welfare aspects of the business, and with the aid of an accountant to help direct the financial aspects of the business. They might conceivably have led to worker control of industry, but the law stipulated that although they had a decisive say in welfare questions, as far as economic questions were concerned their role was only consultative. In fact, it is generally agreed that in practice this measure did not live up to the exaggerated hopes it had inspired. The economic attributes of the committees remained largely theoretical. Their failure was predictable, whether it is imputed to the unco-operativeness of industrial heads, the lack of sophistication of workers, or the impossibility of reconciling by legislation a variety of conflicting interests.

Social security was introduced in principle by the orders of 1945 and these principles were more closely defined by the law of 22 May 1946, and were partly derived from the Beveridge Plan, published in England in 1942. The benefit of social security was to be extended to all, and in the first place for wage-earners, as far as the development of the economy would permit. Insurance was made compulsory and covered illness, disability, old-age, accidents and death. The primary object of the scheme was effectively to guarantee the security of those incapable of providing against a future economic or social crisis. A further aim was to effect a more equitable distribution of national wealth, and thus indirectly increase wages.

The employers accepted the scheme with gloomy resignation. They were at pains to point out the direct relation between the cost of welfare, based on the level of salaries paid, and the selling price of their goods in the world market where they would lose their competitive edge. Wage-earners, on the other hand, liked the idea of social security on the whole, and realized the value of the guarantee it offered.

There are no precise statistics to show if the social security system led to a redistribution of incomes, and to a narrowing of inequalities of wealth. Unquestionably inequalities continued to exist; but were they diminishing after 1946? Some say that there was only a redistribution at the lower end of the income scale, that the 'poor helped the very poor'. What statistics there are tend to confirm this claim. Wages and social allowances represented 53.7 per cent of the total national revenue in 1949. In 1959 this had risen to 60.6 per cent. But there were now more wage-earners, and the duration of work had increased. If any redistribution had taken place, its effects were limited to the group of wage-earners.

There was a determined effort in favour of the family. In the inter-war period, the government had done what it could to encourage more births. The law of 1920 dealt severely with abortion and the advocacy of birth control. The payment of family allowances by employers was made compulsory by the law of 11 March 1932. On the eve of World War II, by the law of 29 July 1939, the government had secured the passage of a Family Code, which raised and extended family allowances, and introduced special grants for first births and loans for the newly married.

The law of 22 August 1946 extended and modified the allocation of family allowances and brought it within the social security system. By this law all workers, or those unable to work (especially the sick, disabled, unemployed or single women caring for several children), whatever their resources, received family allowances, provided that they were responsible for at least two children, until these children reached fifteen years of age although extensions were granted for apprentices, students and the sick. Various other payments were added – for example, grants for pregnant women, maternity grants, and generally to those with families who were unable to work for some reason.

All families benefited from these money allowances, apart from lodging allowances, and all received the same size of allowance, whatever the wealth of a particular family. A determined effort in favour of the family was thus being made in France. Despite the intentions of the founders of the system, the allowances did not keep pace with the rise in the cost of living. Financial support for families has in recent years diminished in relative value. This process is likely to continue with the increased attention being paid to those in greater need such as the aged and the 'economically weak'.

3. Economic take-off and its consequences, 1950—70

The post-war reconstruction of France is usually said to have taken five years to achieve, boosted by a tremendous collective effort and a very considerable contribution from Marshall Aid. In 1950 began a period of economic development without precedent in her history, and which signifies an undoubted moment of 'take-off'.

A 'reconstruction' pattern of fair shares for all of a modest sized cake, of cautious capitalist enterprise, politically ambivalent and not particularly efficient, soothing doses of nationalization and limited state control has been replaced by the ideal of 'modernization', productive rather than distributive, more interested in innovation than social beneficence, more responsive to market mechanisms and aiming at putting the largest possible quantity of material goods in front of the largest possible number of people.

The transition from semi-stagnation to growth has caused deep but generally acceptable change, though occasionally giving rise to tension, dismay or frustration, both in sectors that have lost ground, such as agriculture where the active population has dropped from 36 per cent in 1946 to 30 per cent in 1954, to 16 per cent in 1968, as well as in those that are expanding rapidly, such as technicians and managerial staff. These first consequences of the economic take-off, as experienced in the 'fifties and 'sixties are what immediately concern us.

The 'silent revolution' of the peasants

This phrase was coined by one of the heads of the CNJA (*Centre National des Jeunes Agriculteurs*) to draw attention to the great though long unnoticed changes that had affected the peasants' world. Since then, however, the revolution has become loud enough to compel the attention of the authorities as well as large sections of the general public.

The first demonstrations took place in October 1952 when a farmers' action committee organized road blocks from dawn to dusk on all roads in eighteen *départements*, together with a veto on the sale of all agricultural produce. The organizers claimed a great success, inasmuch as they had really alerted the government and public opinion to the state of French agriculture. The success was illusory: peasant syndicalism took no account of general social and economic problems but was simply concerned with a demand for better prices. Eight years later when more demonstrations in Brittany left town dwellers in no doubt about rural malaise, the younger members, with Catholic backing, changed the direction of the movement, enlarging the context of the problem and proposing more fundamental solutions.

Underlying the change in peasant life was the 'tractor revolution'. After liberation the initiation of agricultural loan societies with the call for industrial expansion led to the rapid spread of mechanization. Agricultural officers in departmental administrations encouraged this and the campaign was boosted by the advertisements of agricultural machinery manufacturers, by the oil companies and by the high powered salesmanship of suppliers. In 1946 there were 46,000 tractors; in 1953, 200,000; in 1956, 400,000; and in 1960, 600,000. The tractor seemed destined to be the saviour of the peasant; it gave the small farmer the impression of increasing the earning value of his land without changing his habits of mixed agriculture.

All too soon he discovered that the tractor was a great absorber of his ready money, involving as it did the purchase of numerous accessory implements needed for the mixed character of his cultivation. After investing his reserves or raising a loan for their purchase he found himself unable to invest in anything else, thus raising again the awkward problem of the profitability of his holding. Having taken this first step on the path of technical progress he had to go further. Faced with competition from more advanced farming in other countries he had to use more and more chemical fertilizers, patent foodstuffs, even more mechanical tools, in order to keep abreast of modern methods. For all of which more and more finance was required.

Peasant attitudes were affected by other pressures – those of a society with an ever rising standard of living. They, and especially their wives and daughters, wanted modern plumbing, washing machines, comfortable homes, less arduous work, holidays. So recourse was had to loans, for home comforts, for agricultural needs, and often for actual land. The newly acquired habit of borrowing, as well as the need for heavy investment, revolutionized peasant life, based as it was on the sale of any excess beyond subsistence. But a peasant paying the interest on a loan cannot hold on to his produce for a good price; he has to sell all his crop at the current rate. Their archaic background made the peasants ill-prepared for the rigours of the trade cycle, and it was the realization of this that caused a fresh eruption of agricultural syndicalism.

In their original form the agricultural syndicates had concentrated on the question of prices alone. They wanted the government to give them guaranteed prices based on industrial price levels. This exactly suited big farmers of good land, well-equipped for large scale production and with good outlets; it suited also the syndical chiefs, big men in their towns or market centres, political operators, with conservative or reactionary views on the perpetuation of the rural status quo. But it was of little help to the smallholder, cramped by the size of his operation, perplexed by technical problems and incapable of understanding or controlling market mechanisms.

The later version of agricultural syndicalism, without abandoning its demand for fixed prices (especially in the context of the enlarged European market) aimed at a wider strategy involving fundamental reforms in methods of trade and in the use of property. The existing commercial set-up left the producer at the mercy of market fluctuations beyond his control. A grower who has adopted modern agricultural techniques has to have assured outlets that the traditional system with its fluctuating prices cannot provide. The remedy is to create a long term policy for agricultural surpluses laid down by bodies under combined state and professional control, with funds at their disposal, who can regulate prices and output. This aim was achieved by the syndicates with the creation of FORMA (*Fonds d'orientation et de régularisation des marchés agricoles*) whose stated intention was to secure 'a proper organization for marketing the main agricultural products' and 'to pave the way for government decisions about markets and the relevant action'. The sort of property reform demanded by the young peasants was of greater social significance. They cared much less than their fathers had about extending the family property, and were more interested in getting a better system of grouping units of land. 'Is ownership of property vital in agriculture? What really matters for the peasant is security. Formerly property meant security. Tomorrow security will be found in other ways: assurance of status, family allocations of land, larger units, better technical education; an assured status for agriculture will replace the notion of ownership' (Debatisse). Indifferent to the mania for ownership the young syndicalists suggested the formation of societies for 'the supervision of property movements' with the aim of preventing the continuous splitting up of properties by multiple inheritance and building up viable holdings by subsidized purchase; preventing the acquisition of cultivable land by non-cultivators or property companies, or the boosting of prices through speculation which blighted the chances of youthful beginners.

These plans were strongly opposed by the right, by the rural establishment and by old-fashioned syndicalists who saw in them a threat of land nationalization and alleged that to lay hands on the property structure would 'split the agricultural world'. In spite of this the agricultural law of 1960 gave some satisfaction to the young syndicalists by its creation of the SAFERs (*Sociétés d'aménagement foncier et d'établissement rural*[1]), whose aim was 'to acquire land or estates that are up for sale, also virgin land, returnable to its owners after cultivation. Their principal aim is to strengthen the basis of agriculture, to increase the area of specific farms, and to facilitate new agricultural enterprise.' But in order to be in a position to forestall property speculators they needed to have a first option on all land put up for sale. The law gave them this right in principle, but it was hedged by so many conditions that its efficacy was much diminished.

The reforms proposed by the young syndicalists seemed very wide-ranging. Their reform of market organization hit at the roots of commercial profit and the laws of supply and demand; planning and annual contracts for produce hit at free enterprise; the change in the structure of property, the separation of landed property from 'exploitation property' hit at ground rents and rights of private ownership. They were symptomatic of a change of mentality among some peasants who wanted to emerge from their traditional isolation and be treated on the same footing as other social groups; to cease leaving political action to their betters and regarding the state as nothing but a provider of subsidies, but to act politically and economically just like any other producer of consumption goods. As Bloch-Lainé remarks

> Agriculture has nothing to gain by living in another world. Peasants can't complain of being treated as outcasts and at the same time enjoy the pleasure of being different. Workers on the land have the same rights and duties as any other kind of worker. The young farmers want to leave their unsplendid isolation, to get together with the industrial unions, be involved in the world of commerce and economic planning.

This struggle for the proper integration of agriculture into the economy explodes the myth of peasant unity sedulously propagated by the old-look syndicalists for the benefit of the large-scale producers. Ranged against them is an emergent 'peasant middle class', farming technicians, conscious of modern economic problems, uninhibited by ideas of social inferiority.

[1] Property management and rural settlement corporation.

Fig. V.3   Exploitation of the soil

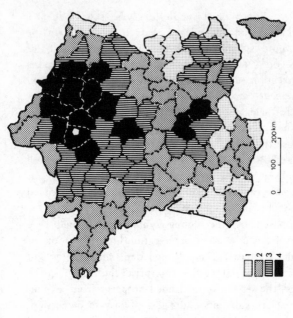

Average extent of land exploited
1. Less than 10 hectares
2. From 10 to 15 hectares
3. From 15 to 25 hectares
4. Over 25 hectares

Types of exploitation
1. Over 25% share-cropping
2. Over 50% tenant farming
3. More than 50% owner farming

Source: A. Labaste, R. Blanchon, R. Oudin, *France et pays d'expression française* (Paris, Colin, 1963).

The gains and losses of this silent revolution are not easy to sum up. One may count as a gain the awakening of the young farmers, and the fact that country folk have not fallen back on passive resistance, but have thrown up militants and leaders. There have been disillusions and setbacks: the SAFERs have through lack of funds been restricted to a very minor role (after eight years of life they had intervened in only 25,000 of the 1.5 million transfers of property that have taken place); the co-operatives have not always been capable of adapting to the rigorous conditions of modern competition or of maintaining guaranteed standards of quality; unfortunately some of the most forward-looking growers, such as those who concentrated on fruit growing, have been badly hit by falls in prices.

More often young farmers now complain that mixed farming, for which they had great hopes, is now obsolete and the future lies with factory farming closely linked with the big firms of the processed food industry, who can control market prices and 'condition' consumers. The disarray of traditional farmers leaves them open to demagogic demands for the maintenance at all costs of the 'family enterprise', and the old demands for guaranteed prices and incomes.

The agricultural population has been a huge reservoir drawn on from all sides, but is now purely residual, and indeed generally aged. There is no doubt that the nation owes this victim of economic growth some help — at any rate for those whose age, lack of skill or equipment have left them straggling in the wake of their more enterprising fellows.

The 'new working class'

This phrase is used by the writer Serge Mallet in connection with changes in working conditions that have deeply affected part of the French working class. But only part: since France is still a sort of industrial museum, and there are many firms whose methods and organization have changed little since the nineteenth century; there are still more that continue to use the production line methods of the inter-war period. The revolutionary technology and automation adopted by the more advanced industries such as petrochemistry, heavy electrics, telecommunications, the motor industry, heavy engineering, has introduced machines that replace not only manpower, but occasionally brain-power. So far this has affected only a few, but among them the most important, and others will eventually follow their example.

Automation calls for a different type of skill — knowledge of a trade acquired through apprenticeship has no place in work which involves surveillance and control. Professional training is gained not for a trade but for a firm. Firms' specialization is getting more and more intensive, and with each firm developing its own production methods and using more and more specialized machinery the worker acquires a specialism that he can only use in that particular firm. The older type of worker had a personal skill which enabled him to change jobs easily, regardless of actual firms; the worker in an automated firm has no individual skill outside the firm in which he is so closely integrated.

Because of this situation the question of what wage should be paid to the worker is more difficult, since skill and qualifications are no longer the significant determinants they once were. The worker's wages ultimately depend on the economic well-being of the firm, and no longer on the quality or amount of their work.

The lack of mobility between various sections of work means that there is more stability of personnel. This, in turn, means smoother production which, in turn, serves to guarantee gradual wage increases. Productivity agreements between workers and employers are thus more common. They naturally suit the employers because of probably increased production. They also suit the workers who, by receiving promises of increased wages, feel more secure. The workers are thus becoming increasingly integrated into many firms. In these same firms the level of trade-union membership is extremely high – between 50 and 90 per cent – whereas in the older type of firms, where workers' qualifications are of more general order, trade-union membership is rarely more than 15 to 20 per cent of the labour force.

The character of the trade-union movement is also tending to change. The basic unit is tending to be the firm itself, rather than a particular trade within firms, or even a particular industry. This tends to lead to some difficulties with the big trade-union groups. The purposes and methods of striking have also changed. Instead of all-out strikes, which would only come to an end with the capitulation of the employers or the exhaustion of the resources of the workers, different tactics are now used. Production is held up by short work stoppages, at vital times or in vital sectors of work. These are less costly for the workers. This requires unity among the trade-union members, and also a degree of knowledge both of economic questions in general and of the running of the firm, so that the maximum effect may be realized from industrial action.

The trade unions now aim beyond wage increases. They seek greater worker participation, and, to some extent, control of the running of a firm. In some agreements with the management in 1960, clauses were inserted giving the unions the right to make sure that the management kept its promises, for example, the promise that working hours would be reduced without wages being reduced as a consequence, and that workers should be consulted on matters relating to the organization of work. In these demands for greater worker participation and even some control over production, the workers' movement has taken a new direction.

But the old form of wage claim, not touching the question of control, still persists among the unions. The workers' movement is thus, to some extent, divided. For many workers 'control' means very little. They only seek immediate material improvement and some protection from unemployment. The division is partly between new and old firms. But it is also found within firms, between 'automated' and 'manual' parts of the firm. This could create a new split in the trade-union movement, setting a wage-claim unionism against a control-claim unionism. The latter might conceivably enlarge its scope to embrace the idea that controlling the policy of firms may lead to controlling the nation's economy.

Such a prognosis has not been borne out by the events of May-June 1968, where the 'new working class' played an unimportant role and strike action was started by workers in the older types of industry. It may be, too, that the impetus of claims for participation in control has been sapped by the concession of longer holidays, more job security, bi-monthly wages, all of which raise the social status of the working man.

The 'new middle classes' and the 'cadres'

Theories about the middle class were much in vogue between the wars when class war seemed to threaten revolution, and the bourgeoisie were looking round for allies. These theories owed less to observation of facts than to political flights of fancy. The group was envisaged as consisting of owners of small factories, landowners, tradesmen, anyone whose interests made him a supporter of property and free enterprise; it included salary-earners such as engineers, who were supposed to share the attitudes of their chiefs, civil servants who allegedly had the same outlook as members of the liberal professions, and the same sense of belonging to a bourgeois élite. Nothing could really unite such a mixed collection except fear of the sort of social collapse that might follow a victory of the workers.

But 'new' middle classes have emerged, in quite different circumstances. Because of technical progress and greater specialization in industry entirely new and very clearly defined structures are called for;

which is why management personnel (*cadres*) plays an increasingly important part in modern society.

They are definable by functional criteria: managers are people with an adequately complete knowledge of their trade and capable of supervising a group of workers or employees (middle management), and people capable of assuming responsibility for running a department or a business (top management). The functional criterion is not enough for the latter, for it does not distinguish between directors and owners. A further criterion is that of status: managers are not principals but salary-earners. They rank at the head of this hierarchy.

The number of these men varies from industry to industry. The older industries tend to have a lower proportion. Three per cent of the total labour force in mining industry belong to this management category, 5 per cent to 6 per cent in the textile, timber, furniture and leather industries. In the engineering and chemical industries the percentage is 12 per cent, 18 per cent in the gas and electrical industries and 19 per cent in the petroleum industries. The number of men in this 'management' category has therefore grown at the same time as industry has developed, but the rise has varied from industry to industry, and has been particularly noticeable in the more rapidly expanding industries.

These 'cadres' are found in both the private and public sectors of industry. In the public sector they form a large percentage of the labour force — probably 18 per cent in banking and insurance. Teachers in secondary schools also fall into this category but it is hard to assess percentages in other branches of public administration.

This is, however, a wide category. Since owners of firms are excluded, the upper limits are easy to define, but defining the lower limits poses difficult problems and the further one goes down the harder it gets. At the top there is a good deal of chair-swapping between the top brass of the public and private sectors, while among technicians it is hard to distinguish between managers and workers.

Statisticians have produced figures for all those forming part of management structure.

Table V.2 Managerial class ('cadres')

	Approximate numbers	% of working population
1954	1 684 000	8.7
1962	2 387 140	12.4
1968	3 172 560	15.5

Over fourteen years the proportion of managerial staff in the population has nearly doubled as has their total number, which is much higher than that of employers and farm owners.

Men are dominant in this category. Although there are two working men for one working woman in France, in top management there are five men for every woman. Obviously the 'management' category tends to be found in the towns. Although half the population lives in the countryside, only one-tenth of the management category lives there. Fifty per cent of the total are to be found in the Paris region. As one might expect, the management sector is better educated than the average. Three-fifths of the upper management ranks have their *baccalauréat*, and half have higher qualifications than this.

They are much better paid than the workers (on average they receive a salary four times greater than that of the worker). In marked contrast with the average bourgeois they are far more interested in income than in wealth. They aspire to a high standard of material comfort and their expenditure ranges from one and a half to two and a half times as much as the average Frenchman. Expenditure on food, though higher in absolute terms, is only 25 per cent of their annual income as against the general average of 31 per cent. But they spend more on travel, holidays, leisure activities, culture. Their pleasure lies in consumption, not, like the bourgeois, in saving.

They spend more because they feel secure, especially in the public sector where there is a good deal of protection against the arbitrary whims of employers or superiors. There is less security in the private sector, though technical skill is always something of a guarantee of constant employment which enables a man to feel independent.

Socially, apart from pursuing similar ways to material comfort, they tend to be individualistic, keen on personal advancement, not openly committed as regards politics and parties, uninterested in ideologies. The majority are not active in the trade-union movement and most of them have never considered joining a union or attempting any form of group betterment. Of the rest, some belong to the *Confédération Générale des Cadres*, which looks on itself as a third force between employers and workers, some to various independent unions, like the teachers', some to the main national unions. Managerial unionism is attracted in two directions, towards working-class unionism because they are wage-earners, and towards the bourgeoisie on account of their sense of professional responsibility and their standard of living. This equivocal attitude has persisted since the crisis of May 1968, though some, feeling that they have no defined position in the general hierarchy, have supported claims for more participation in policy making.

4. Conclusion: society in conflict

Twenty years of rapid progress appear to point to 1950 as the year of economic 'take-off'. Whether one accepts this view or not the society that developed in this period was an affluent one. But since the blessings of this affluence have been unequally distributed, not everyone has accepted it as wholly good. Social malaise, leading to a violent explosion, nearly blew it apart in May 1968. But it turned out to be more solidly based than its detractors expected.

Taken as a whole there are all the external symptoms of a dazzling success. Real national income, after allowing for inflation and monetary erosion, tripled between 1950 and 1970. In purchasing power the working man's pay has increased from 100 in 1949 to 173 for the father of a family in Paris, 210 for a bachelor in Paris, 226 for a provincial bachelor (1968). A more objective criterion is that of 'real' consumption: starting from 100 in 1956 (the first year for which we have reliable figures) and allowing for monetary erosion and rise in prices, the following progress has been recorded:

Table V.3 Increase in consumption by households:
1969 compared with 1956 (basic index of 100)
(N.B. Figures show percentage increases from widely different starting amounts. See text)

	Food and drink	Consumer goods	Total
Industrial chiefs, professions	115	147	139
Middle managers	122	160	144
Industrial workers	120	180	150
Farmers and farm managers	148	176	160
Farm workers	164	194	176

The increases have been inversely proportional to positions occupied in the social hierarchy. Over thirteen years the working classes have increased their total consumption by a half to three-quarters, while at the top of the pyramid the increase has been by one-third only. In this area at least social differences have tended to narrow (though the gross consumption of a wealthy businessman's household is double that of a farm worker). Although the countryman eats much better than ever before, the real all-round improvement is in things that used to be regarded as luxuries, i.e. in clothing, home comforts, leisure activities.

The last have shown the most spectacular increases, and represent some 20 per cent of household expenditure. Although the working week has increased slightly from 45 to 46 hours, more people take a whole weekend off, and the annual holiday has grown from eighteen to thirty days. On the whole, though, the French, unlike the Anglo-Saxons, seem to prefer to take their time off in the annual holiday rather than at weekends. The summer exodus of the French is more complete than in any other country; nearly 20 million, not counting children under fourteen, take off.

The problem of leisure is attracting more and more attention with talk of a policy of 'developing cultural activities' with counter talk of the 'massification of culture' and the threat of an all-pervading mediocrity. Typically, at the very moment when more and more people are getting more and more material comforts, questions are asked about the quality of life. Prosperity always makes the least favoured sections of society more aggressive than poverty does, and rapid modernization produces discomfort at all levels. Hence it is hardly surprising that an atmosphere of criticism and protest has been generated by the intelligentsia, and especially the Parisian intelligentsia. They indulge in rather arbitrary pronouncements about the opulence of modern society, 'so-called civilization', 'soulless, repressive and absurd', threatening both the quality of life and the liberty of the subject. 'Technobureaucracy' manipulates society and conditions the individual. In fact all the values of industrial society are questioned. Their resentment probably springs from the fact that industrial society takes very little notice of them; and they certainly count for far less in a society dominated by technicians and businessmen than they did at the end of the nineteenth century. Wounded pride makes them reject the 'consumption society' in which they feel like strangers, and pine for a purer age.

There is nothing new about this. One only has to look back at 'the spirit of the thirties' to find plenty of familiar echoe. Anticapitalism, antiiliberalism, antimaterialism, antinationalism, and a desperate rejection of the established order. These go back even further than the economic crisis of 1929 to the brief prosperity of the Poincaré-Tardieu government of 1926–8. The difference between the two periods is that when in 1934 the participants took to the streets the forces of conservatism took over, while in 1968 the politicians were so discredited that they proved quite incapable of repeating the operation.

French society in the 'sixties was thus divided and dispirited, labelled by a recent critic 'the stalemate society', constipated in organization and in action, with fear of a confrontation on one side, and on the other an excessively hierarchical view of authority. The inherent contradiction is that the French find this authority both intolerable and indispensable. In an attempt to resolve the difficulty they have developed a system of absolutism, the arbitrary character of which is tempered by its unobtrusiveness. This has the unfortunate effect of raising an awkward barrier between rulers and ruled, between social groups, though all with the praiseworthy aim of satisfying the prevailing desire for security. Such conditions of rigidity make it hard to adapt to change, so that when it becomes essential it comes by way of a crisis — a typically French mode of action.

Hence one interpretation of the events of May 1968, as 'an instinctive revolt against the stalemate society'. Raymond Aron describes it as 'the incredible (*introuvable*) revolution'. Numerous other interpretations have been offered, including the idea that it was simply an accident, an irrational 'happening', a motiveless outburst of extremism. Whatever started it, the young were violently infected (many of them were set in motion by the mere prospect of exams — their first obstacle in a permissive society); so were the intellectuals of Paris, who for a time lived in a dream world of delirious oratory. The movement quickly turned into a violent attempt to overturn the régime, and became controlled by a communist group who used it to make purely material demands. Finally the whole thing collapsed after one speech by General de Gaulle.

The results achieved were hardly what the rioters expected. No revolution, no administrative reform, hardly any political change even. But a few revelations: one, the inability of the 'establishment' to cope in the way it had in 1934; another, that the return of a government of the left to power was quite out of the question for the majority of people. Some thought it a demonstration of mass wisdom, others of apathy on the part of the working classes who rejected riot and preferred the ballot to the barricade. What was quite certain was that historical determinism had led them, all unconsciously, to stick to the 'consuming society'.

The results may have turned on the new prime minister's action (modelled on Kennedy's 'new frontier' and Johnson's 'Great Society') in creating the 'New Society' which was to be 'prosperous, young, generous and liberated', and to replace 'our archaic and conservative social system'. As it moves towards the distant fulfilment of this vast plan governmental action becomes more and more subdued, its everyday policy increasingly devoted to social pacification and the immediate satisfaction of claims from any social group immediately they become embarassingly loud. Such will to appease, with such featherbedding tactics, creates the illusion of a society without conflict and a government without power — a fulfilment of the doctrines of the radical party at the end of the nineteenth century.

documentation

Table V.4 Prices and wages: 1905–1958

| | Prices | | Hourly wages (1911 = 100) | |
	Wholesale	Retail	Paris	Provinces
1905	83	83		
1906	88	83	97	96
1907	92	85		
1908	86	87		
1909	86	—		
1910	92	89		
1911	96	98	100	100
1912	100	97		
1913	98	100		
1914	100	100		
1915	137	119		
1916	185	134	118	
1917	256	160		
1918	332	207		
1919	349	259		
1920	499	357		
1921	338	312	401	502
1922	320	300		
1923	410	333		
1924	479	380	440	563
1925	539	407	472	607
1926	688	530	580	700
1927	604	553	582	720
1928	607	552	597	750
1929	598	586	693	833
1930	521	590	755	883
1931	443	567	751	883
1932	391	517	721	868
1933	373	500	721	846
1934	352	479	721	846
1935	333	439	710	820
1936	388	471	802	961
1937	541	593		1 217
1938	614	673	1 212	1 341
1939	645	717	1 242	1 368
1940	847	851	1 239	1 378
1941	1 038	998	1 376	1 559
1942	1 216	1 199	1 397	1 787
1943	1 412	1 489	1 447	1 974
1944	1 590	1 820	2 552	3 452
1945	2 247	2 700	3 876	5 960
1946	3 874	4 119	5 423	8 060
1947	5 894	6 145	6 590	9 555
1948	10 162	9 752	10 140	15 310
1949	11 341	11 037	10 580	15 890

Table V.4 (*continued*)

| | Prices | | Hourly wages (1911 = 100) | |
	Wholesale	Retail	Paris	Provinces
1950	12 282	12 141	11 950	17 050
1951	15 685	14 116	17 250	24 850
1952	16 433	15 794	17 930	26 000
1953	15 685	15 529		
1954	15 412	15 595		
1955	15 390	15 739		
1956	16 059	16 401		
1957	16 977	16 897		
1958	18 928	19 448		
1959	19 835	20 643		

Source: Annuaire statistique, 1961.

Table V.5 Net monthly salaries: 1938—1959

| | | Single | | Married with 2 children | |
		Paris	Provinces	Paris	Provinces
1938	— October	1 605	1 001	1 793	1 124
1939	— —	1 749	1 077	2 015	1 245
1940	— —				
1941	— —	1 765	1 152	2 326	1 515
1942	— —	1 905	1 328	2 557	1 812
1943	— —	2 169	1 548	2 895	2 039
1944	— —	3 050	2 376	4 528	3 396
1945	— —	4 771	4 222	6 714	5 596
1946	— —	7 124	6 070	11 067	8 793
1947	— —	9 856	8 083	14 330	11 762
1948	— —	16 034	13 108	24 363	20 084
1949	— —	17 206	13 985	25 555	21 388
1949	— Average	17 103	13 937	25 445	21 337
1950	— —	19 843	15 608	28 412	23 106
1951	— —	24 882	19 863	35 614	29 239
1952	— —	28 823	22 884	41 190	33 690
1953	— —	30 507	23 775	42 223	34 074
1954	— —	32 567	25 342	44 794	36 031
1955	— —	34 819	27 250	47 455	38 487
1956	— —	37 109	29 260	49 594	40 694
1957	— —	41 183	31 880	54 044	43 572
1958	— —	44 976	35 221	58 740	47 520
1959	— —	46 964	37 114	61 384	49 778

Source: Annuaire statistique, 1961.

Table V.6 Monthly net earnings of workmen
(from base index 100, 1 January 1956)

Date	Single		Married with 2 children	
	Paris	Provinces	Paris	Provinces
1956	100.0	100.0	100.0	100.0
1957	111.8	109.1	108.7	107.2
1958	125.1	121.4	120.5	117.8
1959	129.5	127.3	124.6	122.3
1960	139.5	138.0	133.8	131.6
1961	153.1	149.3	144.6	140.6
1962	166.3	163.1	156.7	152.9
1963	181.5	179.6	169.5	167.1
1964	193.8	193.7	180.3	178.7
1965	202.0	203.0	188.2	187.3
1966	215.4	216.3	199.2	197.8
1967	226.5	229.0	208.0	207.2
1968	236.6	238.7	214.9	213.5
1969	266.9	274.2	241.0	243.0
1970	283.0	293.3	257.2	262.0
1971	308.8	321.9	278.4	284.1

Source: Ministère du Travail, Statistiques Sociales.

Table V.7 Annual expenditure of Parisian working class families,
1906 and 1936—7

	1906[1]	1936—7[2]
Food and drink	1 460	11 620
Lodging	370	1 480
Heat and light	125	1 580
Clothing	183	2 370
Furniture	65	745
Medicine	20	387
Doctor		999
Dentist		432
Personal	17	492
Tobacco	26	209
Transport	42	730
Reading matter	8	225
Subscriptions (union, insurance)	13	126
Entertainments		154
Miscellaneous	24	781
TOTAL	2 353	22 330

1. Average of 5 families in old francs.
2. Average of 4 families in old francs.

Table V.8 Annual expenditure on food and drink of Parisian working-class families, 1906 and 1936—7

| | Amount consumed[1] | | Expenditure in francs | |
	1906	1936—7	1906	1936—7
Bread	900	600	243	1 220
Meat	128	262	351	2 480
Charcuterie	12.4	49.5	39.5	570
Fish	8.5	40	13.8	325
Butter	52.8	23.5	52.8	515
Eggs	440 (ho)	629 (ho)	66	407
Sugar	75	59.5	54	229
Groceries	—	90.5	6	270
Rice	8	5.7	5	24
Pasta	4	36.6	6	186
Cheese	20	43.6	56.5	508
Milk	280 litres	490 litres	109	720
Potatoes	190	297	28.3	271
Beans	30	25.2	30	156
Fruit	—	211	—	628
Coffee	9.3	14.6	53	284
Chocolate	4.75	12.9	18.9	189
Wine	910 litres	730 litres	204	1 440
Miscellaneous	—	—	123.2	1 198
TOTAL			1 460	11 620

1. In kg.
After HALBWACHS (M.), 'Genre de vie', *Revue d'économie politique*, 1939, pp. 438—55.

Table V.9 Household expenditure in 1969

	1	2	3	4	5
Cereal foods	957	766	896	710	766
Vegetables	839	742	866	712	708
Fruit	382	318	579	501	425
Meat, eggs, fish	3 374	2 917	3 554	2 894	2 722
Milk, cheese	753	634	706	720	690
Fats	617	469	416	393	428
Miscellaneous	326	314	348	324	279
Drink	1 030	1 025	1 308	1 090	1 030
Home grown produce	2 990	1 277	378	219	365
Eating out	527	596	1 446	1 323	861
Food total	11 795	9 058	10 497	8 886	8 274
Clothing	1 848	1 597	3 313	2 934	1 970
Housing	2 799	1 766	5 805	5 246	3 845
Health	1 539	1 115	1 785	2 065	1 506
Transport, communications	2 175	1 466	5 911	4 139	2 247
Leisure activities	918	708	2 764	2 066	1 164
Miscellaneous	2 014	893	4 711	2 992	1 510
Non-food total	11 293	7 545	24 289	19 442	12 242
Total consumption	23 088	16 603	34 786	28 328	20 516
1956 compared					
Food total	4 777	3 241	5 318	4 277	4 083
Non-food total	3 783	2 300	9 582	7 295	3 993
	8 560	5 541	14 900	11 572	8 076

Family averages, in 'new francs', by profession of head of family
1. Farmers.
2. Farmworkers.
3. Heads of industry, big business, liberal professions.
4. Middle managers.
5. Workmen.

Fig. V.4 Sources of income averaged over total population, 1954

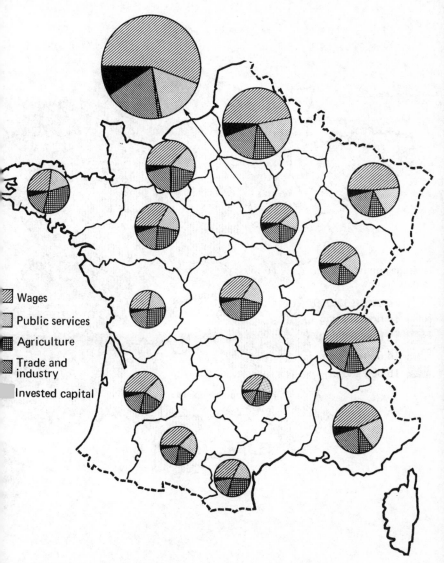

Wages
Public services
Agriculture
Trade and industry
Invested capital

ource: N. Delefortrie, J. Morice, *Les Revenus départementaux en 1864 et en ·54* (Paris, Colin, 1959).

Fig. V.5   Average family incomes by region, 1965

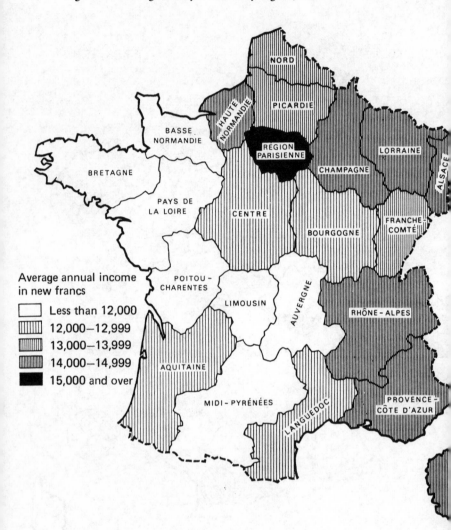

Fig. V.6   Inequality of incomes, 1960, *Monthly family incomes in new francs (from tax records)*

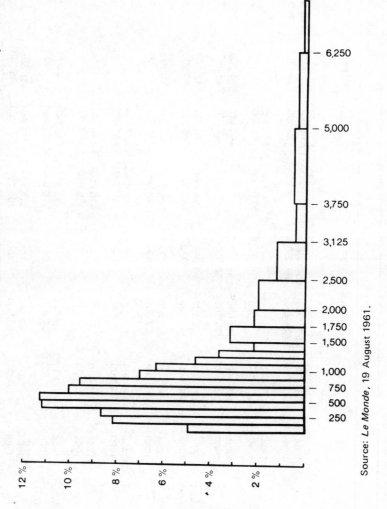

Source: *Le Monde*, 19 August 1961.

Table V.10 Working population, by professions 1954 and 1968 census

		Men				Women		
		Total	Independent or employers	Members of family	Wage-earners	Total	Independent or employers	Members of family	Wage-earners
Agricultural entrepreneurs	1954	2 320 211	1 636 045	684 166		1 645 804	279 519	1 366 285	
	1968	1 527 780	1 229 700	298 080		932 060	169 140	762 920	
Farm workers	1954	987 422			987 422	173 934			173 934
	1968	527 200			527 200	61 000			61 000
Industrial and business chiefs	1954	1 455 298	1 346 688	98 610		856 118	504 255	351 863	
	1968	1 276 940	1 220 360	56 580		685 040	381 360	303 680	
Liberal professions and top management	1954	477 467	102 167	1 056	374 244	76 252	13 149	7 263	55 840
	1968	806 600	116 700	1 040	688 860	186 200	20 800	8 540	156 860
Middle management	1954	704 196	9 602	174	694 420	408 347	16 290	760	391 297
	1968	1 197 360	17 680	840	1 178 840	816 740	16 900	1 780	798 060
Employees	1954	975 894			975 894	1 092 224			1 092 224
	1968	1 188 300			1 188 300	1 841 000			1 841 000
Workmen	1954	5 015 010			5 015 010	1 474 861			1 474 861
	1968	6 128 840			6 128 840	1 569 760			1 569 760
Members of service industries	1954	196 841	15 924	146	180 771	820 948	9 478	397	811 073
	1968	2 245 200	27 600	1 060	216 540	925 860	2 500	2 480	920 880
Armed forces, clergy, etc.	1954	379 687	68 396	161	311 130	134 250	115 898	436	17 916
	1968	417 420	61 380	260	355 780	105 260	85 040	600	19 620
TOTAL	1954	12 502 026	3 178 822	784 313	8 538 891	6 682 738	938 589	1 727 004	4 017 145
	1968	12 315 640	2 673 420	357 860	10 284 360	7 123 520	675 740	1 080 000	5 367 780

Traditional peasant life

(As described by a young woman from a small rural *commune* in the Isère)

I am twenty and I have no friend of my own age. I live in a little village in the Isère and help my father and mother, my brother and an aunt, on our twenty acre farm. My future way of life was decided for me when I was a child, and there has only been one big day for me — when I got my certificate at school. That marked a nasty change. I had to put away my books, though I longed to go on learning. School was a happy time for me, though for my parents it was just a useless waste of two strong arms. When I left school there were four of us to work, and a year later my brother got his certificate and had to join us.

The very day after my exam my books went into the cupboard, never to come out again. I put on an old hat and an apron, like my parents, and started milking Roussette. She was the nicest of our six cows and didn't kick like the others. She was small and didn't give much milk, but it was very creamy. I seemed to have always known Roussette, and when we finally decided to sell her she was so old she couldn't walk.

There is no time to be bored on our farm. Everything it is possible to grow, we grow. This is in order to buy as little as possible. But it also means a great dispersal of effort.

The milk collector comes early in the morning. He comes to our farm first on his rickety cart pulled by his old horse. He collects 500 or 600 litres of milk a day. He always knows the local gossip and comes in to tell us all he knows. We love this and make him stay as long as we can. In winter he only comes every other day and then we watch the milk to make sure it keeps fresh.

After milking we have to feed the animals. This takes up a good part of the day. In summer they remain in the fields for most of the day. But in winter they have to be fed with what one can find. Hay, from permanent pastures, is mixed with dry lucerne. The straw for litter is stacked in an orchard fifty metres away and, come rain come shine, has to be carried daily to the byre by the fork-load. The roots, for fodder, are in an old shed about a hundred metres away together with grain for the fowls. Our well is at the end of the yard. I wheel barrow-loads of roots, and carry buckets of water. My arms and legs are weary with kilometres of fatigue. If we paid someone else to do all this work the cost would be appalling; but this has never occurred to anyone.

In spring the fruit trees and the vines are pruned. There is about a fifth of an acre of vines which yield about a thousand litres of rather acid wine for our consumption and some for our neighbours. In the spring we sow barley and oats for the cattle, and food for the hens. We sometimes mix some clover or lucerne with the winter wheat; but half the time this fails to come up. We also plant a patch of potatoes, sufficient for all the needs of the year. We eat a lot of them. The best are sold. Some are fed to the pigs, cows and poultry.

There are seed-beds of beetroot and maize which are useful as fodder for the cattle when the grazing areas are mowed at the end of summer. Alongside we leave enough room to plant beans, turnips and cabbages. As soon as the cabbages are planted, we harvest the coleseed, which is treated by the local oilman to produce enough colza oil for the whole year.

Then it is time for gathering in the hay from all the fields. This takes several weeks. The grass is left to ripen so that the seed is automatically sown for new grass to grow, or else it is gathered in and the seed is sown on other ground.

The rye is harvested and then the corn. The rye is used to make straw. We hold back the best seed from the corn for next year's harvest. When the harvest is finished we quickly plough a few stubble-fields in order to plant buckwheat which is ripe in October.

Everyone joins in the harvest. The women have to do their housework as well as work in the fields. The neighbours remind us how lucky we are to be able to do the harvest without calling on others. We cope with everything ourselves, although occasionally a neighbour will come and give us a hand in return for the loan of a horse for a day. We do need help for threshing and when this goes on the women work in the kitchen after having tended the animals.

We sell a bit of corn — probably about one ton. We keep some back for seed and some for poultry food, and exchange some for bread. The income from the sale of the corn to a dealer in a neighbouring small town, from the sale of 10,000 to 15,000 litres of milk, and the sale of five or six calves, is more or less the only money which falls into our hands.

This money is carefully put by. It will be used for buying up a plot of land, for equipment — a new reaper, a harrow or a plough.

When we are absolutely obliged to buy new clothes we keep back something from the sale of cheeses, eggs and poultry. But groceries must be bought first.

We sometimes add a little extra to our Sunday lunches by eating one of the older hens, and sometimes rabbits. Very rarely, when we sell a calf, we bring back some butcher's meat. Generally we eat salt-pork with home-grown vegetables, and usually potatoes. We never have red meat. Steak is simply never seen in the house because it is too expensive. We fill up with bread and any unsold goats' cheese. Sometimes my mother brings back some charcuterie and fruit, but only if the poultry has sold well in the market.

Twice a week the baker comes to the village square and sells bread. A grocer comes twice a month. We buy sugar, coffee, rice and pasta from him. He buys eggs and goats' cheese from us. He likes to stay and gossip, too.

We are absolutely cut off from news. We have neither radio nor newspapers. We have few visitors because we are so isolated.

In the nearby village the girls who are older than me have married or have left for the town. The only girl in my class who is left lives at the other end of the village and works in the local factory. She spends some of her money and saves some. Her parents don't want her to be a farmer like themselves. They say that she should not tire herself out farming for little gain at such a dirty job. Every summer she buys a new dress. She goes to the cinema, goes dancing, reads magazines, has her Sundays free and has time to meet her friends. But I never go out, except for urgent shopping. I have only been to the cinema three times. I never read a newspaper and for me Sunday is just another working day.

The household is haunted by constant anxiety and the fear of imminent catastrophe: of illness, of a bad harvest, of frost, of death of one of the beasts, or of a creditor who cannot pay what he owes. There is no money to pay for the care of any of us should we fall ill. This fear for tomorrow makes work even more exhausting. We are a small, isolated world enclosed by our own habits and daily routines, from which there seems to be no escape. My mother has not even been to the capital of the *département* 60 kilometres away.

This is an account of my daily life until I was twenty-two. I didn't exactly suffer, but in a way it was worse because I was used to my life and didn't wish to change it, and never took the opportunities of seeing something new, even if it only meant being away for a few hours. I devoted myself to the needs of my parents, and I never thought that I should do anything else. My life was my work, and all the daily tasks that involved. The thought of change never occurred to me.

M. DEBATISSE, *La Révolution silencieuse. Le combat des paysans* (Calmann-Lévy, 1963) pp. 21–7.

The agricultural revolution in Aquitaine

The last thing one might have expected in 1950 was the modernization of agriculture in Aquitaine. Life there had changed very little; in spite of the 1946 legislation on share-cropping hardly any land had changed hands and the rural population, though increased since 1940, had shown little sign of migrating. But life in the country was not too bad. Although not a great deal was produced the markets were so short of everything that good prices were earned. Very little fertilizer was used, mechanization was hardly thought of, investment was low and living conditions remained simple and unmodernized.

There were no obvious signs of change. The black market of the war years and later had provided many farmers with a certain amount of cash, which tended to be devalued before they knew what to do with it. Banking it was out of the question for those who still remembered the bank failures of 1931. Some way of spending it had to be found and the panic that spread through farms and villages when the 5,000 franc notes were recalled unleashed a rush to buy things at any price. There was not much to buy, and what there was was of poor quality. People would have liked to build, but there was a shortage of steel and cement. So there was a rush for tractors. They were scarce, but they seemed a good investment for the future. This was a slow start, but it might have been much slower. Some of the tractors remained in their sheds, but most of them were used. Sales gradually increased, boosted by competition and concessionary petrol prices.

By 1955 people were beginning to say that tractors had become such an obsession that many small holders were over-equipped. Ten years later when the number of tractors had doubled or tripled the fallacy of this belief became clear. In Lot-et-Garonne in 1945, for instance, among 28,000 farmers there were about 1,000 rather dilapidated machines; by 1952 there were 3,300; in 1955, 5,437; and in 1960, 11,000.

Mechanization was not the answer to all problems. Its effect varied according to the milieu. For the first time in history in the Gers the soil of the clay slopes was regenerated by deep ploughing with heavy tractors. This was a revival in better conditions of the old deep digging which had been given up for lack of labour in the previous century. Moreover it was quick, so that it could be finished while the soil was in just the right condition, something which the slow pace of the ox could never achieve. The ox team was becoming uneconomic. It ate the surplus produce which was needed for sale. By replacing it with a tractor one could use some of the surplus to fatten calves.

It was a considerable investment, and this made the farmer keep proper accounts, which he had never done before. This made him realize the need for increasing his output by using his tractor for spreading fertilizer and sowing some of the new wheats which were appearing — particularly the famous 'Etoile de Choisy'. This, the first of a series of high-yielding strains, produced 3,000 to 4,000 kilos per hectare instead of the 1,000 to 1,200 of older varieties. This unprecedented success gradually did away with the age-old inferiority of Aquitaine to the Paris basin as a wheat-producing area. Yields of 5,000 kilograms per hectare became common, and thanks to deep ploughing and fertilizers the impact of climatically bad years became progressively less serious.

Another difficulty overcome was that of access-roads to farms on marshy ground, which became impassable after heavy rain. A start on improving them was made in 1945 with German prisoner-of-war labour. Then the Ponts et Chaussées helped the *communes* with money and materials to enlarge and improve both main roads and country lanes. This was of course done all over France, but in Aquitaine, the character of soil and slope made it uniquely valuable. The metalled road combined with the new wheat and the heavy tractor to restore the dilapidated farms of the Gers and Agens to profitability. To take a further instance: the repatriated farmers from Algeria could never have undertaken the regrouping and enclosing of small holdings into huge wheat growing estates without their heavy tractors and lorries. The new network of country roads has undoubtedly been a decisive factor in the agricultural revolution that has transformed local life in the years 1955—65.

Another factor which started a further cycle of change in the Adour was the result of American experiments in the hybridization of maize in the years 1930—40. The aim was to facilitate machine reaping by producing plants of consistently equal height. This would also produce, by the use of fertilizers, the heaviest cropping. The first|trials|of this variety were made in the Adour in 1948 and they were immediately successful. In 1949 out of a total of 41,000 hectares 3,000 were sown with this maize, and in 1955 almost half of all growers had taken it up. In the Landes progress was slower and it was only sown on a third of all land used. By 1960 hardly any of the original maize was sown anywhere.

In a land where dyed-in-the-wool conservatives swore — admittedly after a few drinks — that no 'American muck' would go into their soil, this success is astonishing, and it is due to the government's agricultural services and the 'Jeunes agriculteurs'.

ENJALBERT, *Histoire d'Aquitaine* (privately printed, 1971).

Demoralization of the workers

The worker always feels, at heart, that his lot will never improve. A fighter in the Spanish Civil War from 1936 to 1938 put it in his own words. 'We workers are always at the bottom of society. We were at the bottom during the Civil War, then in the emigration both in camps and when we were freed from them, in France or in Mexico. We are the underdogs in the factory – today as yesterday, in the union, in the party and in society, and it will never be otherwise. When I joined the militia, I thought this might change. . . .' Yet the same worker would tell you that when socialism triumphs the workers will run the factories because their political party is in power. Although he has an inborn conviction of what life really holds for him he continues to mouth sentiments he barely understands. Once he stops deluding himself with slogans and takes a dispassionate look at things he becomes disillusioned.

As one worker said, 'When I was young I thought all this would change. I thought that the worker could become a God in society. But as I get older I become more cynical, more disappointed. . . .'

Perhaps there is still hope. Perhaps this disappointment is a temporary set-back. But this is not the case. The worker continues, 'When I was thirty I thought that we had been let down . . . that everything would have to be started again . . . but in the end I realized that this was impossible. The trade unionists believed that revolution would release the workers from their chains of servitude, but there will always be such chains. There will never be equality, not even equality of wages. The revolutionary syndicalists are just dreamers.'

All those former militants are thus in agreement. The workers are convinced that within factories and firms there will always be an administrative hierarchy which hardens into a social hierarchy, and within these hierarchies the ones who really produce will be at the bottom of the ladder while those who do not, but simply direct, will always dominate. The worker found that most of the workers in the factory considered that the very fact of working at their machines destines them to be obeyers of orders rather than givers of orders. They might talk otherwise, but this was their basic point of view.

Work is therefore no longer seen as a liberating force but as a curse. Those who do the most work become instruments of profit, benefiting those who do the least work. Work keeps the worker down. The idea of work as a social liberating force is now regarded as a myth, whereas fifty years ago the idea was sacred. This is the true essence of the change in the worker's attitude to his work.

ANDRIEUX, A., LIGNON, J., *L'ouvrier d'aujourd'hui* (M. Rivière, 1960) pp. 66–7.

The workers' style of life and political attitudes

There have certainly been changes in the style of life and in the political attitudes of the workers. The old terms 'proletariat', 'workers' fight' have lost much of their old emotional significance, although not all of it. The workers do not all live like bourgeois, though a great many wage earners have got drawn into a way of life that sets a premium on material comfort and well being. Militancy has not disappeared, but the sense of values that lay behind it has been sapped.

Before 1950 there was a tendency for the better-paid workers in their forties to assume a 'bourgeois' style of life. But nowadays this happens around the age of thirty.

Ten, twenty or thirty years ago workers would begin to think of relaxing, of spending a bit of money on their families when the head of the household was over forty. But nowadays political and union militancy tends to fade out about ten years earlier. The standard of living is rising at rather a faster pace and promotion at work is rather faster too, since workers come to the top of their particular promotion ladders at a rather earlier age. There is now more security at work, and with retirement pensions the end of the workers' working life is viewed with less apprehension.

Modern industrial society thus quickens the transition from youth to adult life, especially for men. Men earning an adequate wage at twenty already feel themselves to be men. Marriage usually occurs after military service, if it has not already taken place. Women also work more, and the fact that they work is taken for granted. The second wage is usually used to purchase greater material comforts, which are purchased soon in married life, before motherhood obliges the wife to give up her job, even if temporarily.

If one is going to keep up with the neighbours one has to have, by the age of thirty, electrical domestic equipment, a car, a television. The cunning propaganda of modern industry has created these symbols of social standing: one reason why the worker buys a car which he only uses for two months of the year. Of course these manifestations of 'modest comfort' cause further involvements: with a car the family has to be taken out on Sunday; with a television one does not need to think, and one's evenings are occupied; electrical equipment encourages the search for new aids to comfort bought by hire purchase.

These new factors have led to the workers taking up different political attitudes. Militancy is giving way to 'responsibility', in that commitment to a particular political or trade-union ideal is less total than before, and is more likely to be tempered by other factors. The word 'militant' involves a certain largeness of spirit and will to sacrifice hardly consistent with the enervating effect of modern life. The militant battles for an ideal, but the 'responsible' man is not fully committed to the ideal. His commitment is only partial; he limits his activity to chosen objectives. To my mind the dramatic aspect of the French left is that it has overlooked, whether deliberately or not, this descent from a life of all-out vigour to a limited commitment of a pragmatic rather than ideological kind.

A phenomenon which is just as significant as the urge to possess televisions and motor cars is the result of holidays with pay. The French working man spends proportionately more on his holiday than anyone else. The family savings of six months of the year are devoted to it. The annual break from work, lasting for about a month, is regarded as so sacred that one wonders if any kind of political cataclysm occurring between June and September would dent this seasonal indifference to affairs of state not only of workers but even of the average citizen.

These are the realities which have to be faced, and they deserve further analysis. The basic factors affecting working class political behaviour are as follows:

— The development of credit facilities.
— The importance of television and radio, which are to be found in nearly every home. The views expressed are particularly absorbed by those who have no alternative source of information, or by those who cannot read with any great facility and have not got the cultural background which might enable them to evaluate the torrent of pictures and works that pours on them daily.
— Transport developments enabling workers to escape their home *milieu* for the weekend.
— Increasing home comforts which make evenings out less attractive. Union meetings that take place after 8 pm are increasingly thinly attended.

This 'embourgeoisement' of an increasing number of the working class makes them more open to special kinds of political propaganda. Today the urge for revolution, ideological vigour, opposition for its own sake no longer interest people. What matters are certain economic indicators and the likelihood of political parties acting on them – employment, cost of living, economic growth, internal stability, etc.

While the parties of the left only study sociology (rather inadequately) so as to make facts conform to their theories, those of the right draw conclusions about public opinion from investigation and statistics which give practical help in shaping their propaganda. The right determines its policy on these indicators because of their obvious popular appeal, the left (and frequently the unions as well) neglect them in favour of structural reforms, which though vitally necessary are described in jargon that only 'militants' appreciate. The left have not even the credit of having achieved economic reform (social welfare, worker participation, etc.) but have left that to the right. Why did not the government formed after the elections of January 1956[1] think of that sort of reform (which cost the economy nothing)? Whatever one's opinion of the motivation or opportunism of these reforms, they exist, and will survive.

And this goes to show that the increased range of choice earned by the worker and the newly-won power to decide on consumer priorities encourages a strong sense of what is practical. The change from a purely subsistence budget to one where one can actually spend money on one's social standing makes the worker, understandably, more and more concerned with political realities. Household economy is a microcosm of national economy and if the workers are weak on macro-economics they understand increasingly well an elementary version of the subject. The more they know abour national budgetary problems the less impressed they will be by the grand revolutionary utterances of unrealistic demagogues.

This is a subject demanding much more research: why are certain consumer goods given priority, what is the role of advertising and hire purchase? Such an analysis of consumption may throw some light on working class political action. Meanwhile it is no use regretting the disappearance of a type of man we once held dear; we have to try and guide this new and powerful force towards an ideal of life where

---

[1] The *Front Républicain* government under Guy Mollet.

comfort and welfare are only one element in a society of genuinely human dimensions.

DETRAZ. A. 'Consommation ouvrière et attitude politique', *Les nouveaux comportements politiques de la classe ouvrière*, (P.U.F., 1962) p. 248–52.

The mentality of managerial man ('cadres')

The psychology of this go-getting child of modern technical education bears a strangely Parisian imprint. He is a product of the Paris of government, of higher education, of competitive exams, of company boards, a world in itself which has no use for family tradition and in which it is every man for himself. Provincial life has its own narrow viewpoint, its slow and prescriptive way of life. Paris has changed all that and one need not live there to realize it. Cinema, radio and the press never stop telling the rest of France.

To the shocked dismay of the cautious bourgeois he wants to get the best out of life quickly and realizes that others do too: not that this stops him from treading on them if they get in the way of his ambitions. He is completely self-centred in this respect, though he is not incapable of generosity. He shares the bourgeois liking for material goods but not their hoarding instinct. A carefree spender, he feels no need to economize.

Even when he is hard up he likes to make a show of affluence. He has a car, or hopes to have one. It would not occur to him to let his wife have a maid but he will give her domestic equipment unheard of by their parents and which in any case they would not have bought before buying a home. For he likes to be contemporary and he doesn't mind about appearances. If he does buy a house or apartment he stretches his means to the utmost and does it in a big way. In general, though, he is restless. Why stay for ever in the same place? To some extent he vents this feeling of restlessness in travel. The French all go away on holiday and he likes to go far afield visiting foreign countries with car and tent, with an interest less in monuments than new faces. Daily life also provides human contacts, though of a different kind. No more tea parties, a smaller social circle, but a closer one; fewer formal parties but relationships between families, who visit each other without ceremony. The wife of the 'managerial man' has an individuality hardly attained by her bourgeois grandmother. Young men and women mix freely in lecture rooms, on sports grounds and on holiday. They marry while both are young, without fuss over family or dowry. Tastes in common matter more than birth or money. Whatever her qualifications the wife has often had a job before or in the early days of married life; she too is a 'technician' be it a lab assistant, a teacher or a secretary, and only changes it to take charge of her mechanized home. Here she is the boss, and recognized as such by her husband. Their home is a joint enterprise, serving the 'managerial' ideal of efficiency and authenticity.

The 'managerial man' has acquired his sense of values from men and machines, which have taught him that his status in his firm and his ability to control forty employees or three hundred workmen owe nothing to birth. He doesn't think it beneath him to roll up his sleeves and help with the washing up or to open the door to his friends wearing an apron. When he entertains he offers what he usually eats himself. He has no cellar and when he goes out to buy a decent bottle of wine he buys to please himself without considering his company. He spends what he earns without repining and doesn't mind saying how much it is. He insures his life and belongs to a pension scheme. If a windfall comes his way he may buy a few gold pieces, or he may blow it all on some gramophone records or a piece of china. He is not interested in saving capital for an investment income; the only capital he is interested in is a sum sufficient for a deposit with a building society. He may have a little fling on the stock exchange, but if he does he tells his broker he wants capital gain, not extra income. For he is well aware that he is the man who pays surtax. He is rather proud of being the intelligent working backbone of the nation. The writer of these lines, himself a 'managerial man', considers this view not far from the mark.

The bourgeois thinks he earns a lot and cannot understand how he can spend still more. But the managerial wife has the family budget well in hand; she decorated the apartment herself so as to afford a fur coat. At her age her mother would have considered rabbit skin quite good enough and left the paintwork alone. The children's future would be her worry. But he thinks the children will get all the education they need; anyway they'll get by. He rather likes to use coarse language, particularly if he comes from a good family; it shows he didn't need birth and breeding to get a good job.

Self-centred and open handed, good husband and father, though a bit footloose, carefree and pragmatic, unbiased except in favour of his own success, unpredictable, occasionally idle, he is hard to define in systematic terms. It is still not clear what his place in society or his social obligations are. A new sort of world is evolving, and the 'cadre' is one of its first inhabitants. As time goes on the outline of a mentality which is still in its formative phase will gradually become discernible in literature, in politics and in ideological thought.

BLETON (P.), *Les hommes des temps qui viennent* (Les Editions ouvrières, 1956) 200—203.

The Gernelle Agreement (27 May 1968)

1. Increase of SMIG (*Salaire minimum interprofessionel garantie*, national minimum wage) to three francs an hour and relief for depressed regions.
2. Increase of wages by 7 per cent to June 1968 (including in this percentage increases granted since January 1968), increase to be 10 per cent in October.
3. Reduction of hours of work before the completion of the Fifth Plan (i.e. 1970) by two hours where more than forty-eight hours are worked already and by one hour where between forty-five and forty-eight hours are worked.
4. Inquiry into the improvement of family allowances for families with three or more children and those with a single wage-earner.
5. Increase of minimum old-age pension by 1 October 1968.
6. On employment and training: joint trade union and employers' body to explore, before 1 October (a) facilities for classification and retraining, and (b) institution of means for assuring jobs of equivalent status for redundant workers. The government to guarantee to make funds available for employment services and youth advisory services.
7. Social security: reduction of contribution from 30 per cent to 25 per cent and acceptance of a debate over the ratification of the Ordinances.
8. For time worked in recovery of time lost by strikes, payment in advance of 50 per cent of pay for hours worked.
9. Rights of trade unions inside businesses: creation of government plan after a meeting of professional and trade-union bodies to eliminate areas of disagreement.

DANSETTE, A., *Mai 1968* (Paris, Plon, 1971).

The incredible 'revolution'
(i) the facts
The events of May 1968 constitute a unique phenomenon in French political history. They were highly complicated and confused, and the

bare facts ought, therefore, to be summarized, in so far as that is possible, before the question of what it all meant is discussed. The whole affair resembled a conductorless, chaotic, and discordant symphony in three movements. The first, and longest, lasted from 2 to 18 May. At first, only students were involved. Workers' participation (the 'second subject') really came in only from about the middle of the month, and the two sides remained distinct throughout, although less distinct than union leaders wished them to be. There was also an important background of university unrest and of student conflicts with the authorities, going back to the autumn of 1967. But the events themselves really began with the decision on 2 May by the Dean of Nanterre to close the Faculty, following a series of provocative incidents, mainly inspired by the small band of anarchist students calling themselves *le Mouvement du 22 mars*, an organization founded by a sociology student, Daniel Cohn-Bendit.

The following day, after a protest meeting at the Sorbonne against the disciplining of M. Cohn-Bendit and a handful of his supporters, he and a number of students were arrested. The authorities had decided to call in the police, owing to threats of clashes with right-wing extremists, a decision regarded by students – and, indeed, almost all left-wing opinion – as an unacceptable infringement of the tradition of Sorbonne extraterritoriality. There was, consequently, a serious clash between police and students outside the building. Cobble-stones were thrown and the police used tear gas and truncheons. The Sorbonne was closed. On the following two days, students appeared before the court, and four were sent to prison. This, together with student resentment of police behaviour, brought more support for the revolutionaries from junior staff as well as students. A strike called on 6 May in support of the release of the imprisoned students led to clashes with the riot police and to the spread of sympathetic strikes in universities outside Paris and in some Paris *lycées*. By this time, Nanterre, the Sorbonne and the Censier annex to the Sorbonne had all been closed, and some 49,000 students were, therefore, unoccupied and free to demonstrate in the streets.

The night of 10 May (*la nuit des barricades*) saw the most violent clashes so far. The Minister had refused to negotiate and this time the riot police went in in force. The Prime Minister, M. Pompidou, who returned from a visit to Afghanistan on 11 May, immediately decided to make the three main concessions that the students had demanded as conditions for negotiation – the reopening of the Sorbonne, the withdrawal of police from it, and the freeing of the imprisoned students. But it was by then too late. The Centre Censier was occupied on 11 May, and when the Sorbonne opened on 13 May, the students occupied it too. On 14 May, Nanterre and Grenoble declared themselves independent universities. Other universities were demanding self-government, and almost all universities as well as a number of *lycées* were by then occupied.

Efforts were being made by students to associate 'the workers' with the movement. The Sorbonne was thrown open to 'workers' (undefined). But there had still been no systematic support from the trade-union movements for the student revolutionaries. Both CGT and Communist party leaders had, indeed, attacked them. The Communist majority on the Nanterre Municipal Council had issued a statement accusing the *'groupuscules'* — described as anarchists, Trotskyites, Maoists, etc. — of 'serving the purposes of the government, by preventing the normal working of the university'. The acting Communist leader, M. Georges Marchais, had called M. Cohn-Bendit and his supporters 'bogus revolutionaries who ought to be unmasked'. The first systematic contacts between the student union and the CGT and CFDT had originally resulted, on 10 May, in a joint decision to hold a demonstration on 14 May, in favour of *both* an amnesty for the imprisoned students *and* trade-union and political liberties. After the 'night of the barricades', however, this became the general strike of 13 May, in which all three main confederations took part. But the trade-union leaders still tried, though unsuccessfully, to keep the student and trade-union elements of the procession apart.

This date, nevertheless, marked a turning point. The demonstration was followed by an official CGT statement of working-class solidarity with the students. The following day, the first factory occupation took place — at the Sud Aviation plant near Nantes. It was followed by the rapid spread of factory occupations throughout the country. These did not have official CGT support, however, and CGT leaders continued to warn trade unionists against 'Leftists'. CFDT leaders were more sympathetic to spontaneous strikes, regarding them as indicative of growing support for 'workers' power'.

The second phase of the 'revolution' — the slow movement of this chaotic symphony — lasted from 18 May, when General de Gaulle returned from a four-day visit to Rumania, to 27 May. It was characterized by belated Government efforts to contain the movement, and by a continued policy of playing things very cool. By now, unofficial staff—student committees in many schools and universities were busily drawing up new constitutions providing for their joint responsibility in running the university or school, and some actually began to apply these provisional constitutions. Examinations – and in particular the all-important *baccalauréat* – had been postponed. Some of the new 'constitutions' had, indeed, abolished examinations. In Paris, the Odéon had been occupied, and the staffs of the State radio and television services had taken over control of their own programmes. Both in Paris and the provinces, the workers in all the nationalized industries were on strike, and so railways, the underground, postal, gas, and electricity services were all partially or wholly paralysed. It was estimated that, in all, between nine and ten million workers were idle.

Political parties had not, as yet, adopted any official position, except for the PSU, which was openly on the side of the revolutionaries. But on 20 May, the President of the Federation of the Democratic and Socialist left, M. François Mitterrand, called for elections, the Communists called for a joint programme with the Federation, and M. Pierre Mendès France called on the Government to resign. The CGT was still expressing opposition to the students' claims rejecting them as 'empty ideas on workers' control, the reform of society and other inventions', and pressing for specific measures – increases in wages, reductions of hours, guaranteed employment and improved conditions for trade-union activities in factories.

By then the whole affair seemed to have reached a curious stalemate. Neither side seemed to know what to do next. Between the 'night of the barricades' and 23 May, the violent clashes between police and students had ceased. The public was beginning to be more concerned about the effects of the strikes than about the students. On 22 May the Government adopted a Bill to amnesty imprisoned students – a belated and useless gesture, emphasizing the gulf between 'occupied streets, occupied universities, occupied factories and a preoccupied Government'. The National Assembly spent 21 and 22 May debating a motion of censure that failed to interest anyone. 'None of the speeches', wrote a well-known commentator, 'reflected even remotely the reality of a country paralysed by strikes and in which authority, law and the structure of society were all under challenge.' On 24 May, the President broke his silence by a short broadcast declaration promising a referendum on participation. Comprehensibly, this fell very flat, since, in the circumstances, no such referendum could have been held. The night before his broadcast and that following it saw a revival of street violence. On 27 May, after two days of negotiation, the Government and the main trade-union confederations reached agreements on wages and other demands (the Grenelle agreements), only to have them immediately rejected by the rank and file.

Though it was not apparent at the time, Monday 27 May proved to be a turning point. First, on 28 May, following a mass meeting the previous evening at the Charléty Stadium, at which the audience was adjured by one impassioned revolutionary speaker to make the revolution quickly, M. Mitterrand proposed at a press conference that in the event of the resignation of General de Gaulle and of the Prime Minister there should be a provisional Government of ten, and announced that he himself would then be a candidate for the presidency. At a press conference the following day, M. Mendés France, who had been mentioned by M. Mitterrand as his first choice as Prime Minister of such a provisional Government, stated that he would not refuse governmental responsibilities entrusted to him by a united Left. This surprising and controversial development focused attention on the political problem of the future of the régime. There followed two days in which political uncertainties were increased. The first was a day of irrelevancies. The Minister of Education's resignation was finally accepted. The date of the proposed referendum (which certainly could not be held) was given as 16 June, and the *Conseil d'Etat* stated that such a referendum would be unconstitutional. The second was a day of amxiety, during which General de Gaulle's intentions (and even his whereabouts) remained a mystery, and rumours of his impending resignation began to circulate. The day of decision came on 30 May. General de Gaulle made a brief, incisive and authoritative declaration, dissolving the National Assembly and announcing a general election forthwith. The referendum was adjourned *sine die*.

The announcement was immediately followed by a massive demonstration of support for him, in which thousands marched from the Place de la Concorde to the Arc de Triomphe. Though M. Mitterrand had himself called for an election, his reaction to the declaration was extremely hostile, and he even went so far as to describe it as 'the voice of dictatorship . . . a call to civil war'. It was, in fact, a call to normality, and the response was immediate. The Government was reshuffled, Ministers mainly concerned with the events being replaced. Negotiations between Government and trade unions were resumed and successfully concluded early in June. The French public left Paris and other towns in their thousands for the Whitsun weekend, after which strikers returned to work steadily during the following week. On 16 June, the last student bastion, the Sorbonne, was peacefully evacuated. The revolution was over.

(ii) queries and theories

'The French always magnify their revolutions in retrospect into great festivals, during which they experience all that they are normally deprived of, and so they have the feeling that they are achieving their aspirations, even if only in a waking dream.'

RAYMOND ARON, in *La Révolution introuvable; réflexions sur la révolution de mai*

'With the 22 March, the Soviets in the original and integral sense came to France. . . . The 22 March imitates all past revolutions, the Spanish war, the cultural revolution, 17 October, the Paris Commune, but with the aim of living and bringing to life the socialism of councils . . . these Soviets of a quite new kind, the "committees of students and workers".'

EDGAR MORIN in 'Conflict de générations et lutte de classes', *Le Monde*, 6 June 1968

The events left a host of unanswered question in the minds of people outside as well as inside France, uncertainties that the publication of some hundred books and innumerable articles over the following months did not dissipate. They confronted the Government with social and economic problems that took months to resolve, and of which some were not resolved. And they provided academics, politicians, and above all sociologists with material for unending post mortems, theories, arguments and controversies on what actually happened, what it had all meant and what it ought to have meant. Some of the questions call for an attempt at an answer in the political context of this book. Why was the student movement able to take hold so fast and go so far? Why did the Government and General de Gaulle remain inactive for so long? How did the left-wing political parties come to take it so seriously? And why did the disturbance die down so quickly?

An answer to the second question would seem to supply part of the answer to the first. Even a few weeks after the events, many observers who had seemed to take the movement seriously at the time could no longer do so in the light of the massive vote in the general election for General de Gaulle and for law and order. On the face of it, therefore, it looked as if stronger action by the Government could have prevented the movement from ever getting out of hand. In reality, however, the facts are less simple. The reactions of the public, for instance, changed perceptibly, so that what was possible in the later stages might not have been possible earlier. One thing can be said with some degree of certainty. Only in Paris, with its romantic revolutionary myths of barricades and torn-up cobble-stones, and with its traditional tolerance for students' political games, especially in cases of conflict with the police, could a collection of small, quarrelling, Maoist, Trotskyite and anarchist groups have hoped to escalate a university sit-in into a nation-wide threat (or apparent threat) to the State. And even in Paris it would not have lasted more than a token day or two, if it had not been for the existence of a quite exceptional conjunction of circumstances.

Two characteristics of the 'revolution' call for some comment, even if no credible explanation of them springs readily to mind. The first was the rapid contagion of the movement. This cannot be wholly explained away by the influence of radio and television, important as that was. It was a contagion that affected not merely students, but also sections of the community normally credited with a greater degree of level-headedness – a sudden delirium followed by a no less sudden oblivion.

> One after the other [wrote Pierre Viansson-Ponté] writers occupied the Hôtel de Massa, the headquarters of the *Société des Gens de Lettres; cadres* invaded the offices of the CNPF; young architects and young doctors occupied the offices of their associations; film technicians 'contested' the festival at Cannes and brought it to a halt. . . . All France exploded and challenged professional structures.

The second characteristic was the extent to which the 'revolution' engendered an inexhaustible flow of words, few if any of which left any discernible trace. At the Sorbonne (to quote Pierre Viansson-Ponté again):

> Sexuality, publicity, culture, society, art, ideologies, revolution – everything is questioned. People insult each other, get caught up and carried away in eternal blethering. Entry and speech are both free. . . .

The interminable debates in the Odéon, which had become a meeting-place for 'students and workers' – 'a permanent headquarters of creative revolution' – were described as:

> Verbal delirium, a perpetual flow of words, of which all that survived was the fact that it happened . . . a deluge of ideas, a tornado of words. . . . Demagogy, dreams, mad ideas, powerful ideas, new ideas – all drowned in an ocean of verbosity. . . .

Among the theories produced in explanation of this phenomenon, about half-a-dozen deserve some attention from politicians and political scientists, irrespective of the extent to which they carried conviction either then or later. The leading student revolutionaries and a number of academic supporters saw the revolution essentially as a revolt of youth against age and against a social system of which they proclaimed themselves victims. Many of them were sociologists. It was at Nanterre that the movement was launched. Nanterre housed the sociology department, and there were far too many students of sociology who were destined to find far too few jobs at the end of their studies. They saw, or professed to see, 'society trembling and the Establishment on the verge of collapse'. For them, the student revolution was, at the very least, 'a dress rehearsal', 'a pre-revolutionary situation'. It was a rediscovery of 'the essence of Revolution'. 'The *enragés* of 1968 set out to destroy civilization and prevent the victory of technocracy.'

What these revolutionaries sought to put in the place of technocracy and civilization was never made clear, either in the unending debates in the occupied Sorbonne or in subsequent analyses. According to Daniel Cohn-Bendit, there *was* no constructive side (in the accepted sense of that word) to the revolution. In an interview with Jean-Paul Sartre in the midst of the events, he stated categorically that his aim was a series of revolutionary outbursts – 'a succession of breaks in the cohesion of the system' (*des mouvements de rupture dans la cohésion du systéme*) – which he thought would fail, but that would destroy 'bourgeois' law and order in the process. Indeed, for him, the first priority was action, and only in the course of action would it become clear what its purpose was. Action itself was constructive, if it was directed towards the destruction of bourgeois society. He and his supporters put the theory into practice, by reducing parts of Nanterre University to a shambles, and making work impossible for its 11,000 students. 'We do not pretend to represent the majority', he is reported as saying. 'But our ten *enragés* at Nanterre have now become 1200.' One of the theorists of the 'revolution' wrote:

It was Daniel Cohn-Bendit who best understood that the only way to break through the doctrinal and organizational divisions was to fuse all radical groups in direct action with immediate aims. Being contagious, action would mobilize growing numbers of students and the tendency of the *groupuscules* to put theory first and to act according to pre-established patterns would be kept in check by mass participation and direct democracy in action committees, specialized working groups. . . . The practice of direct democracy and action would produce a new type of self-organized vanguard, abolishing all authority and responsibility, abolishing the division into 'leaders' and 'led', submitting the theorists to the criticism and control of the rank and file.

For other academic supporters, however, the 'revolution' was a purely utopian adventure. For Edgar Morin,

Those who believe that its mission was to trigger a workers' revolution and those who feel that it should have restricted itself to university reform have misunderstood its rôle. Precisely because it was utopian rather than constructive it was able to envisage a future which embraced the whole of society.

Offered the choice between, on the one hand, 'constructive destruction' and '*contestation*'[1] carried out on the off-chance that the reasons for them might emerge at some later date, and, on the other hand, a utopian fantasy that, in Edgar Morin's phrase, subsumed 'all the revolutions ever dreamed of, in a "quasi- or peri-revolution" – a "detonator" that would accelerate reform as well as the movement to contest the very basis of society', it is hardly surprising that there were those at the other extreme who dismissed the whole affair as '*révolutionnarisme*', 'a bogus revolution – play acting, which parodies memories of older tragedies, no longer repeatable or playable'. Supporters of this point of view emphasized that, if the student revolution was a demonstration against the 'consumer society', its main inspiration came from the products of it, for most of the students involved belonged to the middle or upper classes. In the words of a commentator looking back on the revolution two years later,

In a world where insurrection stops for the weekend, who would not share M. Waldeck Rochet's fear of this generation which is not revolutionary, but 'Swedish' – ready for any kind of fancy-dress that will provide a rôle for it to play. The crisis of 1968 revealed not so much '*contestation*' as a new kind of practitioner of it, both volatile and hypocritical. . . . The children of May resembled the world they attacked too much to imperil it.

[1] There is no satisfactory English rendering of the student revolutionary concept of '*contestation*'. It is 'disputation' that, in practice, implies the right of students to challenge academic authority by breaking up lectures (and even the university) and to challenge political opponents without tolerance and with no holds barred, as upholders of 'bourgeois' society.

Some of the manifestations of revolutionary enthusiasm were certainly more easily explicable on this thesis than on any other, for instance, what was often called its *'aspect folklorique'*. There was, wrote John Gretton, a sympathetic academic eye-witness,

> something more than a little bourgeois about this aspect of the student revolt (French students are essentially a bourgeois phenom-enon). From being an austere temple of learning (it was built at the end of the nineteenth century as a temple *to* French culture) the Sorbonne became a sort of gigantic theatre, a kind of 'Round House', where total freedom was allowed to everybody to live as they pleased and to express themselves in their own way, where the quadrangle resembled a garden fête . . . this kind of total rejection of normal social values is only possible for those who start off with a secure base in the society that they reject. The 'beat' or 'hippy' movements of the last two decades have recruited their followers almost exclusively among the middle classes.

The attempt to associate 'the workers' (never defined) with this aspect of the revolution was regarded even by some sympathetic academics as not merely bourgeois, but also either spurious or wildly romantic.

> To believe in the possibility of using an available and disorganized working class in order to bring about a fundamental socialist revolution by means of spontaneous action committees [wrote Professor Maurice Duverger] is to indulge in a frightening utopianism. The mass of the workers is not ready for any such thing, and the nation — which is predominantly conservative — would not support it. The nature of an industrial society rules out such methods.

Academic observers emphasized not only the essentially unrealistic nature of *'ouvriérisme'*,[1] but also the essentially non-educative nature of interminable 'teach-ins' — or rather talk-ins — in the occupied university. These were attended by ever-changing, haphazard audiences, spontaneously discussing heterogeneous subjects ranging from 'revolutionary warfare to the social function of orgies in the late Roman empire'. And the committees they set up began, of course,

> with sociology and went on to literature and sex . . . thousands of discussions which expressed and celebrated the vision of a university

---

[1] *'Ouvriérisme'* is an emotive term, meaning the attribution to a notional entity called 'the workers' of special virtues and special claims to leadership.

utopia where true knowledge, stripped of its 'class' content, could be interchanged freely. (Posner)

This was only one side of the picture. If what it describes was harmless, it was all the same unlikely to add to the sum of human knowledge. But there was another side. An example of it is provided by the factual account of what was actually involved in the application of the decision, announced in *Le Monde* on 5 June, to occupy the British Institute in Paris, rebaptize it *Institut britannique populaire* and invite 'workers' to join in organizing it as a 'critical university'. On 15 June, the Director of the Institute, Mr Francis Scarfe, wrote, in a letter to *The Times* (19 June 1968):

> The British Institute in Paris was thus occupied at 4 p.m. on June 4 by an anonymous group of students and non-students of various nationalities, including British, French, American, German, Dutch, Spanish, South American and Cuban. Since then it has proved almost impossible to negotiate with them as they are not students of this institute and the occupying body is constantly changing.
>
> . . . As a group they have turned the institute into a dosshouse for all comers, have fouled the premises, broken locks, destroyed doors and furniture, and written slogans all over the inside walls. They have hoisted black and red flags outside. They have prevented the institute from carrying out its legitimate functions. Apart from some £2000–£3000 damage which they have now done, their occupation has already caused a loss of income of about £10,000 to the institute, which has very limited resources, as well as imperilled its future. . . . Meanwhile the livelihood of 92 employees and their dependents is at stake, as well as the studies of about 6000 students. . . .

Whatever grievances the students had against French universities, they could have had none against this British institution. Clearly, in the revolutionary-student hierarchy, some 'workers and students' were regarded as being definitely less equal than others!

If there were 'hippy', 'beat', and 'squatter' elements among the revolutionaries, the revolution itself was a kind of *Fronde*, in that it had no coherent objectives. This led some observers to conclude that the escalation of the movement was purely fortuitous. It has been suggested that the various revolutionary theories were not a cause, but a consequence, being thought up *en cours de route*, or even after the event. For instance, Jacques Sauvageot of the students' union (UNEF),

Alain Geismar of the teachers' union (SNE-Sup), and Daniel Cohn-Bendit emerged as leading personalities in quite haphazard ways. They were not in any way representative of their respective organizations, and Daniel Cohn-Bendit himself rejected the whole concept of leadership. He did not play an active rôle after the first week or so, and he was actually out of the country for much of the time. The participating movements disagreed on both tactics and aims. Individuals and movements quite extraneous to either the student or the trade-union world joined in both occupations and demonstrations.

Though a number of participants interviewed appeared to have had only the vaguest ideas of what they hoped to achieve, many spoke of the need for reforms in the educational system, and a great many of the student and *lycée* action committees did actively concern themselves with trying to work out provisional plans for reform. For some of these would-be reformers, the spontaneity and licence of the revolutionaries were seen as reactions against the excessive formalism and rigidity of both school and university curricula and methods, and the main aim of the movement was reform of the educational system. Some of the plans that they produced were demagogic and unrealistic, but others were well thought-out and intelligent documents, produced by joint staff and student or staff and pupil committees. This aspect of the revolution was recognized as having made a positive, if only very limited, contribution to the actual reform of university education carried out later in the year.

None of these theories necessarily excludes any other, since the 'revolution' was essentially pluralistic and unorganized. There were also circumstances which exercised an indisputable influence over the development of the movement, but whose importance it is impossible to estimate with any degree of accuracy. Among these must be included the effects of radio and television reporting. It enabled organizations and areas to feel themselves part of a larger movement, directly encouraged imitative adventures, and so contributed to the speed with which strikes and occupations spread throughout the country. The influence of transistors had been much commented on during the 'revolt of the Generals'. Then, it was a factor that certainly strengthened the President's hand. In 1968, it equally certainly assisted the students.

Another factor of importance was the already existing acceptance by much of public opinion of a degree of violence in pressing political demands. General de Gaulle at first attributed the student revolt to 'the immense political, economic and social transformation' that France was going through, and therefore urged the need to adapt institutions to meet these new stresses, especially through participation. A week later, he had decided that it was due to 'intimidation, brain-washing and tyranny carried out by groups which for a long time have been organized by a totalitarian party'. M. Pompidou also emphasized the importance of changing structures, recalling events in the fifteenth century, 'that despairing period when the structures of the Middle Ages were collapsing and when students of the Sorbonne were also in revolt'. The students could quote precedents much nearer at hand – farmers' riots, the violence of small tradesmen's associations, and the concessions that followed the violence. M. Pompidou's own immediate announcement, on his return to Paris from Afghanistan, of concessions to student demands did not pass unnoticed. There had been ample evidence during the ten years of the Fifth Republic that violence paid. Why should it not pay for students and trade unions? 'The revolt of youth' (wrote Philippe Guilhane in *Le Monde*,) 'certainly went too far; but who would have listened to them without barricades, without burnt-out cars, without police batons?' Algerians, farmers, and small tradesmen had also concluded that violence was the only way of forcing the Government to pay attention to them. The Grenelle agreement and the Government's speedy introduction of the university-reform Bill immediately after the election could reasonably be seen as further confirmation of the accuracy of this view.

Nevertheless, although the revolt can be regarded as a 'happening' to which all these factors contributed something, and which evolved in a haphazard way in response to circumstances, without either coherent objectives or even an agreed strategy, it could reasonably be argued that it would not have become the unique phenomenon that it was without the conjunction of a number of political circumstances, none of which was in itself determinant. Two of these circumstances created a potentially revolutionary situation. They were, first, the existence of long-standing political, economic and social grievances, in this case caused primarily by the discontent of two specific sections of the community that seemed to have been left behind in upheavals of the economic and technological revolution. The too numerous – sometimes intellectually inadequate – pupils and students and the underpaid workers in nationalized industries and in under-modernized industries provided two large and permanently dissatisfied classes of the community, both of which had repeatedly proclaimed their grievances during the previous years.

The second circumstance was the underlying fear that the political system itself might be vulnerable. This was never far below the surface.

The fact that Gaullist leaders (and General de Gaulle in particular) so often claimed that the Fifth Republic had eliminated this constitutional vulnerability and established stable political institutions was in itself an indication of the extent to which both politicians and public needed to be reassured on this point and yet, despite reassurances, remained unsure. The frequent predictions of 'a crisis of the régime', when General de Gaulle ceased to be head of the State, frequent disagreements regarding interpretations of the Constitution, the growth of violence among certain sectional interests, the spread of extremist groups (some of them violent) on both Right and Left – all these helped to strengthen both memories of the ease with which in the past political crises had escalated into constitutional crises, and also fears that this might happen again.

To transform what was no more than a potentially dangerous situation into revolutionary action that threatened immediate danger, two additional conditions were required – the spark to ignite the conflagration and the high winds to spread it. The spark was provided by the Sorbonne incident, when what began as merely another in a long series of university incidents suddenly flared into a political challenge, thanks to the accidental conjunction of vacillations on the part of the authorities, traditional resentment of police action against students (both magnified by tactical errors), public apathy, and the presence on the spot of the potential mass support of some 40–50,000 involuntarily idle and resentful students.

The high wind, which enabled a confrontation between students and the authorities to develop rapidly into a nationwide political crisis, was the fact that the situation was capable of being exploited by at least four separate sections of the community. The factory workers used it in order to press their claims for better wages and conditions. Some teachers and students used it to publicize long-standing complaints about educational conditions, while revolutionary student minorities used it to preach 'instant' revolution. Left-wing politicians used it to try to recover the political appeal that had eluded them for ten years. And finally, when the spread of wildcat strikes became serious, the most powerful trade-union movement, the Communist-dominated CGT, was presented with the alternatives of coming in and trying to dominate the movement, or of being itself undermined by undisciplined groups of the ranks and file that it had been trying to control since 1966. All these elements were seeking to manipulate the 'revolution' to serve their own ends, but none of them in reality wanted a successful revolution, as was made clear by the speed with which normality was restored, once the trade unions, whose organizing ability was essential to the maintenance of the revolutionary movement's momentum, had reason to believe that their major demands could be met without its continuance.

Why and how did the Government allow the situation to get out of hand? Allowance must be made for the extent to which Governments in all developed countries have appeared powerless in face of the relatively new problem of direct and violent action by small 'commandos', whether in universities or in industry. In France, there were also a number of specific contributory factors. For one thing, the explosion was entirely unexpected. On 2 May, nobody foresaw its rapid escalation into a national threat. The Prime Minister was absent from 2 to 11 May in Afghanistan, and the three Ministers most vitally concerned (Education, the Interior and Justice) were all relative newcomers to their jobs. In addition, the Minister of Education had inherited from his predecessor the peculiarly delicate problem of a half-completed and highly unpopular reform of the school system. He was young and ambitious and so had not dared to do anything. Nor did he dare to take initiatives in May 1968. The situation of the university authorities was rendered more difficult by the nature of the French educational system, which was so highly centralized that almost all decisions of any importance had to be referred to Paris. Once the students had decided to defy the university authorities, they were, in reality, challenging the State, and what was needed was decisive action from the top. Not only was this not forthcoming from M. Pompidou until too late, but three days after he returned, General de Gaulle himself left on a visit to Rumania, just at the crucial moment when the industrial strike movement was beginning.

The first weaknesses, then, were uncertainties as to where authority really lay and failure to realize soon enough the potential seriousness of the situation. The domination of President and Prime Minister in the French quasi-presidential system inevitably tends to increase the danger of a vacuum of authority at the ministerial level. The result in this case was 'a classic example of how not to manage a crisis, of dithering, crossed lines of authority, flight from responsibility and of too little too late'.

The third question is: Why did the Left, and especially such experienced political leaders as MM. Mitterrand and Mendès France, make the political mistake, at the end of May, of appearing to present themselves as leaders of an alternative Government that would have been brought to power by insurrection and processions in the streets? This question is answerable only in the context of the traditional myths of the Left, and of its political frustration during the past ten years. M. Mendès France had always opposed the régime and had predicted, with what many even on the Left regarded as excessive confidence, that it would not outlive de Gaulle. He also believed that the change would come, 'not from a man, a group of men, parties' but from 'the voice of the people'. It was perhaps comprehensible, therefore, that he should eventually persuade himself that the May marches and mass meetings represented that voice.

M. Mitterrand was in a somewhat different position. As head of the left-wing Federation's 'shadow Cabinet' (*le contregouvernement*) and the former left-wing presidential candidate, he was the obvious candidate for power, if General de Gaulle were either to resign or to be beaten in the proposed referendum. His mistake was, first, to misread the state of public opinion, and second, to couch his statements in terms that could be used as more effective propaganda by his opponents than by his friends. The Left's over-estimate of the political importance of the movement has to be seen, too, against the background of the difficulties of a situation of apparently permanent opposition. The non-Communist Left had spent the past ten years in an effort to do several impossible things at once – to increase its own cohesion, and especially that of the Socialist party; to improve its image in the country, in which the Socialist party's appeal to the electorate had been steadily declining; to obtain a working electoral agreement with the Communist party in order to maximize its parliamentary representation, but without appearing to be dependent on the Communists; and finally, to present to the electorate an agreed statement (failing agreement on a joint programme) that could reasonably be expected to appeal to the electorate as the basis for an alternative Government.

Since these objectives were incompatible, if not unobtainable, the prospects of success, after ten years, still seemed remote. It was comprehensible that some Socialists should, if only for a brief period, allow themselves to be carried away to the extent of becoming the victims of their own myths. Like the revolutionary students, some saw themselves as re-living the revolutions of 1789, 1830, 1848, 1871 and, perhaps, especially 1936, when a general strike had been the prelude to a Popular Front Government. In reality, of course, though the 1936 strike has become part of Socialist revolutionary mythology, there was no resemblance between it and 1968. In 1936, the strike had been called *after* a Socialist electoral *victory*, and so had helped to strengthen the hand of the incoming Socialist Prime Minister, who had a majority for an agreed left-wing programme. The participants in the 1968 events had no common policy. By the end of May, they had also lost the support of the public, and were on the eve of an electoral *defeat*.

These facts in themselves help to provide an answer to the fourth question: Why did the revolution collapse so quickly? The short and simple answer is that it did so when trade-union elements that gave the movement its strength were convinced that they could attain their objectives (namely an improvement on the Grenelle agreements) by normal bargaining procedures. At that point, trade-union leaders could afford to get back to the job of restoring normal trade-union discipline. The announcement of an impending general election brought the left-wing political parties back to political reality with a bang — to the world of electoral tactics, in which they had to appeal to an electorate that they had been ignoring, and that was heartily sick of the effects of the strikes. And trivial though it may seem, it was nevertheless a fact in May 1968, as in May 1958, that even a national crisis was not enough to prevent thousands of French families from streaming away from Paris for the Whitsun weekend holiday. This, too, helped to recreate an atmosphere of normality. When they returned, they were faced with other normal requirements — the need to fight an election and to think about overdue school and university examinations.

DOROTHY PICKLES, *The Government and Politics of France*
(Methuen, 1973) volume II, pp. 126–45.

Interpretation of the Crisis of May–June 1968
. . . we have managed to reduce the vast number of interpretations made to eight:

1. attempted subversion;
2. a university crisis;
3. a revolt of youth, a rush of blood to the head;
4. a spiritual revolt, a crisis of civilization;
5. a class conflict, a new sort of social upheaval;
6. a traditional sort of social upheaval;
7. a political crisis;
8. a series of coincidental happenings.

. . . we have been asking ourselves these fundamental question for two years without ever giving the same solutions, and today we have given up trying. . .

TOUCHARD, J. *Revue Française de Science Politique*, June 1970.

Chronological table

	POLITICAL	ECONOMIC	SOCIAL
1789	May: Opening session of States General	December: *Assignats* issued	July: *La Grande Peur* August: The 'Night of 4 August' November: Confiscation of clerical property
1790	July: Fête de la Fédération	November: New tax system established	March: Decree of redemption of feudal rights
1791	October: Meeting of Legislative Assembly		March: Abolition of corporations and guilds
1792	September: Abolition of the monarchy September: First meeting of the Convention		
1793	July: Robespierre at the Committee of Public Safety	August: Adoption of metric system September: General maximum in restraint of prices and wages	July: Final abolition of feudal rights
1799	November: Coup d'état of Brumaire		
1802	April: Concordat with Vatican and 'Organic articles'	December: Creation of Chambers of Commerce	May: Establishment of lycées November: Inauguration of the *cadastre* (property maps)

1803		April: Value of franc fixed by law	December: Introduction of workers' *livrets*
1804	May: Empire proclaimed		March: Civil Code promulgated
1806		November: Berlin decrees (continental system)	May: Founding of Imperial University
1808		January: *Banque de France* incorporated	March: Imperial titles of nobility instituted
1815	March–June: The Hundred Days · July: Second restoration of monarchy		
1817		Beginning of long period of falling prices (to 1850)	February: Electoral law establishing property owners' suffrage
1824	Death of Louis XVIII; succession of Charles X		
1825			April: Law allotting compensation to returned émigrés
1830	Revolution; abdication of Charles X; Louis Philippe 'King of the French'		
1831			November: Riot of weavers at Lyons

	POLITICAL	ECONOMIC	SOCIAL
1833			June: Guizot's law reorganizing primary education
1841			March: Law regulating child labour
1842		June: Law for construction of main railway lines	
1848	February rising: Republic proclaimed; Louis Napoleon first president	March: First discount houses founded	February: Luxemburg Commission February—June: Organization of National Workshops March: Decree shortening working day by one hour March: Universal male suffrage decreed
1850		Beginning of long period of rising prices (to 1873)	March: Falloux Law, increasing clerical influence in education
1852	December: Second Empire proclaimed	July: *Crédit Foncier* and December: *Crédit Mobilier* founded	March: *Sociétés de Secours Mutuel* regulated by law
1860		January: Anglo—French commercial treaty signed	
1864		*Comité des Forges* founded	February: Manifesto of the Sixty

1871	March—May: Paris Commune		May: Ollivier's law on the right to strike September: Foundation of the Socialist International
1873	October: Failure of attempts at royalist restoration	Beginning of long period of falling prices (to 1896)	
1875	Constitutional Law of Third Republic		
1878		Invention of Thomas Gilchrist steel refining process First large scale use of water power	Pasteur discovers principle of inoculation
1879	Republican majority in Senate:		
1882		January: Bankruptcy of *Union Générale*	Commencement of Ferry's reform of primary education
1884			March: Waldeck Rousseau legislation legalizes trade unions
1891			May: Strike at Fourmies
1892		Méline introduces protectionist tariff	August: Strike at Carmaux November: Law of child and female labour

	POLITICAL	ECONOMIC	SOCIAL
1895			Foundation of Confédération Générale du Travail
1896		Beginning of long period of rising prices (to 1929)	
1898		Law of Chambers of Commerce	April: Legislation on industrial injury and hours of work
1900			
1905	Founding of SFIO Disestablishment of Church		
1906	Clémenceau's ministry		March: Weekly holiday established by law October: Amiens Charter
1908		Nationalization of *Chemin de Fer de l'Ouest*	
1909	Briand's ministry		Strikes of railway and post office workers
1910			April: Legislation for workers' retirement pensions

1914	Outbreak of World War I	Law permitting *Banque de France* to increase banknote issue	July: Income Tax introduced
1919	Treaty of Versailles Victory of Bloc National at election Foundation of Third International		April: Law of eight-hour working day. Founding of CFTC
1920	Socialist/Communist split		
1921			December: Trade union split, CGT/CGTU
1928		Stabilization of franc	April: Social insurance laws
1929		Wall Street crash; beginning of world economic crisis	
1932			March: Family allowances for wage-earners established by law
1936	May: Election victory of Popular Front 'Social laws' voted	Devaluation of franc	May–June: Strikes and factory occupations June: Matignon agreement
1938	Fall of Popular Front government		November: Failure of general strike
1939	September: Outbreak of World War II		July: Family code voted

	POLITICAL	ECONOMIC	SOCIAL
1940	Fall of France June: Vichy government headed by Pétain		August: Creation of 'organizing committees' November: Abolition of all trade-union confederations
1941			October: 'Labour charter' promulgated
1943	May: Formation of National Council of Resistance		February: Creation of compulsory labour service
1944	June: Allied invasion of Normandy August: De Gaulle enters Paris		October: Female suffrage
1945	May: Surrender of German armies	December: Nationalization of north-east coalfields, Renault factories, *Banque de France* and main deposit banks, gas and electricity, followed by nationalization of all coalfields	October: Social security laws, farm laws
1946	October: Second constitution voted		August: Rates of family allowances fixed
1947	May: Dismissal of communist ministers	Adoption of Monnet Plan	April: Strikes at Renault works

1948	April: RPF (*Rassemblement du Peuple Français*) holds first congress	April: Marshall Plan accepted. Franc devalued (twice)	December: CGT/Force ouvrière split. Strikes of miners, civil servants, further miners' strikes suppressed by troops
1951	Electoral reform law General election	Schuman plan for European coal and steel pooling agreed	September: Adoption of minimum wage September: State payment to catholic school teachers voted
1952	Pinay forms government		
1953	René Coty President		August: General strike of public services October: Day of peasant road blocks
1954	Fall of Dien Bien Phu June: Mendès France government July: Indo China settlement November: Algerian revolt		June—October: Numerous collective agreements on wages signed
1955	February: fall of Mendès France ministry	June: Adoption of second Monnet Plan	February: Anti-drink laws August—September: Industrial trouble at St Nazaire and Nantes September: Wage agreement accepted by Renault workers

	POLITICAL	ECONOMIC	SOCIAL
1956	January: General election Mollet government	January: Atomic energy plant at Marcoule starts operating	February: Extension of paid holidays to three weeks June: Old age pension fund established
1957	May: fall of Mollet ministry	March: Treaty of Rome for Common Market ratified August: devaluation of franc	
1958	May: Army revolt in Algeria June: Government of de Gaulle, followed by referendum on new constitution, and acceptance of Fifth Republic. De Gaulle president, Debré premier		
1959		February: adoption of third Monnet Plan	February–March: Iron, coal and steel workers' strikes; demonstrations against unemployment at St Nazaire and Nantes; peasant demonstrations
1960		January: adoption of 'nouveau franc'	January–April: Numerous peasant demonstrations

1961	April: Collapse of army revolt in Algeria	January: Tariff equalization by Common Market members	June: Further peasant demonstrations; occupation of Morlaix sous-prefecture by 5000 farmers
1962	April: Debré resigns. Pompidou premier July: Independence of Algeria proclaimed	June: adoption of fourth Monnet Plan (1962–5)	December: Renault workers gain a fourth week of paid holiday
1963		January: De Gaulle vetos British entry to Common Market	February–April: Miners' strike
1964		March: Decree setting up twenty-one economic regions	
1965	December: De Gaulle re-elected president	July–December: Common Market crisis France abstains for six months November: adoption of fifth Monnet Plan	
1966			June: Law establishing sickness insurance for independent workers

	POLITICAL	ECONOMIC	SOCIAL
1967	May: General election	May: Kennedy round; agreement of Six to lower tariffs on industrial products	March: Wine-growers riot in protest at imports of Algerian wine April: Publication of three orders on participation of workers in the 'benefits of industrial expansion'
1968	'The events of May' July: General election, Couve de Murville premier	July: abolition of all tariffs between the Six	May: Grenelle agreements
1969	April: De Gaulle resigns as result of referendum. Pompidou president, Chaban Delmas premier	August: devaluation of franc December: acceptance in principle of British entry to Common Market	September: The premier announces to the National assembly his plans for a 'new society' December: The National assembly ratifies the principle of workers' shareholdings in Renault
1970	November: Death of de Gaulle	February: Agreement by the Six on finance of agricultural policy June: adoption of sixth Monnet Plan	February: Railway strike March–July: Agreement on monthly payment of wages at Renault and in the iron and steel industry

Bibliography

BOOKS REFERRED TO IN TEXT
(When details are not already in text.)

Chapter 1
BALLOT, C., *L'Introduction du machinisme dans l'industrie française*, (Lille, 1923).
CAMERON, R., 'Profit, croissance et stagnation en France au XIXe siècle', *Economie appliquée*, X, April–September 1957.
—— 'La croissance du revenu français depuis 1780', *Cahiers de l'I.S.E.A.*, series D, no. 7.
—— *La France et le développement économique de l'Europe au XIXe siècle* (Paris, Le Seuil, 1971).
DUNHAM, A. L., *The industrial revolution in France* (Jericho, New York Exposition, 1955).
LEON, P., 'L'Industrialisation en France du début du XVIIIe siècle à nos jours', *Première conférence internationale d'histoire économique, Contributions, communications* (Stockholm, 1960).
MARCZEWSKI, J., 'Le Take-off en France', *Cahiers de l'I.S.E.A.*, series A–D, no. 1.
PALMADE, G. P., *Capitalisme et capitalistes français au XIXe siècle* (Paris, Colin).
PINCHEMEL, P., *Structures sociales et dépopulation rurale dans les campagnes picardes de 1836 à 1936* (Paris, Colin).
ROSTOW, W. W., *Stages of economic growth* (Cambridge University Press, 1971).
WALTER, F., 'Récherches sur le developpement économique de la France de 1900 à 1955, *Cahiers de l'I.S.E.A.*, series D, no. 9.

Chapter II
BOIS, P., *Paysans de l'Ouest* (Paris, Mouton, 1960).
BRAUDEL, F. and LABROUSSE, E., eds. *Histoire Economique et Sociale de la France*, I, (Paris, Presses Universitaires, 1970).
DAUMARD, A., FURET, F., *Structures et relations sociales à Paris au XVIIIe siècle*, Cahiers des Annales, no. 18. (Paris, Colin, 1961).
GARDEN, M., *Lyon et les lyonnais au XIIIe siècle* (Paris, Les Belles Lettres, 1970).
GOUBERT, P., *L'Ancien Régime*, I; *La société* (Paris, Colin, 1969).
GUTTON, J. P., *La société et les pauvres, Lyon, 1543–1789* (Paris, Les Belles Lettres, 1970).
LEFEBVRE, G., *Études orléanaises*, I: *Contribution à l'étude des structures sociales à la fin du XVIIIe siècle* (Paris, Imprimerie Nationale, 1962).
LEFEBVRE. G., *La revolution aristocratique*, (Paris, C.D.U.).
LEON, P., 'Récherches sur la bourgeoisie francaise de province au XVIIIe siècle', *L'Information historique*, no. 3, 1958.
LEON, P. (ed.), *Structure économiques et problèmes sociaux du monde rural dans la France du Sud-Est* (Paris, Les Belles-Lettres, 1966).
LIGOU, D. *Mintauban à la fin de l'Ancien Régime et aux débuts de la Révolution, 1787–1794* (Paris, Rivière, 1958).
PARISET, F. G. (ed.), *Bordeaux au XVIIIe siècle*, vol. V of *L'histoire de Bordeaux* (Bordeaux, Fédération historique du Sud-Ouest, 1968).
SENTOU, J., *Fortunes et groupes sociaux à Toulouse sous la Révolution* (Toulouse, Privat, 1969).

Chapter III

ARMENGAUD, A., *Les populations de l'Est Aquitain au début de l'époque contemporaine* (Paris, Mouton, 1962).

BLANCHARD, M., *Le Second Empire* (Paris, Colin, 1950).

BLANQUI, J. A., *Les Classes ouvrières en France* (Paris, Pagnerre, 1849).

DUVEAU, G., *La Vie ouvrière sous le Second Empire* (Paris, Gallimard, 1968).

GUEPIN, A., *Nantes au XIXe siècle* (Nantes, Sébire, 1835).

LEFEBVRE, G., 'La révolution et les paysans' and 'La vente des biens nationaux', *Études sur la Révolution française* (Paris, Presses Universitaires de France, 1954).

LHOMME, J., *La Grande Bourgeoisie au pouvoir (1830—1880)* (Paris, Presses Universitaires de France, 1960).

PERNOUD, R., *Histoire de la bourgeoisie en France* , vol. II: *Les Temps modernes* (Paris, Seuil, 1962).

SAUVIGNY, B. de, *La Restauration* (Paris, Flammarion, 1963).

VIDALENC, J., *La société française de 1815 a 1848*. I: *Le peuple des campagnes* (Paris, Rivière, 1970).

VIDALENC, J., *Le Département de l'Eure sous la Monarchie constitutionelle* (Paris, Rivière, 1970).

VILLERMÉ, L. R., *Tableau de l'état physique et moral des ouvriers employés dans les manufactures de coton, de laine et de soie* (Paris, Renouard, 1840).

Chapter IV

BOUVIER, J., 'Le mouvement d'une civilisation nouvelle', in Duby, G., *L'Histoire de la France*, III (Paris, Larousse, 1971).

SEIGNOBOS, C., *L'Évolution de la troisiéme République*, vol. VIII of *L'Histoire de France contemporaine*, ed. Lavisse (Paris, Hachette, 1931).

SIEGFRIED, A., *Tableau des partis en France* (Paris, Grasset, 1930).

SORLIN, P., *La Société française*. I: *1840—1914* (Paris, Arthaud, 1969).

Chapter V

ARON, R., *La Révolution introuvable* (Paris, Fayard, 1968).

DEBATISSE, M., *La revolution silencieuse. Le combat des paysans* (Paris, C-Levy, 1963).

MALLET, S., *La nouvelle classe ouvrière* (Paris, Seuil, 1963).

SAUVY, A., *Histoire économique de la France entre les deux guerres* vol. I: *1918—1931*; vol. II:1931—1939 (Paris, Fayard).

FURTHER READING

This represents only a fraction of the reading matter available. Good bibliographies will be found in the three volumes of Alfred Cobban's *History of Modern France* and Dorothy Pickles' *Government and Politics of France*.

Only such French titles are given as are likely to be available in a reasonably well-equipped library.

General

ARDAGH, J., *France today*, London, Penguin.

ARDAGH, J., *The new French Revolution: a social and economic study of France 1945—68*.

COBBAN, A., *A history of modern France*, 3 vols. London, Penguin.

DESMAREST, J., *L'Evolution de la France contemporaine*, Paris, Hachette, 1970).

FOHLEN, C., *La France de l'entre deux guerres, 1917–38* (1966).

JOHNSON, D., *France, a companion to French studies*, London, Methuen, 1970).

WRIGHT, G., *France in modern times* (London, Murray).

ZELDIN, T., *France, 1848–1945, Ambition, Love and Politics* (Oxford, University Press, 1973).

Political

CAHM, E., *Politics and society in contemporary France, 1789–1971* (London, Harrap, 1972).

EISENSTEIN, E., 'Who intervened in 1788?' *American History Review*.

GOGUEL, F. and GROSSER, A., *La politique en France* (Paris, Colin, 1964).

HARTLEY, A., *Gaullism: the rise and fall of a political movement* (London, Routledge and Kegan Paul, 1972).

HAYWARD, J., *The one and indivisible French Republic* (London, Weidenfeld and Nicolson, 1973).

JOHNSON, D., *Guizot, aspects of French history*, (London, Routledge and Kegan Paul, 1963).

MARCZEWSKI, J., The take-off hypothesis and the French experience', in Rostow, W. W., *The economics of take-off into sustained growth*, (London, Macmillan, 1968).

NERE, J., *La troisieme république* (Paris, Colin, 1967).

PICKLES, D., *The government and politics of France*, vol. 1: *Institutions and Parties*; vol. II *Politics* (London, Methuen, 1973).

PINKNEY, D., *The French Revolution of 1830* (Princeton University Press, 1973).

PONTEIL, F., *La monarchie parlémentaire, 1815–48*.

SAUVIGNY, G. B. de, 'Population movements and political change in nineteenth-century France', *Review of Politics*, XIX (1957).

SAUVIGNY, G. B. de, *The Bourbon restoration* (University of Pennsylvania Press, 1963).

SYDENHAM, M. J., *The French Revolution* (London, Batsford, 1965).

WILLIAMS, P. M., *French politicians and elections 1951–69* (Cambridge University Press, 1970).

Economic

BOSHER, J. F., *The single duty project* (London, Athlone, 1963).

CAMERON, R., *France and the economic development of Europe, 1800–1914* (New York, Rand McNally, 1967).

CLAPHAM, J. H., *The economic development of France and Germany, 1815–1914* (Cambridge University Press, 1936).

COHEN, S. S., *Modern capitalist planning: the French model* (London, Weidenfeld 1969).

CROUZET, F., 'Wars, blockades and economic change in Europe', *Journal of Economic History*, 1967).

DUNHAM, A. L., *The Industrial Revolution in France* (New York, Exposition, 1955).

HANSEN, N., *French regional planning* (Edinburgh University Press, 1968).

KEMP, T., *Industrialization in 19th century Europe* (London, Longman, 1969).
Economic forces in French history (London, Longman, 1971).
The French economy, 1913–1939 (London, Longman, 1972).

KEVY-LEBOYER, M., 'La croissance economique en France au XIXe siecle', *Annales*, July 1968.

MILWARD, A., *The new order and the French economy* (Oxford University Press, 1970).

PALMADE, G. F., *French capitalism in the 19th century* (Newton Abbott, David and Charles, 1972).

PILBEAM, P., 'Economic factors in the growth of political opposition in Eastern and North-eastern France on the eve of the 1830 revolution, in Merriman, J., *The social question in France: the revolution of 1830*

ROSTOW, W. W., *The stages of economic growth* (Cambridge University Press, 1971).

SAUVY, A., *Histoire economique de la France entre les deux guerres*, vol. I: *1918–31;* vol. II: *1931–39* (Paris, Fayard).

SEE, H., *Histoire economique de la France,* vol. II.

For the successive Monnet plans see the documents issued from time to time by the French Embassy, and *Documentation Française* services.

Social

ARMENGAUD, A., *La population française au 19e siecle*
La population française au 20e siecle (Paris, Presses Universitaires de France 1965 and 1971).
Les populations de l'Est aquitain au debut de l'époque contemporaine (Paris, Mouton, 1962).

BEHRENS, C. B. A., *The Ancien Régime* (London, Thames & Hudson, 1967).

BOIS, P., *Paysans de l'Ouest* (Paris, Mouton, 1962).

CHEVALIER, L., *Labouring classes and dangerous classes in France*

COBB, R. C., *The police and the people* (Oxford University Press, 1970).
Second identity (Oxford University Press, 1969).

COBBAN, A., *The social interpretation of the French revolution* (Cambridge University Press, 1964).
Aspects of the French Revolution (London, Cape, 1968).
'The vocabulary of social history', *Political Science Quarterly*, 1xxi (1956).

COLLINS, IRENE (ed.), *Government and Society in France, 1814–48* (London, Arnold, 1970).

DAUMARD, A., *La bourgeoisie parisienne, 1815–48* 1970

DAVIES, A., 'The origins of the peasant revolution of 1789', *History*, 1964.

DUVEAU, G., *La vie ouvrière sous le second empire* (Paris, Gallimard, 1946).

FRANKLIN, S. H., *The European Peasantry: the final phase* (London, Methuen, 1969).

GOUBERT, P., *The Ancien Régime* (London, Weidenfeld & Nicolson, 1973).

GURVITCH, G., 'The social structure of pre-war France' *American Journal of Sociology*, p. 535.

HAMPSON, N., *A social history of the French revolution* (London, Routledge, 1964).

HUFTON, O., *Bayeux in the 18th century* (Oxford University Press, 1967).

LABROUSSE, E., *Le mouvement ouvrier et les idées sociales en France, 1815—71.* (Paris, Les cours de Sorbonne, C.D.U. 1948).

LEFEBVRE, G., 'La Revolution et les paysans' and 'La vente des biens', *Etudes sur la revolution francaise* (Paris, Presses Universitaires de France, 1954).

LORWIN, V., *The French labor movement*

MARX, K., *Class struggles in France, 1848—50*

MCDONALD, J. R., 'Labor immigration in France 1946—65', *Annals of the Association of American Geographers*, March 1969, pp. 116—134.

MCMANNERS, J., *French ecclesiastical society under the Ancien Régime* (Manchester University Press, 1969).

MORAZE, C., *La France bourgeoise*

RIDLEY, F. F., *Revolutionary syndicalism in France* (Cambridge University Press, 1971)

TOCQUEVILLE, A. de, *Recollections* (ed. J. P. Mayer) (New York 1970, Doubleday).

WRIGHT, G., *Rural revolution in France: the peasantry in the 20th century* (Stanford University Press, 1968).

ZELDIN, T., *Conflicts in French society* (London, Allen and Unwin, 1971).

WYLIE, L., Village in the Vaucluse (second edition, Harvard, 1967).

Index